Critical Essays on

JOHN MILLINGTON
SYNGE

CRITICAL ESSAYS
ON
BRITISH LITERATURE

Zack Bowen, General Editor
University of Miami

Critical Essays on

JOHN MILLINGTON SYNGE

edited by

DANIEL J. CASEY

G. K. Hall & Co. / New York
Maxwell Macmillan Canada / Toronto
Maxwell Macmillan International / New York Oxford Singapore Sydney

G. K. Hall & Co.
Macmillan Publishing Company
866 Third Avenue
New York, New York 10022

Maxwell Macmillan Canada, Inc.
1200 Eglinton Avenue East
Suite 200
Don Mills, Ontario M3C 3N1

Library of Congress Cataloging-in-Publication Data

Critical essays on John Millington Synge / edited by Daniel J. Casey.
        p.   cm. — (Critical essays on British literature)
    Includes bibliographical references and index.
    ISBN 0-7838-0006-1
    1. Synge, John Millington, 1871–1909—Criticism and
interpretation.   2. Ireland–In literature.   I. Casey, Daniel J.,
1937– .   II. Series.
PR5534.C7   1994
822'.912–dc20   94-2675
                                                                CIP

The paper used in this publication meets the minimum requirements of
American National Standard for Information Sciences—Permanence of
Paper for Printed Library Materials. ANSI Z3948-1984.∞™

10   9   8   7   6   5   4   3   2   1

Printed in the United States of America

Contents

♦

General Editor's Note

♦

The Critical Essays on British Literature series provides a variety of approaches to both classical and contemporary writers of Britain and Ireland. The formats of the volumes in the series vary with the thematic designs of editors, and with the amount and nature of existing reviews and criticism, augmented, where appropriate, by original essays by recognized authorities. It is hoped that each volume will be unique in developing a new overall perspective on its particular subject.

Casey's introduction summarizes the history of Synge criticism and its climax in the plethora of Centenary scholarship in 1971. Casey's forthright appraisals are concise, relevant, and couched in lively prose. His selection of essays offers a general reappraisal of Synge's reputation, with separate discussions of his language, prose essays, and poetry, as well as individual treatments of his best known drama, including four different critical perspectives on *The Playboy of the Western World*.

ZACK BOWEN
University of Miami

Publisher's Note

◆

Producing a volume that contains both newly commissioned and reprinted material presents the publisher with the challenge of balancing the desire to achieve stylistic consistency with the need to preserve the integrity of works first published elsewhere. In the Critical Essays series, essays commissioned especially for a particular volume are edited to be consistent with G. K. Hall's house style; reprinted essays appear in the style in which they were first published, with only typographical errors corrected. Consequently, shifts in style from one essay to another are the result of our efforts to be faithful to each text as it was originally published.

Introduction

♦

DANIEL J. CASEY

A REVIEW OF THE CRITICS

In 1971, the celebration of the centenary of John Millington Synge's birth brought new critical attention to his works. That reassessment spurred a rash of publications, most of which focused on *Riders to the Sea* and *Playboy of the Western World*, Synge's masterpieces of modern theater.

Foremost among the books appearing in the early 1970s were the edited collections: Maurice Harmon's *J. M. Synge: Centenary Papers 1971* (1972) and S. B. Bushrui's *A Centenary Tribute to J. M. Synge, 1871–1909: Sunshine and the Moon's Delight* (1972), both providing long overdue reinterpretations of the Synge canon. Paul M. Levitt's *J. M. Synge: A Bibliography of Published Criticism* (1974) and E. H. Mikhail's *J. M. Synge: A Bibliography of Criticism* (1975) are scholar's tools: Levitt's bibliography misses the furious productivity of the early 1970s, though Mikhail's is more comprehensive and offers an exhaustive list of nearly 2,500 entries.

It seems that, in 1971, every academic in Dublin and in the centers of learning in English-speaking countries and elsewhere was rediscovering the playwright. Following on the success of the four-volume Oxford University Press edition of *J. M. Synge: Collected Works* (1962–68), Robin Skelton produced *The Writings of J. M. Synge* (1971) and *J. M. Synge & His World* (1971) in honor of the revival, "the Synge thing." Ann Saddlemyer contributed "Infinite Riches in a Little Room—the Manuscripts of John Millington Synge," "Some Letters of John M. Synge to Lady Gregory and W. B. Yeats," and "Letters to Molly: John M. Synge to Maire O'Neill" (all 1971). Understandably, *The Shadow of the Glen, The Well of the Saints, The Tinker's Wedding*, and the posthumous and unfinished *Deirdre of the Sorrows*—important yet lesser works, received less attention from the critic-revelers at this Syngefest.

Before 1971, Synge scholarship fell conveniently into three categories: reviews, recollections and commentaries by friends, associates, and early critics

(1900–1930); formal studies by academic critics (1931–1958); and later reassessments based on biographical research and primary sources (1959–1970).

Synge himself claimed to have little interest in the critical response to his work. In fact, in his day there was no apparatus for theater review in Ireland. The *Irish Independent* and other Dublin dailies often dispatched the sports subeditor to cover Abbey performances, and they were covered with all the sensitivity of a commentary on a hurling match. Until Yeats, even the London press had dismissed the Anglo-Irish mainstays as colonials whose work could only come to judgment on a West End stage.

Early personal commentaries by W. B. Yeats, reprinted in *Essays and Introductions* (1961) and in *Explorations* (1962), and by Augusta Gregory, in *Our Irish Theatre, a Chapter of Autobiography* (1913), hold no surprises. Yeats idealizes and celebrates Synge and Synge's works: the tone is that reverent tone of "The Municipal Gallery Revisited": "Think where a man's glory most begins and ends, / And say that my glory was that I had such friends." Yeats's recollections yield a mythologized John Synge, who served as resident dramatist and muse for the renaissance that Yeats created.

In a typically grudging way, George Moore's *Vale*, the third volume of *Hail and Farewell* (1911–14), credits Synge's creative genius, as do other reviews by Synge's contemporaries, such as Padraic Colum and the Abbey regulars. Even John Masefield, an acquaintance of Synge, who once compared him to Shakespeare, wrote *John Millington Synge: A Few Personal Recollections with Biographical Notes* (1915), a little book that reflects Synge's character more than his literary accomplishments.

Though literary and theater histories of the period mention Synge, in *John Millington Synge and the Irish Theatre Movement* (1913) Maurice Bourgeois offers the first full and insightful treatment of Synge from beyond the Abbey circle; it is certainly more incisive than those by Bickley (1912), Howe (1912) and Boyd (1916); and it places Synge in a European context. Bourgeois's remains the soundest of the early commentaries.

By 1931, with the publication of Daniel Corkery's *Synge and Anglo-Irish Literature*, the nationalist bias ignited by *Shadow* and detonated by *Playboy* was regenerated. Corkery's notions—that the Anglo-Protestant Synge was ignorant of the "hidden Ireland" and of the nuances of peasant speech—colored his view. Unfortunately, Irish criticism took its lead from Corkery, whose forte was writing fiction and influencing fiction writers rather than interpreting drama. His *Synge and Anglo-Irish Literature* set Synge criticism back 40 years in Ireland.

The fairest assessment of Synge's work to come out of the 1930s was Una Ellis-Fermor's *Irish Dramatic Movement* (1939). Ellis-Fermor found flaws in the lesser plays but saw *Riders* and *Playboy* as world-class drama, and her judgment was borne out by subsequent criticism from outside Ireland. Edmund Wilson once referred to Synge's plays as "the most authentic examples of poetic drama which the modern stage has seen," and T. S. Eliot's occasional nods to *Playboy* were an indication of his rising reputation among established critics.

Contrary to Alan Price's assertion that "the current of Synge criticism flowed strong and broad" during the decades preceding his own *Synge and Anglo-Irish Drama* (1961), there was little of moment in Synge studies through the 1940s and 1950s. Until the 1959 publication of David H. Greene and Edward M. Stephens's definitive biography *J. M. Synge, 1871–1909*, the only publications worth noting are: a chapter on Yeats and Synge in T. R. Henn's *The Lonely Tower* (1952); four articles in the late 1940s by David H. Greene on *Riders, The Tinker's Wedding, Playboy,* and *Deirdre*; and three articles by Denis Donoghue on *Riders, The Tinker's Wedding,* and Synge's poems, written in the latter half of the 1950s.

Greene undertook his classic biography with the help of Synge's nephew Edward Stephens and, after Stephens's death, wrote a sensitive and introspective study that reproduced the playwright, including his faults, and provoked the first wave of serious scholarly inquiry. It is probably the most significant work ever written on Synge.

Despite the paucity of solid research over the past 20 years, the 1960s were productive. In addition to *Synge and Anglo-Irish Drama,* an intelligent and readable survey of the Synge corpus, Alan Price edited the *Autobiography* and completed the prose volume in *Collected Works* (1966). In fact between 1962 and 1968, the publication of *Collected Works* by Oxford University Press, under the general editorship of Robin Skelton, represents a milestone in Synge scholarship. Skelton brought out volume 1, *Poems,* for Oxford in 1962, and made an excellent case for reanalysis of "Judaslied" and several other pieces. Ann Saddlemyer, who had proven herself in Synge studies with "Synge to MacKenna: The Mature Years" (1964), "J. M. Synge's Aesthetic Theory" (1965), "Rabelais versus À Kempis: The Art of J. M. Synge" (1967), and her monograph *J. M. Synge and Modern Comedy* (1967), edited volumes 3 and 4, *Plays,* in *Collected Works* (1966–68).

The four volumes of the Oxford University Press edition are uneven, because each of the editors has a different agenda: Skelton isolates and defends Synge's poems and translations as *poetry*; Price provides a simplified text "without conflating varying versions of the same phrase or sentence" and establishes an artistic integrity for the prose works; Saddlemyer examines every draft of every play and provides textual variants without elaborate commentary. In spite of its inconsistencies, *Collected Works* provides an authoritative source for subsequent scholarship.

There are several other notable publications from the 1960's: Elizabeth Coxhead's *J. M. Synge and Lady Gregory* (1962), a competent monograph that enjoyed wide circulation; Donna Gerstenberger's *John Millington Synge* (1964), a full study that promotes *Deirdre of the Sorrows* as a significant play; and Thomas Whitaker's *Twentieth-Century Interpretations of "The Playboy of the Western World"*

(1969), a collection of 11 essays on the Synge classic. A number of informative articles also appear: Ronald Gaskell's "The Realism of J. M. Synge" (1963), Donna Gerstenberger's "Yeats and Synge: A Young Man's Ghost" (1965), James Kilroy's "The Playboy as Poet" (1968), and Alan Price's "Synge's Prose Writings: A First View of the Whole" (1968), are among them.

Since the 1971 centenary, the principal writers on Synge—Greene, Saddlemyer, and Skelton (Price died in 1969)—have continued to mine the plays and poems, their sources and influences, and reinterpret the texts, at times with startling discoveries. Ann Saddlemyer's articles: "Synge and the Doors of Perception" (1977), "Synge and the Nature of Woman" (1983), "In Search of the Unknown Synge" (1985), and "Synge's Soundscape" (1992), as well as her two-volume *Collected Letters* (1983–84), have opened new ground for scholarship, though much remains to be done.

After the rush of the early 1970s, the criticism continued apace, younger critics finding and formulating theories to advance new research. The past two decades have produced important critical studies. Nicholas Grene's *A Critical Study of the Plays* (1975), Declan Kiberd's *Synge and the Irish Language* (1979), Eugene Benson's *J. M. Synge* (1982), D. E. S. Maxwell's *Critical History of Modern Irish Drama, 1891–1980* (1984), Seamus Deane's *Celtic Revivals: Essays in Modern Irish Literature, 1880–1980* (1985), and Mary C. King's *The Drama of J. M. Synge* (1985), all reinterpret Synge in light of the recent research. Shorter studies by Grene (1989), Powers (1990), Bretherton (1991), and Roche (1992) are among the best of the current fare.

Between 1979 and 1990, three works edited by Edward A. Kopper, Jr., appeared: *John Millington Synge: A Reference Guide* (1979), *A J. M. Synge Literary Companion* (1988), and *J. M. Synge: A Review of the Criticism* (1990). The *Companion* contains 16 new essays offering a fresh look at the man and his plays—essays by Bowen on *Playboy*, Begnal on *Deirdre*, Fallis on the literary influences, McCarthy on the Renaissance, and by established scholars on other works. The *Guide* has the virtue of being annotated and is thus more useful as a reference; while *Review of Criticism* provides a newer listing that has facilitated contemporary Synge scholarship.

Two essays and a thoughtful book on Synge by Weldon Thornton should be noted here: the first essay appeared in *Anglo-Irish Literature: A Review of Research* (1976); the second in *Recent Research on Anglo-Irish Writers* (1983). Both are useful and significant contributions to the survey of Synge scholarship. Thornton's book, *J. M. Synge and the Western Mind* (1979), offers a uniquely personal and challenging reconsideration of Synge's life and art.

Through the 1980s, A. Norman Jaffares' *Anglo-Irish Literature* (1982), Hugh Kenner's *A Colder Eye: The Modern Irish Writers* (1983), and Harold Bloom's "Introduction" to the edited *John Millington Synge's Playboy of the Western World* (1988), have treated Synge kindly; the recognition of late by important critics continues to add to the playwright's reputation.

REFLECTIONS ON SYNGE

Synge's place in modern Irish drama is secure. He is the acknowledged genius of the Abbey and perhaps the purist of the major Irish writers who, together with W. B. Yeats and Augusta Gregory, brought Irish theater to its brief golden moment. Certainly, with the death of Synge in 1909, the Yeats renaissance fell on hard times, and, notwithstanding protestations from Yeats or the fickle Irish gallery, the Abbey never regained the vitality that Synge's "vast shadow" had cast on it from the wings.

The Synge canon of seven plays, written in whole or in part over 10 years time, brought him a revilement equal to that spewed on Yeats and O'Casey over their considerably longer professional lives. Synge was, until a quarter century ago, an object of suspicion and scorn in Ireland, because he was neither religiously nor politically correct, because he had mocked an impious peasantry at a time when "peasant" carried a notion of "romance" and nationalism was in high gear. Sacred cows make poor mince, and Synge, in serving up his realistic dramas, had clearly offended the masses.

David H. Greene suggests that John Millington Synge was enigmatic— a mysterious loner who shied from public debate and critical argument. Other biographers and critics make much of Synge's childhood infatuations, his adolescent agonies of self doubt, and the melancholy of his later years. Synge was, in fact, a reticent individual accustomed to, and comfortable with, his solitude. He lived far from the crowd, and he did so by choice.

In "A Life Apart" (1988), I make that observation and go on to point out that Synge had to shed an Ascendancy past—after all, the Protestant zealots who had "raped the land" and evicted their tenants were his family. But early in life, the playwright had repudiated his Anglo-Irish birthright and sought a life uncomplicated by a tradition that he believed stifled artistic imagination and demanded too-rigorous adherence to the concerns of class. In spite those repudiations and his anarchistic leanings, he recognized that he was a product of an ascendancy culture. He never switched horses and rode for the nationalist camp. As he explained, "I wish to work in my own way for the cause of Ireland." In that period of political and cultural extremism, he courageously stood the middle ground and called himself "a temperate Nationalist," railing against the extremism on both flanks.

Synge's "atheism" was not at all a proper atheism, but instead a rejection of organized religion, especially the evangelical strain of Christianity hammered home by a family of devotees. He was an inquiring, meditative, deeply religious man, but his sense of religion was pantheistic—encompassing a divine scheme promoting uniformity and cosmic harmony in nature. He dabbled in occultism, read the mystics, and even turned occasionally to Thomas à Kempis for direction.

Synge is thus a complex and interesting figure, and as the master play-wright in a theater movement that reached beyond Ireland to all of modern drama, he is especially significant and central. He has offered a unique comic-tragic blend and a vision of rural Ireland that somehow melds the romantic and realistic without ever jarring. His plays give voice to heightened poetic dialogue that suggests Shakespearean dignity. Always the consummate artist, Synge was faithful to an aesthetic that promoted the language of drama as an extension of the spiritual, but, in reflecting all human life, did not suppress the outrages to the spirit. Accordingly, despotic husbands, tyrannical priests, and greedy shopkeepers were made flesh and offered to audiences that recoiled in horror at their mirror likenesses.

Synge was despised by most Irish and by the Irish critics, and his plays were unwelcome in Dublin and in the Irish enclaves abroad—witness the infamous Playboy riots and the mob scenes in Boston and Philadelphia (the cast was jailed in the "City of Brotherly Love"). Synge's dramas were, after all, seen as "blatant attacks on the Irish peasantry" and "ignominious insults to Irish propriety." In a period of nationalist paranoia, they were the ill-timed strokes of genius. Irish theatergoers were in no way disposed to witness the most perfect tragedy and comedy ever played on the Irish stage, nor were they disposed to tolerate its author. When Synge died at 37, a victim of Hodgkins disease, he was the unsung hero of the Abbey. The tragedy of his life had been played out.

W. B. Yeats, Lady Gregory, and others of the Abbey movement were unable to alter the tide of public opinion in those troubled days. They believed in Synge's great genius, and they defended him in the theater and elsewhere against crass and small-minded attacks, but coming from the ascendancy, their defense went unheeded.

A great deal remains unsaid about the playwright and his plays, autobiography, journals, criticism, essays, and poems. In spite of a reputation as resident genius of the Abbey, scholars and critics have often "missed" on Synge, and have often misplayed works they failed to appreciate.

There is no "Synge industry" comparable to those surrounding Joyce or Yeats. His plays are staged regularly by great companies and directors in theaters around the world. Studies by Synge critics elucidate texts, provide character motivation, or explicate poems. But the prose,—the autobiography, journals, letters, and essays—have become as much the province of anthropologists studying the ways of the Arans and the West, as they are of literary critics; while the poetry, because it is sparse and secondary, has been virtually ignored.

A NOTE ON THE ESSAYS

What follows is a collection of essays that speak to Synge's genius. They are, quite simply, the most direct and informed interpretations of his works that this editor has been able to gather in a single volume. They include classic studies by Greene, Price, Skelton, and Saddlemyer, as well as newer scholarship.

Appropriately, David H. Greene's "A Reappraisal," from *Eire-Ireland* (1971), introduces the volume. Greene asserts, "on the basis of the assumption that we are not likely to have any startling revelations in the future, I have to believe the only fully understandable Synge we are likely to get in the future will be a product of the imagination." An appraisal of Synge must begin, then, with a reappraisal of his art.

Yeats called Synge "meditative." He was also elusive, and his letters, even those to Molly Allgood, disclose a strange soul, emotionally at odds with himself. Greene dismisses the idea that, save for his final year, Synge was preoccupied with his health and explains the playwright's apparent disposition to morbidity as a family trait. He has good evidence, and he speaks to the man rather than the legend. Greene also concludes from Synge's journalistic pieces that his genial observations in prose—in *Wicklow, West Kerry, and Connemara*, for example—belie the darker visage presented by Synge the poet. But, to know Synge's drama and to understand his aesthetic, *The Aran Islands* (according to Greene) is an entirely different affair. "[L]ike the notebooks of Dostoievski or the letters of Keats," he claims it is essential for an appreciation of the plays. Greene makes no excuses for Synge's pedestrian book reviews, conventional lyrics, or his earliest "bad" play. He regards them exercises of a mind on a quest. The Greene essay is to date the most perceptive brief biographical-critical assessment of Synge. It sets a tone for the first part of this collection.

The essays after "A Reappraisal" consider several aspects of Synge's works that Greene raised—Synge's use of the Irish idiom, his poetry, and *When the Moon Has Set* (1968)—his first "bad" play. The prose remains to be considered, including *The Aran Islands*, which Synge calls "his first serious piece of work," and the relationship between Yeats and Synge requires further exploration.

Seamus Deane makes the important distinction between the use of poetic language and the poetic use of language. Given the controversy over "peasant speech" in *Playboy* and the general concern over Synge's "invented" stage language, Deane's observations in *Mosaic* (1971) make eminent good sense. He examines the evolution of the poetry and drama to show that language was to Synge "a sacred joy, just as Ireland became to him a sacred place." "Synge's Poetic Use of Language," not only clarifies the playwright's linguistic intent, it illustrates his method and technique.

Alan Price's essay, "Synge's Prose Writings: A First View of the Whole," from *Modern Drama* (1968), comes after his edition of *Prose* in *Collected Works*. In this summary Price maintains that *Étude Morbide* (c. 1899) and *Autobiography* contain most of the themes in the later writings and that, taken together, the two record Synge's artistic growth from boyhood through the formative years. *Études Morbide* contains jottings of "dreams, ideas, longings, and discoveries" that seem trivial against the richer prose and the somber impressions of *The Aran Islands*. The autobiography, though lean, fills in certain gaps.

Price confirms Greene's observations: that the Wicklow years served as a bonding period with the country people, that the Aran visits were a kind of literary novitiate, that his tours in West Kerry and Connemara elicit evidence of humor and compassion. Price sees a style, integrity, and vitality in Synge's nonfiction that lends them an enduring value. Synge's mature essays and journalistic pieces merit attention.

In his chapter on the poems in *The Writings of J. M. Synge*, Robin Skelton agrees that, while Synge's poems and translations are few, they also advance themes and attitudes that are found in his drama. His attempts at realism in "Queens," "Danny," and "The 'Mergency Man," for example, play on a violence that sets up internal tensions, while in his preface to *Poems and Translations* (1909) Synge writes: "before verse can be human again it must learn to be brutal." There he is working out his theory of linguistic contrasts. The poems have the effect of honing his diction, and they mix images from mythology, lore, and life. According to Skelton, Synge's "gay-grim" verses contrast with the "Celtic Twilight" verses of early Yeats, but seem to intrude tonally on those in *The Green Helmet* (1910) and the later works. Though Synge's poems don't measure up to his drama, Yeats judged them worthy enough to include 12 poems and translations in his edition of *The Oxford Book of Modern Verse* (1936).

When the Moon Has Set is a failure. Augusta Gregory and W. B. Yeats found it abstract and tedious. Synge himself found little virtue in it. There are, however, several versions of the playscript, and according to Mary C. King, in *The Drama of J. M. Synge*, a 1903 rewrite has interesting twists that seem to inform Synge's *Deirdre* and influence the phrasing, ritual, and symbolism of his later plays. King unravels the overworked plot and explicates the text, drawing parallels to Synge's life and art. *When the Moon Has Set* is of no dramatic consequence, though the 1903 script provides early whisperings of Synge's movement toward dramatic genius.

In *W. B. Yeats, 1865–1965: Centenary Essays on the Art of W. B. Yeats* (1965), Donna Gerstenberger's "Yeats and Synge: A Young Man's Ghost" suggests the interdependency of the two literary giants and notes that, though they shared a common Anglo-Protestant background, they were at odds in their approach to their arts. If Yeats dispatched John Synge to the Arans to learn his trade, Synge returned to teach Yeats a thing or two about the making of drama and verse. In an intriguing essay, Gerstenberger shows Synge's influences on Yeats's later poetry.

The first group of essays thus responds to Greene's propositions on Synge's use of language and the enduring qualities of his prose; and to Greene's questions about the virtues of Synge's poetry and his earliest dramatic work. However, Greene advises the reader "to go on to Synge's art . . . for the 'abstract beauty of the person' himself."

Nicholas Grene's "*The Shadow of the Glen*: Repetition and Allusion," from *Modern Drama* (1974), sets aside traditional comparisons with *The Widow of Ephasis*, political and religious concerns, and many other considerations. Grene's analysis works because it focuses on the playwright's deliberate use of techniques that move *Shadow* toward resolution. Repetition allows for mockery, and mockery promotes conflict. The allusions—to sheep, shadows, and mist, and then to Mary Brien, Peggy Cavanagh, and Patch Darcy—establish important contexts beyond the cottage and the stage. Synge's deliberate use of direct language, with repetitions and allusions, allows dramatic interpretations ranging from "situation comedy" to "poetic symbolism." In that sense Grene believes Synge's first stage play exhibits a subtlety and depth that are absent even from his masterpieces.

In my own essay, "An Aran Requiem: Setting in *Riders to the Sea*," from *Antigonish Review* (1972), I pick up on David Greene's thesis that *The Aran Islands* is key to an appreciation of all Synge's drama. The essay begins by considering the notebooks, but ends with a reconstruction of Synge's aesthetic—in his multiplication of symbols, echoes, and allusions, his use of ritual and archetype, his rendering of the Gaelic idiom, and his recapturing "the entrancing newness of the old." *Riders to the Sea* becomes a benchmark for modern tragedy. It contains the elements of Greek tragedy, but in its way, surpasses even the best of Sophocles for its compression and force.

Anthony Roche's "Two Worlds of Synge's *Well of the Saints*," in *Genre* (1979), explores the mythic substratum of the play. Roche's analysis elicits a fuller understanding of the playwright's reliance on myth and lore; it leads from the story Synge heard on the Arans, that served as the frame for *Well*, to the playwright's evolution of a strange black comedy. It doesn't matter that Synge reverses the Christian truth of the tale and plunges Martin and Mary Doul back into their dark world, where visions abound and the harsh reality of their blindness is obscured. What matters are the ironies of the cure and the misery it heaps upon the afflicted. Roche does not rule out other sources for *Well*, though he insists that Synge relies upon his own design.

Kate Powers offers a second perspective. In "Myth and the Journey in *The Well of the Saints*," in *Colby Quarterly* (1990), she sees the play as Martin Doul's dark comic journey ending in his vision; after all, old Martin Doul has a touch of the artist in him. For Powers the myths are meldings of Celtic past and Freudian present that curiously underlie a curious drama.

There is not much published criticism on *The Tinker's Wedding*. Perhaps the best known is Vivian Mercier's essay in S. B. Bushrui's *Sunshine and the Moon's Delight* (1979), which notes that the comedy rests on humor common to Irish tradition, and that Synge was echoing the tone of his Gaelic sources. However, the play is too savage to work its magic. Denis Donoghue's early critical essay, "Too Immoral for Dublin: Synge's *The Tinker's Wedding*," in *Irish Writing* (1955), refutes the charge of blasphemy, arguing that, after all, Synge's portrayal of priest and tinker is realistic, and claiming that the Irish had yet again misunderstood the playwright's intent.

Weldon Thornton's reading of *Wedding*, from *J. M. Synge and the Western Mind* (1979), contrasts tinker and Christian values and cultures, and provides an intelligent analysis of the conflict in the drama. Mercier's essay is being reissued in a volume from Oxford University Press. Denis Donoghue's and Weldon Thornton's fine pieces are reprinted here.

Since its first performance in 1907, *The Playboy of the Western World* has provoked more controversy and attracted more critical attention than any other Irish drama. The riots that raged in Dublin and the irrational Irish critical response heightened interest elsewhere. It doesn't matter that the Irish and the Irish diaspora reject *Playboy* because they fail to appreciate its humor, which is all too Irish. Harold Bloom explains it this way: "What matters is the play's aesthetic originality and power as a kind of phantasmagoric farce, vital in its parodistic drive of rhetoric over the reductive world of the reality principle."

The three essays here offer three different readings of *Playboy*. James F. Kilroy's "The Playboy as Poet," from *PMLA* (1968), looks at Christy's transfiguration from "a talker of folly, a man you'd see stretched the half of the day in the brown ferns with his belly to the sun" to an epic poet with an epic character—with the combined qualities of poet, chieftain, and scholar. Kilroy charts Christy's progression from an apprentice poet to a proper *filé*. George Bretherton's "A Carnival Christy and a Playboy for All Ages," in *Twentieth Century Literature* (1991), examines the carnival atmosphere in the Mayo pub, in which there are elements of surrealism, and where role reversal is the norm. Christy is, of course, a Christ and mock-Christ. But, according to Bretherton, because he is proclaimed messiah and king by the fools of Mayo on a wake night, when there's mischief in the air, he is also a carnival Christy, playing a carnival role. Bill Hart's "Synge's Ideas on Life and Art: Design and Theory in *Playboy of the Western World*," in *Yeats Studies* (1972), reexamines Synge's aesthetic and concludes that *Playboy* is the artistic culmination of all that has gone before. Hart shows how the playwright explains himself to himself through theory, and how the play integrates disparate segments of his artistic creed into a aesthetic whole. The three articles show progressive complexity in the playwright's art manifested in this, his greatest work.

Deirdre of the Sorrows, written for Molly Allgood, was conceived as a literary drama, an interpretation of the tragic heroine from the ancient saga. Ann Saddlemyer, in her *"Deirdre of the Sorrows*: Literature First . . . Drama Afterwards," in *The J. M. Synge Centenary Papers* (1971), sees the work as experimental, a lyric tragedy that, despite its unfinished form, has "proved once again the originality of his genius." Saddlemyer takes Synge at his word, when he says in a letter to Molly, "My next play must be quite different from the *P. Boy*. I want to do something quiet and stately and restrained and I want you to act in it." Synge had already experimented with a translation of

"The Sons of Usnach" while on Aran. In the *Deirdre* play, he was intent on refashioning the ancient saga along new lines that would somehow make it credible as a modern stage drama.

Finally, Ronald Gaskell's essay, "The Realism of J. M. Synge," in *Critical Quarterly*, completes the volume. Though written in 1963, the article sums up the playwright's dramatic legacy, and "the reality and the joy" that Synge recreates in his pages and on the stage. Gaskell offers comparisons with Ibsen, Chekhov, and Lorca, and sets Synge in a European context; he affirms essential aesthetic differences with Yeats. Gaskell also suggests that the dramas finally owe their energy to Aran fisherfolk, farmers, tramps, and tinkers, and notes that Synge, particularly through his women—Maurya, Pegeen, and Deirdre— redefines realism in drama.

If John Millington Synge has been placed in the company of the Greeks; of Shakespeare and Jonson; of Chekhov, Ibsen, and Molière; and of Yeats, Shaw, and Beckett; surely he is worthy of another critical study. These essays, taken together, are meant to provide the reader with a fuller appreciation for Synge's art, and to offer a comprehensive and useful commentary on his works. They are also meant to celebrate a playwright important to world drama.

Selected Bibliography

PRIMARY SOURCES

Synge, J. M. *Collected Works*. Edited by Robin Skelton. 4 vols. Vol. 1, *Poems*. Vol. 2, *Prose*. Edited by Alan Price. Vols. 3 and 4, *Plays*. Edited by Ann Saddlemyer. London: Oxford University Press, 1962–68.
———. *Some Letters of John M. Synge to Lady Gregory and W. B. Yeats*. Selected by Ann Saddlemyer. Dublin: Cuala Press, 1971.
———. *Letters to Molly: John M. Synge to Maire O'Neill*. Edited by Ann Saddlemyer. Cambridge, MA: Harvard University Press, 1971.
———. *The Collected Letters of John Millington Synge*. Edited by Ann Saddlemyer. 2 vols. Oxford: Clarendon, 1983–84.

SECONDARY SOURCES

Begnal, Michael H. "Deirdre of the Sorrows." In *A J. M. Synge Literary Companion*, edited by Edward A. Kopper J., 87–95. Westport, CT: Greenwood Press, 1988.
Benson, Eugene. *J. M. Synge*. London and Basingstoke: Macmillan, 1982.
Bickley, Francis. *J. M. Synge and the Irish Dramatic Movement*. London: Constable, 1912.
Bloom, Harold. Introduction to *Modern Critical Interpretations of "The Playboy of the Western World."* New York: Chelsea House, 1988.
Bourgeois, Maurice. *John Millington Synge and the Irish Theatre*. London: Constable, 1913.

Bowen, Zack R. "The Playboy of the Western World." In *A J. M. Synge Literary Companion*, edited by Edward A. Kopper, Jr., 69–86. Westport, CT: Greenwood Press, 1988.

Boyd, E. A. *Ireland's Literary Renaissance.* Dublin and London: Maunsel, 1916.

Bretherton, George. "A Carnival Christy and A Playboy for All Ages." *Twentieth Century Literature: A Scholarly and Critical Journal* 37 (Fall 1991): 322–34.

Bushrui, S. B., ed. *A Centenary Tribute to John Millington Synge, 1871–1909: Sunshine and the Moon's Delight.* New York: Barnes & Noble, 1972.

Casey, Daniel J. "An Aran Requiem: Setting in 'Riders to the Sea.'" *Antigonish Review* 9 (1972): 89–100.

———. "John Millington Synge: A Life Apart." In *A J. M. Synge Literary Companion*, edited by Edward A. Kopper, Jr., 1–13. Westport, CT: Greenwood Press, 1988.

Corkery, Daniel. *Synge and Anglo-Irish Literature: A Study.* Dublin and Cork: Cork University Press; London: Longmans, Green, 1931. New York: Russell & Russell, 1965.

Coxhead, Elizabeth. *J. M. Synge and Lady Gregory.* London: Longmans, Green, 1962.

Deane, Seamus. *Celtic Revivals: Essays in Modern Irish Literature, 1880–1980.* London and Boston: Faber and Faber, 1985. Reprint. Winston-Salem: Wake Forest University Press, 1987.

———. "Synge's Poetic Use of Language." *Mosaic* 5, no. 1 (1971): 27–36.

Donoghue, Denis. "'Too Immoral for Dublin': Synge's *The Tinker's Wedding*." *Irish Writing* 30 (1955): 56–62.

———. "Synge: 'Riders to the Sea'; A Study." *University Review* 1, no. 5 (Summer 1955): 52–58.

———. "Flowers and Timber: A Note on Synge's Poems." *Threshold* 1, no. 3 (1957): 40–47.

Ellis-Fermor, Una. *The Irish Dramatic Movement.* London: Methuen, 1930.

Fallis, Richard. "Art as Collaboration: Literary Influences on J. M. Synge." In *A J. M. Synge Literary Companion*, edited by Edward A. Kopper, Jr., 145–60. Westport, CT: Greenwood Press, 1988.

Gaskell, Ronald. "The Realism of J. M. Synge." *Critical Quarterly* 5, no. 3 (1963): 242–48.

Gerstenberger, Donna. *John Millington Synge.* Twayne's English Authors Series 12. New York: Twayne, 1964.

———. "Yeats and Synge: 'A Young Man's Ghost'." In *W. B. Yeats, 1865–1965: Centenary Essays on the Art of W. B. Yeats*, edited by D. E. S. Maxwell and S. B. Bushrui, 79–87. Ibadan: Ibadan University Press, 1965.

Greene, David H. "The Playboy and Irish Nationalism." *Journal of English and Germanic Philology* 46, no. 2 (1947): 199–204.

———. "The Tinker's Wedding, A Reevaluation." *Publications of the Modern Language Association of America* 62, no. 3 (1947): 824–27.

———. "Synge's Unfinished Deirdre." *Publications of the Modern Language Association of America* 63, no. 4 (1948): 1314–21.

———. "Synge in the West of Ireland." *Mosaic* 5, no. 1 (1971): 1–8.

Greene, David H., and Edward M. Stephens. *J. M. Synge, 1871–1909.* New York: Macmillan, 1959; New York: Collier, 1961.

Gregory, Lady. *Our Irish Theatre: A Chapter of Autobiography.* New York and London: G. P. Putnam's, 1913.

Grene, Nicholas. *Synge: A Critical Study of the Plays.* Totowa, NJ: Rowman and Littlefield; London: Macmillan, 1975.

————. "Yeats and the Re-Making of Synge." In *Tradition and Influence in Anglo-Irish Poetry*, edited by Terence Brown, 47–62. Totowa, NJ: Barnes & Noble, 1989.

Harmon, Maurice, ed. *J. M. Synge: Centenary Papers 1971.* Dublin: Dolmen, 1972.

Hart, William E. "Synge's Ideas on Life and Art: Design and Theory in *The Playboy of the Western World.*" *Yeats Studies* 2 (1972): 35–51.

Henn, T. R. *The Lonely Tower, Studies in the Poetry of W. B. Yeats*, London: Methuen, 1950.

Howe, P. P. *J. M. Synge: A Critical Study.* London: Martin Secker, 1912.

Jaffares, A. Norman. *Anglo-Irish Literature.* New York: Schocken, 1982.

Kenner, Hugh. *A Colder Eye: The Modern Irish Writers.* New York: Knopf, 1983.

Kiberd, Declan. *Synge and the Irish Language.* Totowa, NJ: Rowman and Littlefield; London: Macmillan, 1979.

Kilroy, James F. "The Playboy as Poet." *Publications of the Modern Language Association of America* 83, no. 2 (1968): 439–42.

King, Mary C. *The Drama of J. M. Synge.* Syracuse: Syracuse University Press, 1985.

————. "Synge's Use of Language." In *A J. M. Synge Literary Companion*, edited by Edward A. Kopper, Jr., 191–209. Westport, CT: Greenwood Press, 1988.

Kopper, Edward A., Jr. *John Millington Synge: A Reference Guide.* Boston: G. K. Hall, 1979.

————. *A J. M. Synge Literary Companion.* Westport, CT: Greenwood Press, 1988.

————. *Synge, A Review of the Criticism.* Modern Irish Literature Monograph Series 1. Lyndora, PA: 1990. (Privately published.)

Levitt, Paul M. *J. M. Synge: A Bibliography of Published Criticism.* New York: Barnes & Noble, 1974.

Masefield, John. *John M. Synge: A Few Personal Recollections with Biographical Notes.* New York: Macmillan, 1915.

Maxwell, D. E. S. *A Critical History of Modern Irish Drama, 1891–1980.* Cambridge: Cambridge University Press, 1984.

McCarthy, Patrick A. "Synge and the Irish Renaissance." In *A J. M. Synge Literary Companion*, edited by Edward A. Kopper, Jr., 161–71. Westport, CT: Greenwood Press, 1988.

Mercier, V. *The Irish Comic Tradition.* New York: Oxford University Press, 1962.

Mikhail, E. H. *J. M. Synge: A Bibliography of Criticism.* Totowa, NJ: Rowman and Littlefield, 1975.

Moore, George. *Hail and Farewell: A Trilogy, III: Vale.* New York: D. Appleton, 1914.

Powers, Kate. "Myth and the Journey in the Well of the Saints." *Colby Quarterly* 26 (December 1990): 231–40.

Price, Alan F. "A Consideration of Synge's 'The Shadow of the Glen.' " *Dublin Magazine* 24 (October–December 1951): 15–24.

————. *Synge and Anglo-Irish Drama.* London: Methuen, 1961.

————. "Synge's Prose Writings: A First View of the Whole." *Modern Drama* XI (December 1968): 221–26.

Roche, Anthony. "The Two Worlds of Synge's *The Well of the Saints.*" *Genre* 12 (1979): 439–50. Reprinted in *The Genres of the Irish Literary Revival*, edited by Ronald Schleifer, 27–38. Norman, OK.: Pilgrim; Dublin: Wolfhound, 1980.

Saddlemyer, Ann. "Synge to MacKenna: The Mature Years." *Massachusetts Review* V (Winter 1964): 279–96.

———. *J. M. Synge and Modern Comedy*. Dublin: Dolmen, 1967.

———. "Rabelais versus A Kempis: The Art of J. M. Synge." *Kosmos* 1 (1967): 85–96.

———. " 'Infinite Riches in a Little Room'—The Manuscripts of John Millington Synge." *Long Room* 1, no. 3 (1971): 23–31.

———. " 'Deirdre of the Sorrows' Literature First . . . Drama Afterwards." In *J. M. Synge: Centenary Papers*, edited by Maurice Harmon, 88–107. Dublin: Dolmen, 1971.

———. "Synge and the Doors of Perception." In *Place, Personality, and the Irish Writer*, edited by Andrew Carpenter, 97–120. New York: Barnes & Noble, 1977.

———. "Synge and the Nature of Woman." In *Woman in Irish Legend, Life, and Literature*, edited by S. F. Gallagher, 58–73. Gerrards Cross, Bucks: Colin Smythe; Totowa, NJ: Barnes & Noble, 1983.

———. "In Search of the Unknown Synge." In *Irish Writers and Society at Large*, edited by Masaru Sekine, 181–98. Gerrards Cross, Bucks: Colin Smythe; Totowa, N. J.: Barnes & Noble, 1985.

———. "Synge's Soundscape." *Irish University Review: A Journal of Irish Studies* 22 (Spring 1992)1: 55–68.

Skelton, Robin. "The Poetry of J. M. Synge." In *Poetry Ireland* 1 (Autumn 1962): 32–44.

———. *The Writings of J. M. Synge*. Indianapolis and New York: Bobbs-Merrill, 1971.

———. *J. M. Synge & His World*. London, Thames & Hudson, 1971.

Thornton, Weldon. "J. M. Synge." *Anglo-Irish Literature: A Review of Research*, edited by Richard J. Finneran, 315–65. New York: The Modern Language Association of America, 1976.

———. *J. M. Synge and the Western Mind*. New York: Barnes & Noble, 1979.

———. "J. M. Synge." *Recent Research on Anglo-Irish Writers: A Supplement to Anglo-Irish Literature: A Review of Research*, edited by Richard J. Finneran, 154–80. The Modern Language Association of America Reviews of Research. New York: The Modern Language Association of America, 1983.

Whitaker, Thomas R., ed. *The Playboy of the Western World: A Collection of Critical Essays*. Englewood Cliffs, NJ: Prentice-Hall, 1969.

Yeats, W. B. *Essays and Introductions*. London: Macmillan, 1961.

———. *Explorations*. Selected by Mrs. W. B. Yeats. London: Macmillan, 1962.

J. M. Synge: A Reappraisal*

David H. Greene

J. M. Synge was a strange man whose personality has always struck me as being unchangingly enigmatic. This is perhaps an unusual admission for a biographer to make. But on the basis of the information we have about him and the assumption that we are not likely to have any startling revelations in the future I have to believe that the only fully understandable Synge we are likely to get in the future will be a product of the imagination. My admission will come as no revelation to anyone who has read the Greene and Stephens biography. In the introduction to that book I quoted Synge's own conviction— "the deeds of a man's lifetime are impersonal and concrete, might have been done by anyone, while art is the expression of the abstract beauty of the person"—and then advised my reader to go to Synge's art, and not his biography, for the "abstract beauty of the person" himself.[1]

I suspect that if I had actually known Synge I would still have found him an enigma. John Masefield, one of the only two men who knew Synge well, the other being Stephen MacKenna, observed that Synge "gave one from the first the *impression* of a strange personality."[2] "I do not know what Synge thought," Masefield wrote. "I don't believe anybody knew, or thinks he knows."[3]

Very few people in Synge's life came even reasonably close to knowing him well. His mother quite clearly did not understand him, although she seems to have thought she did. Other members of his family saw only one side of this complex man. As a creative artist he was completely outside their world. None of them ever saw a play of his performed during his lifetime. Of course this fact alone is not so unusual—one thinks of the remark James Joyce made that only two people in his life, his wife and his aunt Josephine, both women of extremely modest intellectual equipment, had any understanding of what he was trying to do.

Synge was a silent man, and silence is not one of the normal forms of communication. Masefield and others confirm the fact of his reticence. To Yeats he was "meditative." Masefield, to be sure, asserted that Synge's talk to women had a lightness and charm. But Masefield believed that all men

*This essay first appeared as "J. M. Synge—A Centenary Appraisal" in *Eire-Ireland*, 6, 4 (1971), and is reprinted with permission.

talked their best to women, an assertion which might be challenged especially as far as Irishmen are concerned. The letters to women which Synge wrote do something less than overwhelm us with their lightness and charm. In fact they reveal him as very much an ordinary human being but not a particularly eloquent one. As a letter writer he is quite clearly more in Joyce's class than Yeats's.

Admittedly not many of Synge's letters to women have survived. Excluding his letters to Lady Gregory, which were not personal, the only substantial collection we have are those to Molly Allgood, whose stage name was "Maire O'Neill," published under the editorship of Professor Ann Saddlemyer.[4] The impression of Synge which appears in the letters to Molly is of a man deeply but unhappily in love with a young woman whom he seemed to have nothing in common with except the theatre. The letters do not on the whole make pleasant reading, and they give the impression that Synge believed he was writing to a child.

I talked to Molly Allgood only once, in 1939, thirty years after Synge's death and after she had been married to two other men. Naturally I found it difficult to find in her anything of what I assumed would have been the Molly of 1909. Her recollections of Synge seemed indistinct, although I was aware of the possibility that she preferred to keep them to herself. Of course none of her letters to Synge which were returned to her after his death, appear to have survived. So we have only one side of the correspondence, and it reveals an aspect of Synge which is not only unattractive but also incompatible with the complex personality of the man who wrote the plays.

The real Synge has evaded us, and even the discovery of more letters is not likely to alter this fact. One of the discoveries I made about him was the fact that none of the people to whom I talked who had known him personally— Molly and Sarah Allgood, Jack Yeats, W. G. Fay, R. I. Best—seemed able to give me any very clear impression of what he was really like. Sarah Allgood told me, for example, that she had a vivid recollection of Synge sitting in the empty Abbey Theatre watching the company rehearse and looking exactly the way he does in the pencil sketch which J. B. Yeats did of him called "Synge at Rehearsal." As useful as this observation was it was actually an endorsement of somebody else's impression. Impressions which other people gave me seemed to come more from the published record than from personal observation or knowledge. Synge's fame has now, of course, submerged the man in the legend. He has become his admirers, as W. H. Auden wrote of W. B. Yeats— "scattered among a hundred cities, and wholly given over to unfamiliar affection."

One accepts the fact of Synge's reticence. I find it difficult, however, to accept the assumption by Yeats and others that Synge was an unhealthy man, sick and in pain during much of his writing career. "And that enquiring man John Synge comes next, / That dying chose the living world for text." It was Masefield, however, who was responsible for suggesting that Synge's view of reality was abnormal because of his ill health. "His relish of the savagery," Masefield observed after hearing Synge read one of his ballads about a murder, "made me feel that he was a dying man clutching at life, and clutching most wildly at violent life, as the sick man does."[5] But the fact is that Synge was a physically powerful man, who spent much of his life outdoors, walked vast distances and was capable of riding a bicycle sixty miles in a day. He did of course suffer from asthma, though not I believe, excessively. It bothered him when he slept under a thatched roof in Kerry or on Inishmaan, but it did not interfere with his life in any other way. He was also, as we know, operated upon in December of 1897 for the removal of swollen glands in his neck, which was the first appearance of the disease which destroyed him eleven years later. Although he occasionally spoke to friends about his glands there is no indication that he did not recover fully from his operation or that he was aware of the fact that he had an incurable malignancy. Of course he was a very sick man, for the last year of his life and his writing career was over.

In the summer of 1907 there was a recurrence of the swollen glands. In August of that year Synge met Dr. Oliver St. John Gogarty on the street in Dublin and later reported in a letter to Molly that Dr. Gogarty had noticed the enlarged glands and suggested to Synge that they be removed. In 1956, forty-nine years later, Gogarty recalled the incident instantly when I spoke of it to him and told me that he had diagnosed Synge's condition on the spot as Hodgkins disease. But he also remembered that he was very careful not to mention this to Synge. Since Dr. Gogarty was a distinguished eye, ear, nose and throat specialist, even such a curbstone diagnosis is probably not so remarkable. When I asked him if he thought it likely that Synge knew what disease he had Gogarty said that he probably would not have known, that it was not a general practice at the time for a physician to tell a patient that he was not going to recover. I found Gogarty's testimony remarkable because in 1956 only Edward Stephens knew the actual cause of Synge's death. The usual explanation given in print about Synge was that he had died as a result of tuberculosis. I find it difficult therefore to believe that Synge was not a reasonably healthy man for most of his career. He was certainly not in any way prevented from living a life which called for a sound constitution, physical robustness and a state of mind which one can only describe as enviable.

If I am right about this—you are thinking—what about Synge's well known morbidity, the preoccupation with death which is characteristic of much of his work? Here I am still inclined, as I was in 1959, to credit the testimony of Edward Stephens who felt that it was a family characteristic. One of Synge's ancestors in the seventeenth century, as Stephens pointed out, was described by Ware in his account of the Irish bishops as being *vir gravis admodum et doctus*[6]—an extremely grave and learned man. There is ample evidence, according to Stephens, that the words describe a type which recurred in the Synge family through two centuries. Masefield, incidentally, used almost the identical phrase in describing Synge—"his face was dark from gravity.

Gravity filled the face and haunted it, as though the man behind were forever listening to life's case before passing judgment."[7] I am also inclined to believe that the fear of death which Synge's mother had planted in him as a child by her religious teaching, which he eventually recoiled from, provides a possible explanation for his morbidity which is more easily accepted in the age of Freud. It would be quite wrong, or at least misleading, to think that Synge's morbidity, in any case, gives us anything more than an oblique, though authentic, view of the man who wrote one of the most ebullient comedies in the modern theatre.

Where in Synge's art can one hope to catch a glimpse of the abstract beauty of his person? Playwrights, as we know, submerge themselves in the characters they create. One naturally likes to think that there is more of Synge in Christy Mahon than in Shawn Keogh but one can never be certain. All we know is that Synge created both of those gentlemen out of something in himself or his own experience. Drama is the art of externalization, and we must accept the characters as characters and not self-portraits.

Poetry, on the other hand, particularly lyric poetry, is a personal utterance. Masefield wrote that Synge's poems gave a direct impression of the man speaking—"They are so like him that to read them is to hear him."[8] But Masefield, unlike us, was fortunate enough to have heard Synge reading his poems, and naturally they *were* the man speaking directly. As Synge himself once observed when he was comparing the modern experience of reading poetry to the ancient one of hearing it, "The modern poet composes his poems with often extremely subtle and individual intonations which few of his readers ever interpret adequately."[9] Writing verse was only an occasional activity for Synge, in any event, and his verse represents only a small portion of his output. His early verse is conventional and derivative. His ballads and poems of Irish rural life are of course personal statements and one is grateful for the revelations they make. Many of them, to be sure, display a preoccupation with death and violence. But what young poet at the turn of the century was not similarly preoccupied with death—"As for living, our servants will do that for us." And the violence may reflect not so much a natural appetite as a conviction Synge had about contemporary poetry. In the preface to his poems he argued that "before verse can be human again it must learn to be brutal."

Synge's prose writings tell us a great deal about him, and sometimes quite directly. The narratives published under the title of "In the Congested Districts" were written on commission from *The Manchester Guardian* and are little more than mere reporting. For that reason Yeats wanted to exclude them from the canon of Synge's works and when he was not allowed to exclude them withdrew as editor of the works and published his introduction elsewhere. They are interesting and accurate observations about life in a poverty-stricken part of Ireland because Synge did his job like a good journalist. Almost all of the Wicklow pieces similarly appeared in various magazines and newspapers and like the *Guardian* articles attempt objectively to describe the people of the Wicklow mountains and glens. In "The Vagrants of Wicklow," however, he romanticizes the life of the tramp as he was to do in "In the Shadow of the Glen," and thus justifies an important side of his own personality. He thought of himself as a kind of vagrant and he usually signed his letters to Molly "Your Old Tramp." Synge's vagrants were a colourful feature of the Irish countryside, but whether many of them were gifted, younger sons, driven by their frustrations and creative urges to a life on the road, as Synge imagined, is a theory which obviously would not stand up under real scrutiny.

"A Landlord's Garden in County Wicklow" is almost a counterpiece to "The Vagrants of Wicklow" because it expresses sympathy for the tragedy of the landlord class. In fact Synge casts himself in the role of a combatant in the class war by expelling from the garden an invader who turns out to be a relative of the "small boy who came to the house every morning to run messages and clean the boots."[10]

The narrative entitled "In West Kerry"[11] is based upon four visits Synge made to the north and south peninsulas and to the Great Blasket. One can see how relaxed Synge was among the country people, beginning with the crowded train ride from Tralee through Kilgobbin and Anascaul to Dingle. The train is jammed with a confused mass of country people, the floor littered with sacks of flour, cases of porter, chairs rolled in straw and other household goods while a drunken young man sings songs and begs. Synge is happy to be part of it as he watches and listens to everything. Eventually he strikes up a conversation with a young woman—"one of the peculiarly refined women of Kerry, with supreme charm, whose every movement is an expression," who seems "to unite the healthiness of the country people with the greatest sensitiveness," and whose "face and neck flush with pleasure and amusement." When the train arrives in the evening at Dingle, he makes the long journey by side car over the hills to the house in Ballyferriter where he is to stay. He is delighted with the mountain scenery, and Smerwick Harbour is "a wild bay with magnificent headlands beyond it." But his landscape descriptions take on their vitality when there are people in them. Thus, the next day when he lies on the grass looking out to the Blaskets, enjoying the grayness of the atmosphere and the silence over land and sea, his enjoyment reaches its peak when he notices in the distance a procession of people crossing the olive-coloured bogs. "The sight seemed to ring me with an emotion that is partly local and patriotic, and partly a share of the desolation that is mixed everywhere with the supreme beauty of the world."

Several days later, after a walk to the top of Sybil Head, where the air is "like wine in one's teeth," he falls in with two men and sits with them under a hedge to take shelter from a sudden shower and all three of them have a wonderful conversation about "fevers and sicknesses and doctors" and traditional cures and especially about a miraculous local plant which in the old days "the women used to be giving . . . to their children till they'd be growing up seven feet maybe in height."

But his trip out to the Great Blasket is of course the high point in the narrative. The ride in the *curagh* gives him "indescribable enjoyment" and reminds him of Aran. On the Great Blasket he stays with the "king" of the island, but it is the king's daughter, his hostess, who interests him and becomes the model for Pegeen Mike. His account of the accommodations in the house of the king and the joy with which he gives it make one wonder how a morbid and unhealthy man could have volunteered for such an experience. The room in which he sleeps has two beds. The hostess balances the lit candle on the end of the bedpost, takes off her apron and hangs it over the window as a curtain, lays another apron on the earthen floor for him to stand on when he takes his shoes off. After he has retired for the night the "king," who apologises for neglecting the guest, joins him and gets into the other bed, lights up his pipe and, writes Synge, "we had a long talk about this place and America and the younger generations." The next morning he wakes up at six o'clock. He and the "king"—like bardic poets of old—salute the new day with a glass of whiskey and a pipe and a long conversation in bed before breakfast. Perhaps one can be excused at least for preferring to believe that this, and not the author of the poems, was the man who wrote *The Playboy*. The Kerry narrative is not nearly as important a work as *The Aran Islands*, but it is less self-conscious, less controlled. The author of it is no longer a lost apprentice searching for a medium. He is not only enjoying himself but willing to acknowledge it to his readers.

Although I find "In West Kerry" important because it reveals Synge in a way no other work of his does I would hasten to add that *The Aran Islands* is the essential book for anyone who attempts to understand him as a dramatist. The Aran experience was crucial. *The Aran Islands* is a less personal work than "In Kerry," even though it records the experience which transformed Synge into a writer of genius. Like the notebooks of Dostoievski or the letters of Keats it is therefore an important document.

In the introduction to *The Aran Islands*[12] Synge offers his reader a disclaimer. "I have given a direct account of my life on the islands, and of what I met with among them, inventing nothing, changing nothing that is essential." This would give the impression that he had written a travel book, to acquaint us with life in a distant and unfamiliar clime. But to take Synge's statement too literally is to oversimplify. Despite what he says, he was selective in what he chose to record or to publish. A study of the notebooks and diaries upon which the Aran book is based shows how he excluded anything which tended to make revelations about himself. Most significant in this respect are the passages in the notebooks which reveal how he felt drawn to, and was disturbed by, some of the young women. "I saw suddenly the beautiful girl I had noticed on the pier, and her face came with me all day among the rocks."[13]

The islanders were friendly to Synge, as they were and still are to everyone. They must have looked upon him as a rather harmless visitor, a Protestant gentleman from Dublin come to the islands to study Irish. Masefield supposed, from something Synge said to him, that the islanders had the impression "that he was a linguist who had committed a crime somewhere and had come to hide."[14] The islanders knew all about linguists, folklorists and antiquarians. The islands had once been visited *en masse* by members of the Royal Society of Antiquaries. Martin Coneely told Synge that he had known George Petrie and Sir William Wilde and had taught Irish to two European philologists named Finck and Pedersen—Finck published a study of the dialect of Aran in Marburg in 1899. Synge himself tells us that during one of his visits to Aran a French priest-philologist was also on the islands studying Irish. In fact the frequent visits of philological students to Aran, Synge noted, had led the islanders to conclude that linguistic studies were "the chief occupation of the outside world."

The islanders observed that in addition to learning Irish Synge also was interested in copying down the stories of the *shanachie*. He was therefore a folklorist like Jeremiah Curtin who had also visited Aran. But they did not suspect that Synge's real purpose was neither to learn Irish nor to record folktales or that they would provide the inspiration and the medium for his plays. They certainly never became aware of the fact that he was more interested in their English than their Irish.

Although *The Aran Islands* is organized simply into four parts, each part corresponding to one of the four visits Synge made to the islands between 1898 and 1901 and the narrative follows a straightforward chronological plan, it is nevertheless managed so as to achieve a dramatic effect in places. Consider for example the ending of Part III. The boat leaves Kilronan after 4 p.m., having discharged a very large cargo. It is dark when she docks in Galway. The only man Synge can find to carry his baggage is drunk and complains goodnaturedly about the weight of the bag—"It's real heavy she is your honour. I am thinking it's gold there will be in it." At midnight the train leaves for Dublin. It is the evening of the celebration honouring the eighth anniversary of the death of Parnell and the train is crowded with intoxicated people, all going to Dublin to participate in the commemoration. A young girl who sits beside Synge finally loses her shyness and they strike up a conversation while he points out the sights to her through the grey of early dawn. "This presence at my side contrasted curiously with the brutality that shook the barrier behind us. The whole spirit of the west of Ireland, with its strange wildness and reserve, seemed moving in this single train to pay a last homage to the dead statesman of the east."

Synge's train moves between two worlds—the west with its wildness and reserve and the east, paralyzed by the downfall of its leader, the vital past and the prostrated present. One is reminded of Frank O'Connor's story "In the Train." O'Connor's trainload of country people returning to their village from a murder trial in Cork City are also passing between two worlds, one urban and one rural, each with its values, each incomprehensible to the other. One is also reminded of James Joyce's masterpiece "The Dead," in which the west, epitomized in the image of the "dark mutinous Shannon waves," is expected to revitalize and inspire the living dead of a paralyzed Dublin.

One observation which should be made about *The Aran Islands* is that it tells us where Synge got the dialect which became his hallmark. The first audiences to hear it believed it to be entirely synthetic, a language which no one in Ireland spoke, and that impression has to a certain extent persisted until today. William G. Fay, the first stagemanager of the Abbey Theatre, who directed and acted in Synge's plays, wrote of Synge's language, "The dialect used was entirely strange to us, which was hardly surprising seeing that Synge had invented it himself . . . I was quite at home with the traditional 'stage Irish' of the 'Arrah' and 'begob' and 'bedad' school as well as the stage Irish of O'Keeffe, Boucicault and Whitbread . . . it was all the more disconcerting for me to encounter an Irish dialect that I could not speak 'trippingly on the tongue.' "[15] It need hardly be observed that the stage dialect Fay *was* familiar with was as phoney as anything Synge might have invented.

The actual fact, I prefer to believe, is that the dialect of Synge's plays was a real language, actually spoken by people whose primary language was Irish and whose exposure to normal English was extremely limited. It was in fact the English spoken until the end of the nineteenth century by the people of Inishmaan, who had learned it in the Cromwellian period. Evidence of Cromwellian influence on Aran still exists in the remains of Arkin Castle on Inishmore and in the presence of Cromwellian names on the islands. In fact my friend, James Goulden, tells me that there is no evidence that the Cromwellian garrison on Inishmore was ever recalled. It would probably be as impossible now to determine how English was spoken on Irishmaan seventy years ago as it would be to determine how English was spoken in Shakespeare's day. But a theory which enjoys some acceptance among Shakespearean scholars today is that Elizabethan usage and pronunciation survived in the west of Ireland until comparatively modern times.[16]

It is obvious. I think, that as the flood of English-speaking visitors to Aran increased in the twentieth century and as island life changed after 1922, spoken English yielded rapidly to modern influences. My own impression is that Inishmaan people today, to the extent that they speak English at all, use an idiom which is common to the west of Ireland. But in 1898 this was not the case. As Synge observed within a few hours of his landing at Kilronan, the people spoke English "with a slight foreign intonation that differed a great deal from the brogue of Galway." Synge was if anything a sensitive observer, especially of language. He was surprised, he tells us, at discovering how many people in Kilronan spoke English with "abundance and fluency" and that Irish "seemed to be falling out of use among the younger people of the village." In the neighbouring village of Killeany, however, the linguistic picture was drastically different—"English was imperfectly understood." Some men he talked to were uncertain about what the word *tree* meant. After a hurried consultation in Irish they asked if it meant the same as *bush*. Considering the treeless landscape of Inishmore one would have to concede that this example is something less than conclusive.

On Inishmaan Synge discovered that considerably less English was spoken. His hostess, old Mrs. McDonough, had no English at all. Young Martin McDonough—the Michael of the published narrative—was the only member of the family who could read or write English. The women, Synge suspected, had learned some English in school but since they had had no occasion to speak with anyone who was not a native of the islands they used English only when speaking "to the pigs or to the dogs." The children, Synge observed, were taught some English in school but outside the schoolroom spoke only Irish. The men of Inishmaan, however, were all bilingual and most of them were surprisingly fluent. They used Gaelic idioms continually, however, and when their English vocabulary failed them they used "ingenious devices to express their meaning." Furthermore he noticed that foreign languages were a favourite topic of conversation and that the men had "a fair notion of what it means to speak and think in many different idioms." In fact it was their ability to handle two languages so well which led him to admire their self-sufficiency and the variety of their skills. "Each man can speak two languages. He is a skilled fisherman, and can manage a *curagh* with extraordinary nerve and dexterity. He can farm simply, burn kelp, cut out pampooties, mend nets, build and thatch a house, and make a cradle or a coffin."

Twenty-five letters which islanders wrote to Synge survive among his papers. Some of them are in Irish. Five of them, with changes and deletions by Synge, were used in the book. Fifteen are from Martin McDonough, ten from other correspondents including two young girls. But the differences between oral English and the written language of a people unaccustomed to writing a great deal would be substantial. Synge's correspondents, for example, greeted him with such salutations as "John Loyal Friend," or "Old Loyal Friend," or "Old Friend John," or "Friend of My Heart," or "Dear Loyal Sir"—which are Irish vernacular forms of address. Despite the fact that the letters are stilted and self-conscious Synge nevertheless found nuggets to mine. Thus the closing words of Pegeen Mike's letter to "Mister Sheamus Mulroy, Wine and Spirit Dealer, Castlebar," echo a phrase in a letter from Inishere— "Hoping you are quite well and enjoying your music, wishing you the best compliments of this season, from your little friend, Barbara Coneely."[17] Maurya's great speech in "Riders to the Sea" similarly echoes a passage from a letter in which Martin McDonough mediates on the tragic death of his brother's young wife. "Ann was visiting the last Sunday in December, and now isn't it a sad story to tell? But at the same time we have to be satisfied because a person cannot live always."[18]

The reality that Synge's language was neither exotic nor synthetic but based literally and directly upon English as he had heard it spoken on Inishmaan is, fortunately, substantiated by Synge himself in a letter he wrote to a correspondent named Spencer Brodney in 1907. "I look upon The Aran Islands as my first serious piece of work—it was written before any of my plays. In writing out the talk of the people and their stories in this book, and in a certain number of articles on the Wicklow peasantry which I have not collected, I learned to write the peasant dialect which I use in my plays."[19] Of course the language of literature is always to a certain extent synthetic. Imagine what the real Molly Bloom would have sounded like without that avalanche of poetry in her famous monologue. The chief reason why Synge's dialect mystified W. G. Fay and Synge's audiences of the time was the fact that obviously very few of them had ever heard English spoken the way it was in Aran. Because of the isolation of the islands—Synge comments on the fact that steamer service to Aran was only a recent innovation—there is reason to believe that the English spoken by the islanders would indeed have sounded strange to urban Irishmen. In 1898 Synge was witnessing, before it disappeared for good, a linguistic survival from the seventeenth century.

Nobody with the linguistic training necessary has yet to my knowledge made a definitive study of the language of Synge's plays. A. G. Van Hamel, a philologist of reputation, in 1912 published the results of a modest study he had made of Anglo-Irish syntax in *Englische Studien*.[20] He categorized Synge's language as "a very realistic and vigorous western Anglo-Irish." We need to know first what relationship Synge's idiom bears to Irish. We need to know something about the English spoken around the turn of the century on Aran or in other parts of the *Gaeltacht* where there is a clear record of Cromwellian influence as there is on Aran. Possibly enough letters written at the time to relatives in my native city of Boston, Massachusetts, where so many Aran people live, could be assembled so as to provide more of the kind of evidence which exists in the letters of Synge's friends on Inishmaan.

For the present at least I would like to contend that Synge's landing on Inishmaan in 1898 was the making of him. If it had been only a question of his immersing himself in Irish rural life before he discovered his latent talent, it would have happened without his going to Aran at all. He knew the countrypeople of Wicklow long before he discovered the west of Ireland. His family had its roots in Wicklow. He had spent his summers in Wicklow, and as a young man had walked over every foot of it. But the Wicklow man was a monoglot English speaker, and the Wicklow experience, though it made its contribution as Synge acknowledged in his letter to Brodney, was not crucial.

One of the persistent questions which the facts of Synge's life impel is how could the man who wrote those pedestrian book reviews, those early poems derived from all that is conventional in the poetry of Wordsworth and the English romantics, that very bad play "The Moon Has Set" and those morbid—the word is Synge's—fragmentary abortions "Etude Morbide" and "Vita Vecchia" be the man who wrote the best one-act play in the English language and the incomparable *Playboy*? The fact that most of these effusions were unfinished indicates how clearly Synge saw that he was on the wrong track altogether. Except for one short speech of the mad woman in "The Moon Has Set," where is there any foretaste of the torrent of language which bubbled below the surface until it surfaced on Inishmaan?

There is no record of what the islanders thought of Synge's book about them when it was published in 1907. One can assume, I think, that they were not pleased by it. Significantly Synge did not return to Aran after it was published. Despite his attempts to avoid giving offence and his tactful editing of the letters which he published it is not likely that they enjoyed seeing even a sympathetic account of their daily lives given to the world as though they were a subject of curiosity. Synge however published a portion of his narrative, under the heading "The Last Fortress of the Celt," in the New York *Gael* in 1901, and the consequences of this we learn about from a letter Synge's mother wrote to her son Samuel. It seems that the long arm of Aran intelligence reaches far. Some expatriate Aran man in New York saw Synge's article in the *Gael*, recognized Martin McDonough's letter which Synge had reproduced, and sent it to Martin who was deeply offended. Whether he communicated his anger in a letter to Synge or not we do not know—this is one letter Synge might have been careful not to preserve—but Synge received the message loud and clear and told his mother he would not return to the islands. "I am very thankful," Mrs. Synge writes, "John heard of it before he went to the islands, as it might have been very unpleasant to have found himself among an angry set of islanders quite at their mercy."[21] Whatever Synge's apprehensions were, he went back to Inishmaan nevertheless and patched up his friendship with Martin McDonough.

Since Synge's time many other people who have written about Aran have learned that the islanders have their agents in all the principal cities of the English-speaking world. If they were angry about Synge in 1907 they are now at least willing to accept him as an attractive legend. Visitors to Inishmaan are shown "Synge's chair," a pile of rocks on a cliff overlooking the ocean, and when this isn't enough to satisfy one's interest other fictions can be produced. Island life has changed so much since 1898, with calor gas, automobiles on Inishmore and most recently regular airplane service during the winter as well as the summer months, that the Aran islander of today would be the last person to know if Synge's account of life there seventy years ago was accurate or not. Obviously what has to be said, at least by me, is that Synge's account of what he saw so clearly and described so factually has the ring of truth about it.

Synge's interest was in people, the way they lived and talked and looked at life. There are many things he saw but did not bother to describe because they were not significant in his view. He has almost nothing to say about the spectacular stone ring-forts on Aran or even the remarkable collection of early Christian remains. He probably noticed that the people themselves took them for granted and paid little attention to them. He seems also to have been unaware of the fact that the islanders were all Roman Catholics and that their religion must have had an influence upon their attitudes. I find it hard to believe that this can be attributed to his obtuseness. How could anyone, much less a member of the Ascendency, be unaware of a fundamental fact of class in Ireland? Quite clearly it was his judgement that religion, which the people probably wore like a glove since it was so much a matter of habit, was not really as significant a fact in understanding them as most people would have believed. And Synge was not like most people. He was a great dramatist, which means that he understood human beings.

In discussing Synge's achievement I have talked not at all about his plays, which are his real achievement, but about the man himself and how he suddenly and miraculously discovered his capabilities when he went to Aran. One reason why I have not had anything to say about his plays is that some of my colleagues will have a good deal to say about them. But I would like to conclude what I hope has been a tribute to a great dramatist by making one observation about his influence as a dramatist. The usual theory among historians of the Irish dramatic movement is that Synge was viewed by his contemporaries as a realist and that his influence impelled the dramatic movement away from the direction Yeats had charted for it towards realism. Thus it was Synge and not Yeats who was responsible for Lennox Robinson, Brinsley MacNamara, Sean O'Casey, Paul Vincent Carroll and Brendan Behan. Yeats and Lady Gregory talked about the folk, and yet the Abbey Theatre produced only one folk dramatist—George Fitzmaurice—whom it then proceeded to ignore. Earlier critics claimed that Fitzmaurice was a disciple of Synge, but it would have been more accurate to have described him as a casualty of Synge's influence. After Synge, it seemed, realism counted.

Synge, of course, wrote one play—"In the Shadow of the Glen"—which romanticized an authentic folktale. But the audience were unable to recognise the fact that the play *was* based on a folktale and insisted upon seeing it as a realistic treatment of loveless marriage among the country people. No wonder Synge was puzzled by the violent reaction his work received. His unfortunate statement in the preface to The Playboy about lying with his ear to a crack in the floor listening to the servant girls talking in the kitchen of a County Wicklow house and his defense of the authenticity of the language of that play not only made things worse but diverted attention from his real purpose. Synge, as we know now, was not a realist. His vision was unique, personal, poetic, romantic. His view of Irish rural life was, in its own way, just as romantic as Yeats's. Yeats wrote nonsense about the peasant being the key to the collective unconscious of the race. Synge indulged in no such fantasies, but he nevertheless tended to idealize Irish rural life. He could, for example, convince himself that tramps were all artists or that when he listened to Pat Dirane reciting an ancient Gaelic poem he could hear the intonation of the original voice of the ancient poet. These are of course more acceptable myths, but myths nevertheless. And one is reminded of Yeats's reply to a questioner in New Haven, Connecticut, who asked him at his lecture why he read his verses in a sing-song manner. "Because that is the way Homer read his verses," the poet is reported to have replied. "But how do you know, Mr. Yeats, in what way Homer read his verses?" Yeats replied, "Because the merit of the man justifies the assumption."

Synge's influence encouraged Irish dramatists who followed him to look closely at the realities of Irish life, urban as well as rural, and to use the poetic resources of the language to the full. It is this particular characteristic which has made—and continues to make—the work of Irish dramatists unique in the modern theatre. And that fact above all others is what impels us to honour Synge's memory on this, the one-hundredth anniversary of his birth.

Notes

1.   David H. Greene and Edward M. Stephens, *J. M. Synge, 1871–1909*, New York, The Macmillan Company, 1959, p. X.

2.   John Masefield, *John M. Synge: A Few Personal Recollections With Biographical Notes*, Letchworth, Garden City Press Ltd., 1916, p. 6.

3.   *Ibid.*, p. 14.

4.   *Letters to Molly: John Millington Synge to Maire O'Neill, 1906–1909*, London, Oxford University Press, 1971.

5.   *Ibid.*, p. 22.

6.   Greene and Stephens, p. 70.

7.   Masefield, p. 6.

8.   *Ibid.*, p. 24.

9.   Unpublished manuscript in the possession of the Synge estate. See Greene and Stephens, p. 84.

10.   J. M. Synge, *Collected Works, II, Prose*, ed. Alan Price, London, Oxford University Press, 1966, p. 233.

11.   *Ibid.*, p. 237ff.

12.   *Ibid.*, p. 47ff.

13.   *Ibid.*, p. 54, fn. 1.

14.   Masefield, p. 29.

15.   W. G. Fay and Catherine Carswell, *The Fays of the Abbey Theatre*, New York, p. 137.

16.   In his review of Lady Gregory's *Cuchulainn of Muirthemne* in *The Speaker*, June 7, 1902, Synge observed that "The peasants of the west of Ireland speak an almost Elizabethan dialect . . ." *Collected Works*, II, 367.

17.   Greene and Stephens, p. 103.

18.   *Ibid.*, p. 105.

19.   *Collected Works*, II, 47, fn 1.

20.   XLV, 274.

21.   Greene and Stephens, p. 118.

Synge's Poetic Use of Language*

SEAMUS DEANE

I would call attention at once to my title. My subject is NOT Synge's use of poetic language but his poetic use of language. The difference is important. One consistent feature of the Romantic revival in literature, in all its phases, has been its assertion of the inescapably subjective nature of language itself; and through that, the inescapable relation between language and truth which the scientific tradition had denied. As Roland Barthes has said, "No language is innocent." In the late nineteenth century Mallarmé said something similar when he announced that "A poem is written with words." Synge said much the same thing in his preface to *The Playboy of the Western World*. His concentration from the beginning is on "speech" which "should be as fully flavoured as a nut or apple." To appreciate Synge, therefore, we should learn to take his words on their own terms—as linguistic structures each of which has as its object, not its content, but its own form. I adopt that last phrase from Roman Jakobson, a man devoted to the explanation of the links between oral and literary tradition. There is no need to labour the relevance of his remark to Synge's work.

So, we experience the work of Synge as language, not as a system of ideas or as a collection of themes. It is helpful to note straightaway that Synge's language assumes a revolutionary stance towards European culture. He describes this very clearly in the *Playboy* preface. On the one hand, we have language as joy and richness; on the other, we have language dealing with the reality of life in joyless and pallid words. Here is a basic opposition. Synge regards as dehydrating the notion that language is a medium for the transmission rather than as the incarnation of experience—the word made flesh. If we are to understand his language we must recognise this underlying tension, and recognise further how that tension creates a number of subsidiary binary oppositions which ramify throughout his work. We read the language by identifying the recurrent signs of opposition and, in doing so, we experience the conflict between them. Experience and language in a state of fission are transmuted by his effort into a state of fusion.

Ireland was particularly important to Synge because it retained the faith linguistically. In its oral Gaelic traditions it had preserved that joy in words

*This essay first appeared in *Mosaic*, 5, 1 (1971), and is reprinted with permission.

which Europe seemed to him to have very largely lost. He perceived, with Yeats' help, what Marshall McLuhan has since chartered as a tenet of twentieth-century literature; that "only people from backward oral areas had any resonance to inject into the language—the Yeatses, the Synges, the Joyces, Faulkners and Dylan Thomases." Synge recognized this; but he also recognized that a place like the Aran Islands epitomised the conflict between a native language of riches and joy, and a cosmopolitan language of pallid joylessness— one fading, the other encroaching. His work is an assertion of the vitality, not of the Gaelic language as such or any Anglo-Gaelic hybrid, but of the attitude towards the connexion between language and truth which Gaelic incorporated.

This brings us to the problem of the folk (or folksy) element in Synge's language. I think it pointless to argue about the presence or absence, the vulgarisation or the transcriptive accuracy, in Synge's English of the Gaelic idioms and indeed of the Gaelic tales which he heard from the people among whom he lived. Folklore, committed to paper, is radically transformed, even if it is written down by a collector. The oral ceases, the written begins. The new context changes the function of the words. How much more deeply, then, is it transformed when an artist like Synge deploys it for his own particular purposes?—especially when we remember that those purposes were revolutionary? He was going against the grain of his time. Pushkin had done something similar with Russian folk-tales and idioms. Again, to quote Roman Jakobson: "A writer may create in opposition to his milieu, but in folklore such an intention is inconceivable." Synge's language is not state-Irish; it is Irish language staged for polemical purposes which his Dublin audience totally misunderstood. The speech of the Irish peasants gave Synge a linguistic model for which he had been vainly searching in Paris, a model adaptable by virtue of its range and power to his own urgent sense of life. This model language was poetic in the sense already spoken of; it was Synge's achievement to use it for his own purposes by exploiting its own nature.

He used it, but he did not abuse it. For the joy implicit in that language was to him a sacred joy just as Ireland became to him a sacred place. At one point in his *Autobiography*, speaking of his teenage loss of faith in Christianity, he says: "Soon after I had relinquished the Kingdom of God I began to take a real interest in the kingdom of Ireland. My politics went round from a vigorous and unreasoning loyalty to a temperate Nationalism. Everything Irish became scared . . ." A glance at the page from which this quotation comes reveals a whole series of references which indicate the emergence of a personal language that was to find its social home in the language of the Irish peasantry. In a short space we have the following sequence of words: radiance, beauty, intangible glory, transfigured, pilgrim, divine ecstasy, puberty, primitive people, adoration, divinity, kingdom, God, Ireland, sacred, human, divine, goddess. Synge's personal language is innovatory, and his search was for a public language with which it could fuse. Ferdinand de Saussure, the founder of the modern school of linguistics, speaks of this phenomenon in other terms; their relevance to Synge's case is striking. De Saussure spoke of this innovatory, private idiom as *la parole*, the public institutionalised language as *la langue* and the two together as forming *le language*. Synge's language can thus be understood as a merging of his own idiom of erotic joy and pagan ecstasy with the Gaelic tongue's long-learned capacity to embody such experiences.

It may perhaps already be clear how this intermarriage between the artist and his chosen society was going to produce a language tensed by oppositions. We have already noticed the opposition between joy and joylessness which Synge detailed; we can also see how the opposition breeds others. Anyone who reads *The Aran Islands* will quickly become aware of Synge's emphasis on the pagan quality of the people as it is expressed in sexual candour, stoicism or in a nude and terrifying grief at the fact of death—all of these impressions reinforced by the antiquity of their stories, their rudimentary way of life, the exposure of the human to the natural forces of land and sea. This paganism has of course been overlaid by Christianity. So, we have pagan energy expressing itself in a Christian idiom: the language of the peasants, redolent of the language of the great myths which a man like Pat Dirane relays to them, is braided in with the language of Christianity, producing a colorful combination in which, for example, pagan Irish idioms of respect for royalty, nobility and fame blend in with Catholic idioms of respect for sainthood, the Papacy and salvation. The language, in its richness, expresses a tension between two traditions; and again one can see how this public tension was characteristic of Synge's own private experiences. In the *Autobiography*, he describes how, at the age of ten, he wandered in the woods at Rathfarnham with his first girl friend after hearing of the death of an aunt:

> The sense of death seems to have been only strong enough to evoke the full luxury of the woods. I had never been so happy. It is a feeling like this makes all primitive people inclined to merry making at a funeral.

> We were always primitive. We both understood all the facts of life and spoke of them without much hesitation but (with) a certain propriety that was decidedly wholesome. We talked of sexual matters with an indifferent and sometimes amused frankness that was identical with the attitude of folk tales. We were both superstitious, and if we had been allowed . . . we would have evolved a pantheistic scheme like that of all barbarians . . . The monotheistic doctrine seems foreign to the real genius of childhood in spite of the rather maudlin appeal Christianity makes to little children. . . .

If we remember those two major oppositions in Synge's language, joy and joylessness, paganism and Christianity, we can find them suddenly crystallising in those of his poems which manage to avoid a wan derivative tone typical of the aesthete tradition to which most of them belong. Take, for instance, the poem editorially titled "Abroad":

> Some go to game, or pray in Rome
> I travel for my turning home.
>
> For when I've been six months abroad
> Faith your kiss would brighten God!

This was written in 1908 and may, as Robin Skelton says, be a deliberate variation upon a Gaelic original which Frank O'Connor has translated thus:

> To go to Rome
> Is little profit, endless pain;
> The master that you seek in Rome
> You find at home, or seek in vain.

Note that Synge has only retained the opposition between the rhymes Rome and home; otherwise his poem turns on a different axis. There is the opposition between "Some" and "I"; the opposition between "game" and "pray," the different associations of these words linked by the similarity of their central vowel sounds; the opposition between simple "go" and the more purposive "travel," one which is extended to the prepositions "to," "in" and "for" which are controlled by these verbs. "For" emphasises the purposiveness of the movement of "travel;" it arouses a wider expectation which the final lines fulfill. The crossed rhymes obviously confirm the oppositions—Rome / God, home / abroad; Rome is abroad, home is with God. But God is naturally associated with Rome; so "God" is a religious term that has to be converted to the poem's secular purpose: this is done by the kiss (phonally anticipated in the precision of "six") given the returned lover who uses the word God as a condescending metonymy for the world abroad, the world of Rome which he repudiates for the kiss. The condescension is amused: the word "Faith" stands at the poem's heart, a pun embracing the secular and the sacred together. The poem is, then, a series of verbal pirouettes, some sexual and consonantal, some sacred and open vowelled. Taken together they form a total choreographic figure. That figure is the poem. We know it by its oppositions and balances.

The notion of God, the divine, brightened by the human, is one which Christy Mahon exploits in his courtship of Pegeen Mike. Synge has it in another poem, "Dread," written between 1906 and 1908, in which the final line runs "The Lord God's jealous of yourself and me." And in the early sequence *Vita Vecchia*, written in 1896 and revised in 1907, we have the four-line poem "In Dream":

> Again, again, I sinful see
> Thy face, as men who weep
> Doomed by eternal hell's decree
> Might meet their Christ in sleep.

This once more is a love-poem, or a poem of lost love in which the religious idiom is converted to secular purposes. The phonal basis of the poem is simple and effective; we have the homophonous words "see, weep, decree, meet, sleep"; the soft alliteration of "sinful see," "who weep," harder alliterations of "might meet," "doomed . . . decree" all creating a pattern which is suddenly entranced into unexpected shape by the voiced sibilant "Christ." The balance between opposites like "I" and "thy face," "men" and "their Christ," is struck suddenly so that the dream's private whisper couched in the first and second person singular is suddenly amplified into the poem's public language couched in the third person plural. So the dream of the beloved, lost love and the moment of sleep are transposed to the public idiom of the beatific vision, hell, and death. All are harmonised by the simile which poses an opposition between an "I" and "men," and then resolves it. In the other poem "Abroad," "I," and "some" had the same function.

Even in poems as short as these we can see that Synge is fond of retarding the experience by sponsoring its opposite and then converting that opposite into a culmination. If we remember this principle of retardation as a governing device in his language then a great deal of its inversions and figurative delays can be understood as something more than stage-Irishry or untrained exuberance. When we turn to the plays the oppositions already noticed are heard in a more fully orchestrated language, written, as the dramatic form demands, for many voices, but audible in one dominant key.

Synge's poetic use of language depends for its effects, particularly in his plays, upon a system of verbal oppositions which recur periodically throughout a text. These oppositions are to be found rooted in certain base words or morphemes which then breed derivatives or allomorphs. In *The Playboy of the Western World*, for instance, the two basic words which form one part of the pattern of opposition are "lone" and "fear," and all their allomorphs. The word "lonesome" occurs as often as 25 times in the course of the play; "fear," "fearing," "afeard" and "fearless" occur almost as often, and almost always in the company of an only slightly less important morpheme "dark" or its allomorph "darkness" or its cousin "night." The orchestrations on these basic words are founded upon a natural connexion—lonesome-fear-dark-night. The orchestration can be understood as a series of variations upon a basic sentence pattern or what in transformational grammar is known as a kernel. That basic pattern in Synge is a noun phrase plus a verb phrase plus a participial modifier. Shawn Keogh gives an early and simple example when he says: "It was a dark lonesome place to be hearing the like of him." Pegeen gives an orchestrated version or, in the modern grammarian's term, a transform of the basic pattern when she says: "If I am a queer daughter, it's a queer father'd be leaving me lonesome these twelve hours of dark, and I piling turf with the dogs barking and the calves mooing, and my own teeth rattling with fear." The basic pattern is contained in the phrase "it's a queer father'd be leaving me lonesome"; the transformation on that pattern is achieved by the four participial modifier clauses which bring us from one base word "lonesome" to another "fear." We do not therefore simply have an idiom, a characteristic kind of language in Synge; we have a characteristic structure of language in Synge. Further, we can notice the strength of the participial clauses because the main verb is so often a variant of the verb "to be." The frequency with which Synge begins a sentence with a phrase like "It is," "It's," "It is not," "It's I," "It is not I," or "That is," "There is" lends to his language a certain ritual or, in Alan Price's word, "liturgical" quality. Each statement which begins in this assertive manner is invested with the grandeur of conviction, a conviction which is either amplified or modified by the inevitable participial clauses which follow. The conviction of the statement is extended by its being launched into a context which gives that conviction a continuity, a pathos and a landscape in which it can operate. To be lonesome is to hear the dogs barking, the cows mooing, etc. while one is piling turf. The word takes flesh, the morpheme begins to reverberate in a syntax carefully construed to give full acoustic effect.

Yet in the *Playboy*, I have so far only given one part of the dual pattern it possesses. The morphemes "lone" and "fear" which are cast in those sentence structures I have just tried to describe, are opposed throughout the drama by the morphemes "decent" and "saint." Each of these has its own genealogy; "Christian" and "sacred" are the first cousins and the connection expands from them to include God, Pope, Cardinals, Bishops, Father Reilly, Justices of the Peace, peelers, police. We have, in other words, a social idiom set against an idiom of loneliness. Yet the oppositions stated initially in this form do not remain static. As the play progresses we begin to see the opposition resolved; and then after an intermediate resolution branch out again, but now with a renewed power and a different meaning. I am arguing therefore that it is precisely through the opposition between the basic morphemic units of the play that they each, in the end, suffer a semantic change. The change comes about in this way.

Lonesomeness and decency are not, as far as Christy Mahon is concerned, necessarily opposites. Decency indeed is what the lonesome man craves. Shawn Keogh and Christy, the two orphans in the play (even if they are orphans in different senses) have this much in common; they want to get married, settle down and be acknowledged in the social world. They want to leave the dark of anonymity and come into the light, even if only the turf-light, of identity and respectability. This is the turning point of the play. In what way do their respective notions of decency differ? Pegeen has, of course, from the beginning made that difference plain. At an early point in the play she compares Shawn Keogh and the society generally to the great heros there used to be in the past. Christy appears to her, and more belatedly to himself, to be their reincarnation: ". . . and I a proven hero in the end of all." Or again, this time to Pegeen, ". . . you're setting me now to think if it's a poor thing to be lonesome, it's worse maybe to go mixing with the fools of earth." Here lonesomeness rejects decency and respectability. The opposition which had appeared to be offering one as the alternative to the other is repudiated completely. Christy is at first involved in and finally transcends that opposition by his gift for language. And his gift for language is related to the fact that he is not an actual but a symbolic murderer. He transforms the actual into a myth. The real murderer in the play is the Widow Quin, who killed her husband. She offers herself to Christy as an alternative to Pegeen. In doing so she reveals what the decent has to offer the lonesome. As the main figure in the play's sub-plot, a witch woman who nevertheless speaks the social language of shrewd materialism as against Christy's heraldic lyricism, she represents the obverse of decency which is notoriety. And notoriety, for an actual murder, is the provincial form of fame; and fame, for a symbolic murder, which is a matter of words, is what Christy finally seeks and finds. So the progression of the play's key-terms, lonesome and decency, finally yields in the end to a semantic shift whereby the decent is identified with the anonymity which the lonesome had once known, and notoriety is rejected for the sake of fame. The contrapuntal rhythms of loneliness and decency define the village society; the speech of the villagers is caught between those two poles. The tension between them is resolved in terms of gossip and notoriety. Christy goes beyond the village sphere because he speaks a large mythic language of heroic deeds, a language which embraces the great wide vistas of the world beyond. When he first appears Michael James, Jimmy, Philly and Pegeen try to guess what terrible deed he has done; but their imaginations cannot rise to the occasion. Christy dismisses them peevishly. His imagination is already making a myth out of his action. "You'd see the like of them stories on any little paper of a Munster town." Only Christy can get beyond the stock liturgical responses of the village speech to the point where the base words "lonesome" and "decent" begin to give way to others—the others being "wonder" and "madness." Wonders belong to the great world beyond; they are associated with travel and the exotically distant. Madness belongs to the village which is divorced from that world, a world represented for it primarily by Catholicism in its hierarchical, colourful aspects: Pegeen says to Shawn: "It's a wonder Shawneen, the Holy Father'd be taking notice of the likes of you; for if I was him I wouldn't bother with this place where you'll meet none but Red Linahan, has a squint in his eye, and Patcheen, is lame in his heel, or the mad Mulrannies were driven from California and they lost in their wits. We're a queer lot these times to go troubling the Holy Father on his sacred seat." The world, envisaged as geography or history, shrinks to provincial idiocy in the impoverished village frame. Shawn Keogh, of course, is completely subjugated by the notions and the language of respectability and decency. As regards the pagan past, he can only think of Father Reilly's "small conceit" for heroes; and the Christian present centres itself in the dispensation Father Reilly is reputed to be receiving from Rome. Christy, on the other hand, subjugates the Christian idioms of respect to the purposes of his joyfully pagan love-making; despite their names he is less Christian and more pagan than Pegeen; religion is only a metaphor of human love; if he takes it literally, it is to condescend to it. We noted this same feature in Synge's poems: ". . . till I'd feel a kind of pity for the Lord God is all ages sitting lonesome in his golden chair." The base-word "lonesome" is now related, not to darkness or fear, but to splendour and condescension. Christy's next outburst has the Christian mitred bishops and holy prophets peering through the bars of paradise for a glimpse of the pagan Lady Helen of Troy. Similarly, the word "darkness" begins in the course of Christy's love-making to release itself from the binding oppositions which have trapped poor Shawn Keogh. ". . . and I abroad in the darkness spearing salmons in the Owen, or the Carrowmore." "Abroad" and the sonority of the exotic place names again identify Christy, as he identified himself, with a world beyond the one in which the villagers, like Pegeen, are living. Christy's language opens out in a series of geographical, liturgical and historical references to the western wordly horizons of fame. Fame is the theme which swivels on the axis formed by anonymity and notoriety. It is the language of the poem-vagrant who speaks of travelling abroad in the dews of night while Shawn Keogh speaks of staying safely at home. The play's theme is incarnate in the language. Christy's emergence from the unreal oppositions between lonesomeness and decency to the new world of wonder (which the village thinks of as madness) is the emergence of a Gaelic pagan myth hero from a Christianised, anglicised and therefore impoverished community. Lonesomeness is not finally a condition but a choice. Christy goes through a series of evolutionary mutations from the sub-human to the heroic; each stage of his evolution is marked by an intensification of language, and finally by the release of language from the oppositions which had compressed its force.

Synge is by no means extraordinary in his use of a rural or isolated community as a metaphor of vanishing value. This is an old romantic and even utopian tradition—Wordsworth and Hardy are two names that come readily to mind. Further, the Catholic idioms of Irish peasant speech, although they had their own uniqueness, were to be met with in different forms in the tradition of French literature represented in Synge's mind primarily by Baudelaire and J. K. Huysmans in particular. The literary roots of his language and preoccupations are there—in the rural nostalgia of the English romantic tradition, the Catholic decadence, so-called, of the French tradition. The roots flowered in Irish air, because the Irish oral tradition was still sufficiently alive to give Synge's language the resonance of myth.

The County Mayo village which was briefly paganized by Christy Mahon loses its myth and its joy—as Pegeen too late realizes—because it clung too slavishly to Christianity and fact. The elaboration of the language is such that we can see various triadic movements operating on a number of levels— anonymity via notoriety to fame, christianity via superstition to pagan myth, loneliness via decency to triumphal wonder, flight via stability to a chosen vagrancy. All of these facets of the play swing into view as it turns on its central linguistic axis.

This is even more clearly true of the short play *In the Shadow of the Glen*. All of Synge's dramas involve a transformation in which the infinite nature of human desire, confronted with the finite nature of reality, converts the limits of that reality to the infinity of its desire. Thus we have at the centre of the plays conversion motifs like mock-deaths, hallucinations, a miracle, a marriage; and in the tragedies the symbolic and the actual deaths fused together. Through these conversations the natural overcomes the deficiencies of the social, the human triumphs over the deficiencies of the actual. The transformation has to take place in the language itself, and there it almost always takes a triadic form. *In the Shadow of the Glen* offers us two morphemes as base words—again we have "lonesome" and its opposing word "queer," each occurring more than a dozen times in the brief text. The opposition is resolved by the intermediate term "afeard" which occurs with the same frequency. We can then read the play as showing that the queer (which may mean mad or wonderful) are the victims of a loneliness which they fear, the loneliness for lost beauty, for a lost hero like Patch D'Arcy, the loneliness of old age and of death. Again, the play transforms that fear and loneliness into an act of choice—the choice epitomised in the tramp and his chosen vagrancy; his freedom, his promise of youth and mobility being set against the solidifying force of social respectability and old age. The spinelessness of Michael Dara and the old age of Dan Burke are finally accommodated at the expense of the vital Nora and the fine-talking tramp. The basic figure of the play is the movement from heroism and myth to convention and impoverished realism. One other way of tracing this development would be to trace the interactions between the basic morphemes of the play and the multiple references to mountain ewes, sheep and mist. That interaction reveals the structure which gives the play its compact form.

Similarly, in *The Well of the Saints*, a traditional opposition between sight and vision is expressed in terms of an opposition between the word "fine" and all its many derivatives (beautiful, splendid, splendour, grand, great, nice) and the work "pitiful" with all its cognate words (wretched, poor, cold, etc.). "Fine" undergoes a semantic change as a result of this opposition. At first it refers to illusory beauty; after the conflict with the world of ugliness it refers to imaginative beauty. Again, we have the triadic rhythm; again we have the symbolic truth defined in a language which embraces and goes beyond fact. The various forms of colour symbolism which distinguish *Deirdre of the Sorrows* and *Riders to the Sea* could be similarly seen in the light of this technique of conversion through opposition.

It is obvious that Synge's drama is more truly seen as a severe critique of the defects of Irish peasant society than as a glorification of it. He found in the richness of the language of the Irish peasants an inbuilt critique of the poverty of their social conditions. He transformed the language into a code, elaborate in its complication, simple in its principle. The code was deeply indebted to the oral tradition from which it emerged. But it differed from it in that the code took the image of an heroic language living in an impoverished environment as its basic metaphor of heroic human vitality fading under the pressure of institutional forces. But it was a metaphor of decay which he transformed into an assertion of vitality. Synge's linguistic code finally highlights in dramatic terms the myth of heroism which impregnated the language of the peasantry. He radically transformed the oral tradition and simultaneously transformed the modern tradition of the Ibsenite-Shavian problem play. In the Preface to *The Tinker's Wedding*, he said "The drama, like the symphony, does not teach or prove anything." The simile is apt. His drama incarnates its meaning in its language and like the symphony that language can be understood in terms of various devices of composition. My concern here has been to show what some of those devices are and how they operate as linguistic structures.

Synge's Prose Writings:
A First View of the Whole*

ALAN PRICE

The publication recently of the Oxford University Press definitive edition of *J. M. Synge: Collected Works, Volume II, Prose* enables the non-dramatic writings of Synge to be seen as a whole for the first time. The sight is impressive and should further increase his standing which has been steadily going up since the publication of the official biography by David H. Greene and Edward M. Stephens in 1959.

It shows that like Wordsworth, whom he admired and in some ways resembled, Synge the man brooded upon the experiences of his childhood and adolescence, and from this produced autobiographical studies which not only throw singular light on the artist and his work but also provide rare insight into human growth generally. The impulses and fears of a child in an exclusive community, the opening excitements and compensations given by birds and natural scenery, the yearnings and frustrations of passionate adolescence cramped in an obsolete code, are exactly registered by Synge. He apprehended what is valid in the recapitulation theory, the links between the child and primitive man, long before his visits to the Aran Islands, and in his awareness of the interaction between sex and religion, art, and nature, and of the ways in which dedications to the latter three may be expressions or sublimations of sex he foreshadowed Freud. His grasp is further seen in his stress on the value of being part of a community that has not lost touch with the rhythms of nature and traditional crafts and that is not so fragmented as to give insufficient scope for the several-sided development of an individual. In this, and in his dismay at stereotypes and abstractions and at the coarsening and debilitating effects of commercialism, Synge has kinship with Yeats and D. H. Lawrence. Again, Synge's documentation of his growth from a rather precious art-for-art's-sake romanticism to a more realistic vision, mingling compassion and irony—the progress from the simple lyric to comprehensive drama—is typical of the evolution not only of Yeats and Joyce but of many ordinary people. The experiments and investigations of modern psychology and sociology have

*This essay first appeared in *Modern Drama* 11 (December 1968) and is reprinted with permission of *Modern Drama*.

established and gone beyond Synge's intuitions, but these remain valuable since they exist not in clinical generalizations but in terms of individuals in particular localities and in a medium that carries truth alive into the heart by passion.

The advantages and disadvantages of Synge's position can now be seen. In some ways he was well placed to write about Ireland. His roots in an influential family, his education, his cultivated acquaintances, and his travels gave him a range of experience and standards of judgment beyond the provincial, while his wise passiveness, his extraordinary capacity for establishing relationships with different people led him to the heart of uniquely valuable but doomed folk cultures. He attained the right point for creativity: involved enough to feel Irish life profoundly yet sufficiently detached and skilled to crystallize it in literature of concern to people both inside and outside Ireland. Like the Tramp in *The Shadow of the Glen* he appeared and spoke at the crucial time. And the idealized image of the Tramp is noteworthy in Synge. His letters to Molly Allgood he signed "Your Old Tramp," and he saw resemblances between the position of the gifted person in peasant society and that of the artist in bourgeois society. But whereas the peasants (who had "chosen infinite riches in a little room") tolerated if not welcomed the Tramp (who had "chosen penury with a world for habitation") thus enabling him to become a creative outsider, the bourgeois scorned the artist. This was the disadvantage of Synge's position. His family felt that he was wasting his substance and harming his body and soul in associating with artists and peasants and in writing. Hence Synge was driven to justify himself. And one now perceives running through all his work this salient theme—the attempt of a person who wishes to become or has become creative in an original way to demonstrate his vision and values to an indifferent or hostile audience.

The attempt is usually a failure, perhaps because of a flaw in the artist, perhaps because he has been unnaturally forced into theorizing and constructing systems and rationalizing his own work, or perhaps because the audience refuses to collaborate. Here are some examples of this theme. At the age of seven Synge, while reading his earliest poem to the company in the drawing-room of his home, broke down and felt fear for the first time. When Synge was playing his violin for Cherry Matheson he was interrupted by his young nephew, Edward Stephens, and was so disturbed that he had to rush out. At the beginning of *Vita Vecchia* the fiddler similarly trying to impress an attractive woman has nightmares foretelling failure, and in performance this occurs. In *Étude Morbide*, after practising all summer, the violinist collapses at the public concert and consequently his mistress goes mad and dies and his life is altered decisively. In *The Shadow of the Glen*, Nora's attempts to disclose her deepest hopes and fears and to justify her behavior meet with indifference from Michael and violence from Dan (though here the Tramp, significantly, offers rehabilitation), and in *The Well of the Saints* Martin encounters censure and insuperable difficulties in presenting his fresh vision to the people who patronized him when blind. In *The Playboy of the Western World* Christy is always interrupted and deflated when he is boasting of his deed, but because he has a sympathetic audience and the admiration of a handsome young woman his imagination becomes creative and he is inspired actually to become what he was only fancied to be at first, so that by the end he has realized himself and become strong enough to withstand hostility and to triumph. In *The Playboy* the spell of failure in public is finally broken. Paradoxically, however, at its first performances there was a famous breakdown in communication, and Synge, distraught, was led to deny his achievement and to say it was merely an extravaganza. For a space it seemed that the refusal of a clamant part of the audience to contemplate Synge's vision of Irish life had produced his most serious public collapse, but aided by Yeats and the Abbey company he recovered and demonstrated that the play is true and serious.

The importance to Synge of the autobiographical element in writing becomes apparent when one studies *Étude Morbide*, which contains most of the themes of his later writings, and the *Autobiography* which shows his aims as a writer and how art may have the universality of a natural force. It is only when a person is fulfilling his best potentialities that his life becomes really significant and valuable, Synge affirms (a similar view is seen in Hopkins, "As kingfishers catch fire" and in Yeats, "Among Schoolchildren"), and Synge shows, particularly in his autobiographical writings and in an early play, *When the Moon Has Set*, not published until 1968, how formidable are the agencies thwarting this fulfillment. In life Synge rarely found it outside the Aran Islands and this is why they seemed to contain "spiritual treasure . . . every symbol of the cosmos." They became part of the harmony germinating in Synge. Believing that music is the purest art he drew analogies between the movements of a symphony and the major phases of an individual's life, and he stressed that the constant function of the artist was to draw out his peculiar harmony and to give it a living artistic shape enjoyable and meaningful to various people. Apart from this his life was of no consequence.

There are romantic elements in this belief but it hardly ever led to undue rhapsodies. A kinship with Eliot and Joyce even appears in the idea of the eventual separateness of the man who suffers and the artist who creates, and the successive drafts of Synge's prose show how unremittingly and finely he worked. Purple passages can be found, but through their context and the eager piling-up of words into elaborate rhythms a genuine though disordered feeling emerges that has force and merit of its own. Usually, however, Synge presents the precise particular that conveys reality and creates appropriate emotion. Edward Stephens records in his amazingly detailed and comprehensive typescript life of his uncle (page 1846), that when asked to explain realism Synge replied that it was a way of conveying impressions by mentioning significant details instead of attempting to describe feelings, and that, for example, the impression of a very wet day in town would be conveyed far more effectively by saying "the drops were falling one by one from the point of the policeman's helmet" than by any description of how wet the day seem to the writer.

This hold of Synge's on actuality can be noted in his literary criticism. He is practical, and by a close consideration of the words on the page he can, for example, indicate the nuances of Lady Gregory's "Kiltartan" speech or expose the shams of stock Irish sentimentality and humor. Yet this analysis of particular texts did not preclude imaginative grasp of larger issues. Synge knew well that the particular and the universal are related, and in his magnifi-cent onslaught on the Gaelic League it is the poverty of their diction, their soiling of a great (though unfortunately obsolescent) language by inserting into it jargon and attitudes from the popular press that appalls him. It signified too the League's blindness to the fact that English is the mother-tongue of nearly all Irish people and that if it were supplanted Ireland would probably become detached from the more important achievements and movements of modern life. Synge's understanding of this at a time when the Gaelic revival seemed likely to emancipate and nourish the best features of Irish life and to contain the seeds of the future is amazing. Connected with this, and equally valid, is his presentation, in "The Old and New in Ireland," of the justification and principles of Anglo-Irish literature and its relation to Irish. In these statements, which are an essence of most of what can be said about English as the chief medium of language and literature in Ireland, Synge appears as a true prophet, one who comprehends so profoundly the main trends and pressures of his time that the outline of the future becomes discernible.

Ireland was of the highest worth to Synge. Ultimately, as Yeats divined, all that he did or said drew strength from contact with that soil and people, and from them he created high and enduring art; he brought "Everything down to that sole test again, / Dream of the noble and the beggar-man." The leading importance of this is reinforced, and the shape, the consistent dedication, in Synge's life revealed, when the prose is studied as a whole. The Continental episodes and influences were valuable but they had to be transcended, and this process, this abandonment of the esoteric for the plain local mood, can now be traced in such items as Synge's preference for Anatole France over Loti and Huysmans, and in *Étude Morbide* where the author, sunburnt and healthy, plays his fiddle for the peasants, and his skin shivers "to see that in spite of the agony of the world there are still men and women joyous enough to leap and spring with exultation." It is a development from the cloying nineties—"reptile godheads of the East . . . caverns of undulating gloom . . . strange stars . . . and purple feathers"—to the mature art of the descriptions of merry-making on the Blaskets and of the eviction and funerals on the Arans. The end of Synge's exploring was to arrive where he started and know the place for the first time. Through the unknown remembered gate he entered Aran. It was a revelation, but also it led back creatively to his beginning in Wicklow.

Previously, in discussions of Synge, his debt to the various parts of Ireland he knew has not been accurately calculated. His move to the Arans is so well known through Yeats, his experiences there were so dramatic, so clearly climacteric, and so well shaped into a notable book published in Synge's life-time, that it has hardly been realized that what he gained there was not essentially different from what he gained in Wicklow, Kerry, and Connemara, and that, all being considered, it was probably the county of his birth that meant most to him.

Now, however, it can be appreciated how vital Wicklow was to Synge. His understanding of it was remarkably full and intimate, and he knew it far better than any other part of Ireland. In Wicklow his most formative and creative years were spent. There friendships such as that with Florence Ross were made, and his enjoyment and study of the natural world and of wild creatures begun and sustained. With Wicklow the intense anxieties and aspirations of adolescence about religion, sex, music and literature were tightly interlaced, and there was a background and solace for his vain longings for Cherry Matheson. He gained his first understanding of country people and their way of life in Wicklow, and it provided the subjects for his earliest writings. Even during his Continental period he maintained fruitful contact with it. Then for his final years, when he produced his best writings, and love for Molly Allgood grew, he lived most fully in Wicklow.

Synge had a profound reverence for life. His sympathies were strong, flexible, delicate enough to comprehend with abundant and appropriate relish whole and varied ranges of existence—moist fertility, decaying romance, public debate, elemental austerity, the slums of Dublin, the domesticity of the Rhine-land, the board-room of the Abbey Theatre, the ballet-dancers of Paris, the old people of Wicklow, the shanachies of Kerry, and the doomed fisher-folk of Aran. Always there was compassion blended with irony and intellectual strength, and a ready tolerance that did not compromise principle, and shot through it all, though never paraded, an immense distress at the short while we have to experience all the wonder.

The agency which mainly promoted and nourished this creative inter-course, which helped to free Synge from the confines of self and enabled him to enter and understand other lives, was the imagination, "the great instrument of moral good," in Shelley's wise definition. It was also through activity of his imagination that Synge shaped so much of life into his work, as the new Oxford volume affirms. Because of their connection with his plays and poems, Synge's prose writings are uniquely valuable. But quite apart from this they possess an intrinsic worth that would remain even if he had written nothing else. For they have vitality and significance independent of any particular relation, and are not means but ends, created things with a life of their own, offering that extension and refinement of sensibility peculiar to works of art. And as such they merit lasting attention and appreciation.

The Poems*

ROBIN SKELTON

Synge's poems are few, and they do not have the thematic richness and profundity of his mature drama. Nevertheless they take up themes and attitudes which are present in his other work and tackle them from a different point of view, and his thoughts about poetry are as interesting and seminal as his thoughts on other matters.

When W. B. Yeats wrote, in a letter to his father, on 5 August 1913, "There are always two types of poetry—Keats the type of vision, Burns a very obvious type of the other," he was repeating views he had read in a notebook of Synge's. This 1907 notebook, which Yeats saw when he went through Synge's papers after his death, makes the point at greater length. The passage runs: "Poetry roughly is of two kinds the poetry of real life—the Poetry of Burns, and Shakespeare, Villon, and the poetry of a land of the fancy—the poetry of Spenser and Keats and Ronsard. That is obvious enough, but what is highest in poetry is always reached where the dreamer is leaning out to reality or where the man of real life is lifted out of it" (I. xiv–xv). Synge made a similar point in a letter of 1908: ". . . if verse, even great verse is to be alive it must be occupied with the whole of life—as it was with Villon and Shakespeare's songs, and with Herrick and Burns. For although exalted verse is the highest, it cannot keep its power unless there is more essential vital verse at the side of it as ecclesiastical architecture cannot remain fine, when domestic architecture is debased" (I. xv–xvi). These two passages seem to me to cast a good deal of light upon Synge's poetry, and upon his view of the poet's task. The first is from a rough draft of a possible preface to his poems, long before he finally decided to publish. The second is an extract from the letter he wrote to Yeats in September 1908, asking him for his opinion upon an enclosed group of poems. Yeats quotes his own version of this letter in his preface to Synge's *Poems and Translations*, and the difference between what Synge wrote and what Yeats *said* he wrote is extremely illuminating. The Yeats version of

*This essay first appeared in *The Writings of J. M. Synge* (London: Thames and Hudson, 1971) and is reprinted with permission. Extracts from the poetry of W. B. Yeats are reprinted with permission of Macmillan Publishing Company and are from *The Variorum Edition of the Poems of W. B. Yeats*, ed. by Peter Allt and Russell K. Alspach. Copyright © 1957 by Macmillan Publishing Company. Copyright renewed in 1985.

the above passage runs: ". . . if verse is to remain a living thing it must be occupied, when it likes, with the whole of a poet's life and experience as it was with Villon and Herrick and Burns; for though exalted verse may be the highest, it cannot keep its power unless there is more essentially vital verse— not necessarily written by the same man—at the side of it" (I. xxxi). Synge's original letter also included the sentence, which Yeats entirely omits: "Victor Hugo and Browning tried in a way to get life into verse but they were without humour which is the essentially poetic quality in what I call vital verse" (I. xvi). It seems clear that Yeats was not only intent upon preventing Synge's memory being tarnished by the presentation of shaky critical judgments (Browning without humour, indeed!), but also concerned to clarify the meaning and limit the dogmatism of Synge's original. In doing this he changed the whole direction of the statement. The elements of Synge's attitude which he chose to suppress were, in fact, the most essential ones.

The notion of a poetry which is "domestic" rather than "ecclesiastical" which is "vital" because of its "humour," and which is "occupied with the whole of life" is an important one in the history of English poetry. Synge chose Villon, Herrick, and Burns as illustrations, but he might equally well have picked on several members of the Tribe of Ben, and on the Cavaliers. It was the Cavalier poets' strength to make poetry look full of "careless ease," to make it seem as if each poem were an impromptu, or, at the most, the work of an hour or two of pleasurable industry. The greater part of Carew's work looks as if, in the middle of a full life, he every now and again turned to poetry—for fun, or in a passing mood of affection or malice. Many of the poems refuse to take their own statements seriously; pretentious sentiment may be presented, but it is liable to be mocked before the poem's end. Poetry is a by-product of living, and not a god in whose service life should be spent. The Cavalier poet is, essentially, a "man of real life," who is occasionally "lifted out of it" by some fantasy born of strong emotion or transfiguring thought.

If we think of Synge as a poet in this tradition, we can perhaps understand the force and significance of that word "domestic." The "domestic architecture" is made to cope with the daily business of living; the "ecclesiastical" is concerned to provide a place for exhortation, praise, and high sacrament. Poetry can involve itself in the daily business of living in two ways, either by observing it, or by becoming a part of it. Synge's poetry takes the latter course; it is used in the course of living, and in the furtherance of living. There are curses—poems which are constructed as if poetry could alter reality. There are inscriptions—poems made for the flyleaves of books and for tombstones, as if the poet really had a social function as a maker of sentences for special places and occasions. There are poems which are stray thoughts versified, spasms of the heart or intelligence. And there are several poems which tell an anecdote in the kind of language which presumes the existence of a listening audience. Synge, as a poet, succeeded in making for himself a persona which few poets have been able to imitate in the twentieth century. Perhaps only

Yeats could make full use of it after Synge had died. It is this persona which is, to my mind, Synge's greatest contribution to the poetry of our time; it was also quite certainly an immensely formative influence upon the poetry made by Yeats after 1908.

It is not easy to define this persona accurately. It is partly that of the Cavalier, as I have described it. It is also, however, partly that of the poet who saw his vocation as a social function, and who had a strong sense of his role as orator. Synge may not, like Ben Jonson or John Skelton, run to making Masques. He may not produce elaborate complimentary poems, or appropriately orotund elegies. He does, however, in his balance of literary with vernacular diction, and in his counterpointing informal thought with formal manners of speech, continually remind us of the sense of genre which was once so important a part of a poet's equipment. His verse is usually written in the context of this understanding of genre; the success of his translations of Petrarch is, to a great extent, due to his setting a much simplified diction against a highly elaborate construction of thought; it is also due to his bland refusal ever to question or even indicate his premise that poetry of this kind is a natural rather than a falsely sophisticated activity. In the world in which Synge's poems are written it is still possible, if not to write a sonnet to my lady's eyebrow, to send her upon her birthday a verse which in all essentials could have been written in Elizabethan England, medieval Italy, or ancient Greece:

> Friend of Ronsard, Nashe and Beaumont,
> Lark of Ulster, Meath and Thomond,
> Heard from Smyrna and Sahara
> To the surf of Connemara,
> Lark of April, June, and May,
> Sing loudly this my Lady-day.   (I. 60)

Synge's own sense of tradition was as strong as his sense of mortality. Many of his poems are concerned with the passing of time, and with the inheritance of the past by the fleeting present. This is not very surprising in an Irishman, of course, for the habit of looking back upon legend and history was well established as a national literary characteristic before Synge came on the scene. Nevertheless, Synge's use of this theme is inimitable, and connects up directly with his view of the poet's task. A poem written at Coblenz goes:

> Oaks and beeches heath and rushes
> You've kept your graces by the Rhine
> Since Walter of the Vogelweide
> Sang from Coblenz to the Main
>
> But the great-great-great-great bastards
> Of the queens that Walter knew

Wear pot-bellies in the breach
And bald heads are potted too   (I. 61)

The tradition of singing is over. The glory has departed. It is an old and perpetually recurring cry, but Synge was before all else interested in those recurring cries of love or dread which each generation must make again. His deliberate renewal of tradition can be seen in the following poem which is so reminiscent of a well-known poem in Gaelic that one might even call it an "imitation."

Some go to game, or pray in Rome
I travel for my turning home

For when I've been six months abroad
Faith your kiss would brighten God!
(I. 62)

The balance of passion and mortality in Synge's mature poems is almost Jacobean. Kiss and coffin are near neighbours. "To the Oaks of Glencree" begins with an embrace and ends with the worms. "In Kerry" places the wild, ecstatic, delight of the lovers alongside a stack of human bones. There is a continual resentment of the tricks of fate and the inevitability of death. The following quatrain could be the cry of any man against the President of the Immortals:

You squirrel angel eel and bat
You seal, sea-serpent water-hen
You badger cur-dog mule and cat
You player with the shapes of men
(I. 65)

This anger finds expression over and over again in Synge's poetry, and while it must be seen as the expression of a deeply personal agony of mind, it must also be seen as a traditional cry, echoing down from whatever poet it was that first saw a life and feared for himself, and thought to curse the gods. Earlier in this book I quoted one example of Synge's use of this attitude. The poem was written in 1896–7.

I curse my bearing, childhood, youth
I curse the sea, sun, mountains, moon,
I curse my learning, search for truth,
I curse the dawning, night, and noon.

Cold, joyless I will live, though clean,
Nor, by my marriage, mould to earth
Young lives to see what I have seen,
To curse—as I have cursed—their birth.
(I. 14)

This intemperate rage and despair is typical of Synge's early poems, in which (after an early attack of Wordsworthianism) he is clearly adopting a somewhat Byronic attitude. The verse is fevered, sub-hysterical. There are too many pieces of pretentious high-mindedness. Every now and then, however, the poems take on a knotted strength, a hardness of outline which Synge was usually able to seize upon and improve when he revised his early work. His revisions were almost always in the direction of making the poem more concrete in imagery and more brusque in statement. One poem of 1898 read originally as follows:

> I waited and walked in the rue des Ecoles
> And thought to see you arise from the West
> And many a rake and rouged troll
> Jeered my frozen zest
>
> And when your hour was rung at the last
> I stood with a shiver to watch the turn
> And met two creaking coffins that past
> Oh God! I am slow to learn.   (I. 21)

Synge's revisions of 1906–8 altered this to:

> *Rendez-vous manqué dans la rue Racine*
>
> When your hour was rung at last
> I stood as in terror to watch and turn,
> And met two creaking coffins that passed.
> Lord God, I am slow to learn!   (I. 21)

Another instance of Synge's revision of early work is even more indicative of the way he regarded poetry at the end of his life. In 1907 he revised a poem of 1896 to read:

> *In the City Again*
>
> Wet winds and rain are in the street,
>   Where I must pass alone,
> Where no one wayfarer I meet
>   That I have loved or known.
>
> 'Tis winter in my heart, the air
>   Is willing, bitter cold,
> While I am wailing with despair,
>   As I have wailed of old.   (I. 16)

In the autumn of 1908 he tackled the poem again and produced:

Winter
With little money in a great city

There's snow in every street
Where I go up and down,
And there's no woman, man, or dog
That knows me in the town.

I know each shop, and all
These Jews and Russian Poles,
For I go walking night and noon
To spare my sack of coals.   (I. 63)

The significant change here is the movement from the general to the particular. The poem has become almost over-particular and limited by being so specific about the "Jews and Russian Poles." Others of Synge's mature poems have the same quality. "The 'Mergency Man" refers specifically to "Coom" and "Coomasaharn." "Danny" is even more detailed geographically. "In Kerry" refers to "Thomas Flynn." "To the Oaks of Glencree" refers, not to some indefinite graveyard, but to "Mount Jerome." This deliberately narrowing use of detail is a part of the "domestic" element in Synge's verse. The poems must be seen as being a part, not of any generalized life, but of a particular life in a particular place. One should be able to walk where the poem has been. It is one of poetry's tasks to show how the commonplace can be suddenly a miracle; to do that you need to identify the commonplace fairly precisely.

The interest in the passionate transfiguration of the commonplace led to Synge's balancing one kind of diction against another just as did his interest in tradition. In an unfinished poem of 1907–9 we find that while there is the expected use of "romantic" language in such phrases as "splendour of your eyes" and "Stretched beneath a hazel bough," there is an unexpected use of detail in lines like "Kissed from ear and throat to brow," "Kissed from ear to ear," and "Since your fingers, neck, and chin." These are real, not fancy, kisses. The physical situation is clearly described *as* physical, even while it is being also attached to notions of paradisal splendour.

Is it a month since I and you
In the starlight of Glen Dubh
Stretched beneath a hazel bough
Kissed from ear and throat to brow,
Since your fingers, neck, and chin
Made the bars that fenced me in,
Till Paradise seemed but a wreck
Near your bosom, brow, and neck,

And stars grew wilder, growing wise,
In the splendour of your eyes!
Since the weasel wandered near
Whilst we kissed from ear to ear
And the wet and withered leaves
Blew about your cap and sleeves,
Till the moon sank tired through the ledge
Of the wet and windy hedge?
And we took the starry lane
Back to Dublin town again.   (I. 52)

This poem, perhaps because it was never really finished, shows the balance of explicit and implicit, factual and fanciful, simplicity and sophistication very clearly. It also hints at that use of hyperbole which Synge made his own, and which, lurking here behind the prison bars of the sixth line, emerges fully in "In May."

In a nook
That opened south,
You and I
Lay mouth to mouth.

A snowy gull
And sooty daw
Came and looked
With many a caw;

"Such," I said,
"Are I and you,
When you've kissed me
Black and blue!"
                    (I.53)

The absurdity, the wild fancifulness of the exaggeration qualifies the poem's whole tone, making it more affectionate, but also more passionate because less restrained verbally. This is the humour that gives vitality. We see it again in the "stack of thigh-bones, jaws and shins" in the poem "In Kerry" (I. 55), where the near-surrealistic image, however bitter, gives an air of almost savage exultation to the speaker's expression of joy. The perception of reality does not necessarily spoil the fantasy; it may enhance it.

The chiffchaff and celandine
The blackbird and the bee
The chestnut branches topped with green
Have met my love and me

> And we have played the masque of May
> So sweet and commonplace and gay
> (I. 54)

It is commonplace but gay, and who cares if it is no more than a passing show? In Synge's poetry the cries of rage and despair must always be countered by expressions of gaiety, ecstasy even. In *The Death of Synge*, Yeats wrote: "In Paris Synge once said to me, 'We should unite stoicism, asceticism and ecstasy. Two of them have often come together, but the three never.'" Whether or not this statement is a reliable report of Synge's words, the feeling behind it is certainly one we find in these poems. Life and death, birth and decay are often in balance here. Synge's world is one where time is always nudging mankind. In the poem "Samhain" we read:

> Though trees have many a flake
> Of copper, gold, and brass,
> And fields are in a lake
> Beneath the withered grass;
>
> Though hedges show their hips
> And leaves blow by the wall
> I taste upon your lips
> The whole year's festival.
> (I. 42)

In his preface to his *Poems and Translations* Synge wrote: "In these days poetry is usually a flower of evil or good, but it is the timber of poetry that wears most surely, and there is no timber that has not strong roots among the clay and worms. Even if we grant that exalted poetry can be kept successful by itself, the strong things of life are needed in poetry also, to show that what is exalted, or tender, is not made by feeble blood. It may almost be said that before verse can be human again it must learn to be brutal" (I. xxxvi). This has usually been taken as referring to such poems as "The 'Mergency Man," "Danny," and "A Question" in particular, and with some justice. These poems are more violent in expression than those of any other poet of the period save Masefield, though it was not until 1911, after Synge's death, that he made use in "The Everlasting Mercy" of that ultra-realistic colloquialism for which he became famous. Synge first used vulgar colloquialism in his poetry in 1895 when he wrote a ballad in which a vagrant talks to a "Horney" (policeman). The policeman tells him that he would be wiser to steal something and go to prison where he would be taught a trade than to go to the "House" (i.e. the Workhouse or Union) to be a "pauper." The tramp calls the policeman a "great dunder head," and uses such colloquial phrases as "hold your whist" and "by Jabs." The poem is heavily ironic, but its vitality is beyond question. It ends:

By Jabs I niver had beleeved
It was a Horney spoke
Your comin nice and easy on
Wid us young thinkin folk!
Its deuced stiff a cove must steal
To grow an honest man
But Gob I'll do't if you think
It is the best I can!　　(I. 9)

Synge took up the colloquial ballad again in 1907 when he wrote "Danny,"
based upon an anecdote he had heard in West Kerry. It is relentlessly savage,
and the climax is grotesque.

Then Danny smashed the nose on Byrne,
He split the lips on three,
And bit across the right hand thumb
Of one Red Shawn Magee.

But seven tripped him up behind,
And seven kicked before,
And seven squeezed around his throat
Till Danny kicked no more.

Then some destroyed him with their heels,
Some tramped him in the mud,
Some stole his purse and timber pipe,
And some washed off his blood.

And when you're walking out the way
From Bangor to Belmullet,
You'll see a flat cross on a stone
Where men choked Danny's gullet.

Not surprisingly, Elizabeth Yeats found this poem too strong for her stomach
and apologetically excluded it from the Cuala Press edition of Synge's poems.
She also excluded the equally forthright "The Curse."

Synge was doing more in "Danny" than telling a crude story crudely.
He was attempting to give a folk verse-form a content appropriate to the wild
peasant folk he knew. He was implying, by this means, that most of the
ballads of his day and even of earlier days, had got out of touch with the oral
culture from which they originally sprang, and accusing them of a gentility
wholly inappropriate to the genre.

"Danny" is the most violent of all Synge's colloquial poems, and the
most obviously "brutal." It should not, however, be taken as illustrating all
that Synge meant by the word "brutal" in his preface. It is important to
recognize that the violent juxtaposition of literary with colloquial language

also has a brutal effect, and can be found in many poems. In point of fact, I'd suggest that the brutality Synge was after, though it finds one kind of expression in the ballads, is also clearly present in "Queens" where the literary language does not so much counterpoint as come into a headlong clash with the vernacular. I would also suggest that the physicality of "Samhain," or the poem beginning "Is it a month," is another aspect of that brutality, that sense of the vigorously animal, which Synge felt to be as essential as humour to vital poetry.

"Queens" is, however, central to the understanding of Synge's poetry. It was worked out with immense care over many drafts, and the occasional apparently haphazard quality is the product of most careful craftsmanship.

> Seven dog-days we let pass
> Naming Queens in Glenmacnass,
> All the rare and royal names
> Wormy sheepskin yet retains,
> Etain, Helen, Maeve, and Fand,
> Golden Deirdre's tender hand,
> Bert, the big-foot, sung by Villon,
> Cassandra, Ronsard found in Lyon,
> Queens of Sheba, Meath and Connaught,
> Coifed with crown, or gaudy bonnet,
> Queens whose finger once did stir men,
> Queens were eaten of fleas and vermin. . . .
>
> (I. 34)

The listing of great names in this manner is a habit of medieval poets rather than of modern ones. Moreover, the celebration of queens itself is somehow at odds with our century. The speaker of the poem, however, is looking back, not only upon the queens, but also, by implication, upon the days in which it was possible to list them and celebrate them with the appropriate high seriousness. Now, however, the list is bitter, crude, vulgarized; yet it still keeps "in touch" with the old feeling of reverence, and partly by means of its own over-protestation of antiromanticism. Thus in "Queens" we get a curious fusion of the old with the new, of the professional Court-poet with the declassed functionless poet of today. It is a part of the poet's divine arrogance that he can still dare, in this twentieth century, to use and to abuse the old manner with the old confidence. As the Goliards implied reverence of the notions they caricatured so Synge suggests a persona by thus ostentatiously rejecting it, in this poem at any rate.

Reverence for the royal and legendary is as much part of the persona of Synge's poetry as is the rejection of the merely fanciful. The reverence is rather for great exemplars of human feeling, however, than for any notion of aristocracy. Synge could dismiss AE's mystical fairy-land as nonsense. He rejected the "plumed yet skinny Shee" (I. 38). A "man of real life," he was interested in celebrating the human vigour of the peasant in such poems as "On an Island," "Patch-Shaneen," "Beg-Innish" and "The 'Mergency Man." His view of peasantry in these harshly gay-grim verses must have struck Yeats as a challenge, when he first read them in 1908. Yeats' own gentle picture of the haunted peasantry must have appeared odd beside Synge's, and the ballads of "Patch-Shaneen," and "Danny," must have seemed almost like criticisms of Yeats' own ballads of "The Fiddler of Dooney," "The Host of the Air," "Father Gilligan," "The Foxhunter" and "Moll Magee." The way in which several of Synge's poems treat of themes already treated by Yeats does look suspicious, certainly. "On an Island" is, perhaps, the "man of real life's" retort to the fanciful man's "Lake Isle of Innisfree," and how many of Yeats' poems of sorrowing love can be considered answered by Synge's "A Wish"? Here the lover's tears of frustration are regarded as a sauce for the dish. The poem suggests the speaker's agreement with John Donne that: "Who ever loves, if he do not propose / The right true end of love, he's one that goes / To sea for nothing but to make him sick." Synge, moreover, transfers the tears of frustration from the cheeks of the sighing lover to those of the beloved. Indeed, in the early version, sent to his fiancée, Molly Allgood, on 26 March 1907, the phrase "well of pleasure" suggests that the beloved is sexually aroused. This version goes:

> May one sorrow every day
> Your festivity waylay.
> May seven tears in every week
> From your well of pleasure leak
> That I—signed with such a dew—
> May for my full pittance sue
> Of the Love forever curled
> Round the maypole of the world.
>
> Heavy riddles lie in this,
> Sorrow's sauce for every kiss.
>
> (I. 51)

In the revised version published in 1909 the first lines read:

> May seven tears in every week
> Touch the hollow of your cheek,
> That I—signed with such a dew—
> For a lion's share may sue
> Of the roses ever curled
> Round the May-pole of the world.
>
> (I. 51)

Synge indicates the riddling element of the poem explicitly enough for us to suppose him fully aware of the phallic and punning significance of the word "maypole." No one aware at all of the rose image in the early work of Yeats, and in much other work, could possibly avoid perceiving its sexual implications. The phrase "lion's share" suggests something of the predatory, as well as implying (possibly) that there were other shares to be had. Indeed the poem-riddle suggests that the Beloved is not completely adorable, that she deserves to suffer somewhat for this particular lover, and that, far from being masochistically romantic, her man is inclined to relish her discomfort as being both an enhancement of his sense of conquest and a betrayal of weakness in the sex war.

If we turn from "A Wish" to Yeats' love poems of this period, or to those about the "Red Rose," we cannot help feeling that Synge had written his own poem in revolt against the conventional dreamy melancholies of the older poet. It seems not altogether impossible that Synge was himself keenly aware of this aspect of his work. He certainly did not let Yeats see his poems until George Roberts had already asked to publish them, and he showed John Masefield his ballad of "Danny" over a year before he showed it to Yeats. Synge was a reticent man, but he worked in close harness with both Yeats and Lady Gregory; his silence about his poems must, surely, have been a conscious decision, even, perhaps, a strategy. Whatever the reason for Synge's not showing Yeats his verses until 1908 it is clear that once Yeats had read them he began to learn from them. It is extraordinary how much all the poems that Yeats had first printed after September 1908 and that appeared in *The Green Helmet* of 1910 differ from the poems printed before this date. Of the poems published in earlier collections only one or two have the faintest hint of that brusque hardness of tone which emerges so clearly in the 1910 collection. There are some poems in which the persona is that of the poet talking of himself as if his profession had social significance and an accepted stature, but these are almost apologetically couched in comparison with the 1910 verses in which this persona is used. Compare the poem "Never give all the heart" and its use of both vocabulary and metre with "At Galway Races." The former was first printed in December 1905 and the latter in February 1909. The original version of the first began:

> Never give all the heart; for love
> Will hardly seem worth thinking of
> To passionate women, if it seem
> Certain and they never dream
> That it fades out from kiss to kiss,
> For everything that's lovely is
> But a brief dreamy kind delight . . .[1]

The original version of the second began:

> There where the racecourse is
> Delight makes all of the one mind

> The riders upon the swift horses
> The field that closes in behind.
> We too had good attendance once,
> Hearers, hearteners of the work,
> Aye, horsemen for companions
> Before the merchant and the clerk
> Breathed on the world with timid breath . . .[2]

The increase in gusto is formidable. The different view of the nature of delight is obvious. The imagery of the first could find a place in Pre-Raphaelite literature; the imagery of the second reminds me of nothing so much as of Jack B. Yeats' drawings in illustration of the race in *The Playboy of the Western World*. Of all the poems in *The Green Helmet* of 1910, only one was printed before September 1908. This is the first poem in the collection and differs from the remaining poems markedly, especially in its decorative prolixity in its first version, in which we read:

> There on the high and painted stern
> I held a painted steering oar
> And everywhere that I could turn
> Men ran upon the shore . . .[3]

It includes the word "painted" again in the fifteenth line: "And fish and crowd and painted ship"; and it ends with a, by now familiar, reference to "the sweet name of Death."

The "sweetness" in the other poems in the collection is quite different:

> For she had fiery blood
> When I was young
> And trod so sweetly proud
> As t'were upon a cloud . . .
> —*A Woman Homer Sung*[4]

> we that had thought
> To have lit upon as clean and sweet a tale
> —*King and No King*[5]

> Such a delicate high head,
> All that sternness amid charm,
> All that sweetness amid strength . . .
> —*Peace*[6]

The change is not, however, merely in a fresh perspective upon habitual epithets, a new muscularity and concreteness of imagery, a harsher use of the vernacular, but also in the presentation of a new version of the "poet." Pre-1910 Yeats could never have written:

> You say as I have often given tongue
> In praise of what another's said and sung
> 'Twere politic to do the like by these,
> But where's the wild dog that has praised his fleas?[7]

Originally grouped with several other poems under the general heading "Momentary Thoughts," this quatrain was later given the even more significant heading "To a Poet, who would have me praise certain bad poets, imitators of his and mine." The persona of the professional poet, the poet who is at once the Court-poet and the Cavalier, the conscious craftsman and the impromptu wit, is emerging.

I do not wish to describe here the way in which this persona was exploited in Yeats' later work. I have done that elsewhere. It is easy enough, however, to notice its presence, and to claim the superb "Under Ben Bulben" as a masterwork in the tradition. It is easy, too, to see how Yeats learned from Synge to balance kinds of diction against one another, so that many poems derive much of their excitement from the tension between pedantic and colloquial locutions. One might even maintain that the savage humour of Yeats' later short plays, as of some of his later poems, derives from his reading of Synge. An argument along these lines would be long and fruitless, for no one not already convinced of the truth of it could possibly be persuaded; the evidence in these matters is always wildly circumstantial and inconclusive. A careful reader might notice, with a smile, the number of words Yeats spent upon Synge as man, and as playwright, over the years, and the way in which he elevated him into his private pantheon of heroes. Such a reader might also notice that, at times, Yeats seems almost obsessed with the need to establish Synge's greatness; his claims on his behalf are those made for a prophet.

I would like to come out into the open here and admit that I am one who feels that Yeats owed more to Synge's poems than has ever been adequately recognized. I believe that he did not only learn a new forcefulness and clarity of diction, and a new way of balancing the literary against the colloquial, but also the use of a persona which he made central to his work as a lyric poet for the remainder of his life. I would add, also, that this persona provided by Synge was one which enabled Yeats to speak as a member of a long tradition of poets and scholars. He himself looked back at Goldsmith and Swift. Synge looked back to Herrick, Villon, Ronsard, Burns, and Petrarch. He might equally well have looked back to Ben Jonson, John Skelton, or, perhaps most of all, Dunbar, whose complaints, curses, and keenings have much in common with those in his own book, and who also knew how to balance the ornate against the vulgar, the literary against the colloquial. Moreover, Dunbar, like

Synge, was "occupied with the whole of life." He, like Synge, was a "man of real life" lifted out of it by passion and humour, just as Yeats learned to be a dreamer who leaned out to reality.

Perhaps the best comment upon Synge's poems, and upon the persona he rediscovered and renewed, with however careful a recognition of the way the mask must be worn, the strategy admitted, is one by Jack Yeats. In an essay "With Synge in Connemara," which was printed as a part of W. B. Yeats' Cuala Press volume *Synge and the Ireland of his Time* (1911), he wrote: "If he had lived in the days of piracy he would have been fiddler in a pirate-schooner, him they called "the music"—"The music" looked on at everything with dancing eyes but drew no sword, and when the schooner was taken and the pirates hung at Cape Corso Castle or the Island of Saint Christopher's "the music" was spared because he *was* "the music." This is the persona, all right. It has the ultimate gaiety described by Yeats in "Lapis Lazuli": "All things fall and are built again, / And those that build them again are gay."[8] Synge built again, and with that Yeatsian gaiety which can exist in the middle of despair and suffering. It is, perhaps, gaiety born of courage, of rebellion, of pride in the ability to face the real. In one of his very last poems Synge expressed in a fragment, most movingly, the rebellion that lies in the sense of mortality. In this poem he is both the representative of a tradition in which such poems are numerous, the representative of every man that faces death, and also his own most private, most local, most particular self. Person and persona are one; The voice, now fully achieved, ends in the middle of a task which Yeats was to take up and make into the greatest work of twentieth-century poetry.

> I read about the Blaskets and Dunquin,
> The Wicklow towns and fair days I've been in.
> I read of Galway, Mayo, Aranmore,
> And men with kelp along a wintry shore.
> Then I remembered that that "I" and I,
> And I'd a filthy job—to waste and die.
>
> (I. 66)

Six months later he was dead, but he left behind him a couple of dozen poems that will always keep his name in mind as one of the great renewers of tradition.

Notes

1. Peter Alt and Russell K. Alspach, *The Variorum Edition of the Poems of W. B. Yeats*, Macmillan Publishing Company, 1957, p. 202

2. *Ibid*, p. 266.

3. *Ibid*, p. 253.

4. *Ibid*, p. 255.
5. *Ibid*, p. 258.
6. *Ibid*, p. 259.
7. *Ibid*, p. 262.
8. *Ibid*, p. 566.

Text and Context in *When the Moon Has Set**

Mary C. King

That Synge's first play, *When the Moon Has Set*, was rejected by Lady Gregory and Yeats is well known, as is the fact that his premature death left *Deirdre of the Sorrows* incomplete, with the task of preparing a text for performance and publication falling to these two Abbey colleagues assisted by his fiancée, Molly Allgood. Less well known are the various versions of the first work, especially the early two-act typescript (Item 4351, ff 1–43 in the Trinity College Dublin Collection), believed by Ann Saddlemyer to be the version brought by the dramatist to Coole Park in September 1901. The text included in the Oxford University Press *Collected Works* is a conflation of two separate and later one-act drafts.[1] The title of the play does not occur in any of the typescripts. It appears in Synge's diary entry for 23rd May 1903, in relation to a one-act version completed in that month.[2] The one-act versions and the conflated text differ in many respects from the two-act play. Although she is referred to in the two-act typescript, Mary Costello does not appear therein as an on-stage character. The climax of the first act occurs when Columb Sweeny is shot by an off-stage character, assumed to be Stephen Costello, brother of Mary and uncle of the Sweenys' servant girl, Bride Kavanagh. Stephen, we are told, had taken an oath to "shoot the next heir, cousin or descendant" (p. 20) of Columb's uncle. Yet a further distinguishing feature is the framing of the two-act play by substantial readings from a philosophical / aethetic manuscript written by Columb Sweeny. This reflects on the relationships and affinities between music, art and life. It draws heavily on passages in Synge's *Autobiography*, in the *Vita Vecchia* and in the *Etude Morbide*. The play is the most explicitly autobiographical of Synge's dramas. Indeed, we shall argue that the manuscript, together with the other metatextual devices, the letters from and to Columb's Parisian friend and fellow artist, O'Neill, and the letter from Columb's dead uncle to his heir, may be regarded as an inscription into the text of a life-history which the play attempts to explicate, or to release into dramatic action. It thus anticipates the metalinguistic and metadramatic features which are characteristic of all of Synge's later work.

*This essay first appeared in *The Drama of J. M. Synge* (Syracuse, New York: Syracuse University Press, 1985) and is reprinted with permission.

* * *

The setting for the first play is the library of the Big House. The scene therefore foregrounds immediately the metatextual dimensions of the drama. As it opens, Sister Eileen is preparing a bow of crepe, a sign of mourning for the dead master of the house. The first words are *read* from the aesthetic manuscript by Sister Eileen; they compare life with a symphony. As the play progresses, the traditional moral and ethical as well as religious values of the landlord family are called into question by the uncle's posthumously revealed love for a Catholic peasant woman, Mary Costello, and his self-confessed philosophical agnosticism. The challenge to the old values becomes even more explicit in the radicalism of his nephew and heir. Responsibility for the tragic outcome of the uncle's love does not rest solely with himself, or even with the family's traditional class attitudes or religious prejudices. Mary Costello, the poor woman whom he wished to marry, refused his offer because of her own Catholic faith and her inability to accept her lover's agnosticism. If we are to understand the more than purely autobiographical significance of this conflict, we need to note certain parallels between the women in the early play and Deirdre in *Deirdre of the Sorrows*.

By the time Synge came to write his last drama, Deirdre was already well established in the mythology of Irish nationalist aspirations as a typological figure whose tragic fate represented that of Ireland. Lady Gregory included the story of "The Sons of Usnach" in her *Cuchulain of Muirthemna*. George Russell and Yeats had each written plays based on the legend and performed at the Abbey in 1902 and 1906 respectively. Indeed, there is evidence to suggest that Synge first began to consider his own version of the Deirdre legend in reaction against the treatment of the material in these earlier plays. Turning to *When the Moon Has Set*, we find that Sister Eileen, the object of Columb's matrimonial hopes, is a Catholic nun who plays the harp and sings the Gaelic song, the "Cuilfhionn," and that she exchanges her nun's habit for a green wedding dress which was originally intended for Bride Costello. It would indeed be obtuse to ignore the political significance of these features and to see Sister Eileen as simply the distant cousin of the landlord family or a conflated analogue for Florence Ross and Cherrie Matheson.[3] She is as obviously a representation of Ireland as Deirdre, or as Yeats's Cathleen Ni Houlihan. There is a consistent, if formally unsuccessful, effort being made throughout to dramatize the autobiographical material in such a way as to explore its social, historical, political and cultural determinants.

The society represented in *When the Moon Has Set*, like Conchubor's Emain in *Deirdre of the Sorrows*, is growing old and becoming painfully aware of its obsolescence.[4] With Columb's uncle lying on his death-bed, the atmosphere in the house and the surrounding countryside is one of degeneration, morbidity and incipient madness. Conchubor, likewise, is a "man is ageing in his Dun, with his crowds round him and his silver and gold" (IV, 211). By his own confession, he brings to Deirdre as a marriage gift "wildness and confusion in my own mind" (IV, 195). In both plays a form of escape into the natural world from the constricting paralysis of the respective dying generations is considered—although in neither case is this offered uncritically as a simple, or simplistic, alternative to life in society. Whereas, however, *When the Moon Has Set* insists on discovering an aesthetic order and pattern in the lives of its characters and imposing this on the historical and natural processes, the last play questions, and finally refuses, a too easily harmonious or aesthetically satisfying solution to the challenge of the "filthy job—to waste and die" (I, 66).

In *When the Moon Has Set* the hero, Columb Sweeny, is a writer-musician with a mission. In personal terms, this takes the form of a proselytizing determination to win his distant cousin from the celibate life which she regards as the highest form of religious expression. He attempts to convert Eileen from the asceticism of religious dogma to a dogmatic, if confused, aestheticism, which is expounded in the play's aesthetic manuscript. In the passage which Sister Eileen reads at the outset, life is envisaged as part of a cosmic work of art. The function of art is to make the playing of each part as perfect as possible and to reveal the ultimate perfection by expressing the abstract cosmic persona concealed beneath the impersonal, concrete deeds of a man's life-time. The aesthetic debate continues when Columb reads to Sister Eileen a letter from his friend, O'Neill, in Paris. The friend, an *alter ego* of Columb and of Synge, emerges as one who has dedicated himself not just to writing about the fin-de-siecle romantic agony, but to living the part: "He lives in a low room draped in black from the floor to the ceiling. He has a black quilt on his bed and two skulls on his Chimney-piece with girls hats on them. His matches are in a coffin, and his clock is a gallows. He sits there whenever he is not at work and drinks absinthe and vermouth" (p. 21). When Sister Eileen judges this behavior as bordering on the insane, her cousin quickly points out that "in the life of the cloisters and in this life of Ireland, men go mad every hour" (p. 21). Decadence, aesthetic and religious, is thus provided with a local, and Irish, habitation.

The musical references throughout the play are at best inexact. At times they seem to assert an identity between the individual life, general life processes and a mystical, cosmic symphony; at others they suggest tropic analogies. Robin Skelton has described these philosophical passages as "confused, over-emotional, and sloppy in terminology."[5] The vagueness and imprecision of the language, the lack of any convincing testing out of the concepts through dramatic action, make it difficult to determine with any consistency Columb's philosophical / aesthetic position. Part of the play's weakness may be attributed to the tediously repetitive apostrophizing of music's divine power and unifying impulse. The obsessive use of musical tropologization to support, or to mask, the conceptual preoccupations of the drama is suspect, not just as a-historical music criticism. The emphasis on ultimate form is an attempt to transcend process and change. Ideal, discontented form offers an escape from the horrible concretions of history, time, and context-bound identity, which intrude upon the effort to express life, or the life-force, through media as uncomfortably referential as the language-using arts. The philosophical-aesthetic insight to which such a vague statement as "every life is a symphony" (p. 17) pretends remains unarticulated, and in *When the Moon Has Set* the desire or motive to avoid articulation is strong.

The down-grading of language complements, throughout the main plot, the thematic elevation of form. It is part of the impetus towards dis-content-ment which characterizes the ascendancy sequence and is symptomatic of an effort to escape from the linguistically mediated, or the referential. In his final sermon to Sister Eileen, Columb dismisses the incarnate *logos* and celebrates instead a wordless metamorphosis: "It is the beauty of your spirit that has set you free, and your emancipation is more exquisite than any that is possible for men who are redeemed by logic. You cannot tell me why you have changed, that is your glory" (p. 38). The verbal expression of escapist metaphysics, with its risky praise of freedom from the necessities of logic or language, leads all to readily to the act of escape itself. Columb calls on Eileen to forsake history and tradition and to go with him to a green world of unadulterated arboreal beauty:

COLUMB: The world of habit is diseased. . . . We will go out among the trees.
          The red glow is faded and day is come. . . . In the Name of the
          Summer, and The Sun, and the whole World I wed you as my wife
          (p. 38).

By an act of will, the forest world is made to become the whole World, but it fails to accommodate as part of its cosmology the diseased world of habit. Their departure is a solipsistic attempt to "circumscribe all of objective reality with their own subjectivity"; retreat into this second world "removes the ego from history" and "protects the protagonists from historical change, from transformation".[6] There is no trace, in Columb's final speech, of the compas-sionately ironic skepticism about ultimate solutions to the challenge of decay and mortality which may be detected in *Riders to the Sea* and *In the Shadow of the Glen*, nor any of the controlling self-reflective awareness of language and situation which subverts, in the later comedies, the impulse towards evasion or escape.

Yet the conclusion that *When the Moon Has Set* is totally committed to an escape from history into an aesthetically harmonized universe must be qualified. The play's embryonic sub-plots—the posthumously revealed affair between Columb's uncle and Mary Costello, and the relationship between Bride Kavanagh and Pat Murphy—are offered as contexts for the Columb-Eileen relationship. They are variations on the declared theme of the symphony, the dual "facts of love and death" (p. 23). As such, they attempt to restore a kind of contrapuntal content to the main sequence. The uncle-Mary Costello episode has as its theme the way in which love when denied leads to despair, insanity, violence and death. The relationship between Bride and Pat Murphy, by way of contrast, shows the couple accepting the death of the older generation and entering into their inheritance as the starting-point for the legitimization of their life together as man and wife. Love and death are defined and discussed abstractly by Columb, as the subjects of the symphony. Yet once they are treated in the sub-plots in a partially successful dramatic, rather than generalized polemical, manner, they prove to be uncomfortable bedfellows of transcendental idealism. The open challenge to the guilt-ridden problems of inheritance and generation which are masked in the main plot by the musical terminology comes from the peasant-aristocrat Costello family, descendants of "Old Castillian" (p. 19) stock. Stephen Costello both violates and absolves the House of Sweeny by his murderous attempt to shoot Columb because he is heir to the uncle. Stephen thus vicariously slays, but does not slay, the uncle / father, in the name or persona of Columb, who rises from this assault and is enabled to legitimate and successfully conclude his relationship with Sister Eileen. Eileen remains with the "resurrected" Columb ostensibly to nurse him back to health, but in effect to enable him to pursue and consummate his courtship.

The continuum between plot and sub-plot is strengthened if we accept that Sister Eileen "is" also both Mary Costello, the uncle's lover, and Bride. This is suggested by the fact that Eileen, persuaded by Bride's example to wed Columb, appears on-stage wearing Mary Costello's wedding dress at the end of the play. We can, then, observe a struggle in the play, through this complex net of relationships, to develop the theme of cathartic atonement, an attempt to dramatize the expurgation of the ascendancy sense of guilt through the transference of that guilt to Stephen Costello. Stephen is the mad twin brother of Mary. He also resembles, we are told, both Sister Eileen and Columb's *alter ego*, the 'cellist O'Neill. Stephen shoots Columb in revenge for a wrong presumed done, but not "really" done, to Mary by the defunct landlord uncle. This same uncle "really" intended marriage, which Mary's religious scruples, possibly Ireland's, or Eileen's, Catholicism, made impossible. "If you love a woman," Columb's uncle writes, "subdue her," but, he rapidly adds, "you will not love a woman it is not lawful to love. No man of our blood has ever been unlawful" (p. 35). This posthumous, purely assertive, attempt at absolution from generational guilt clears the way, in terms of legitimacy, for Columb's union with Eileen. Removal of the shadow of guilt from the hero's association with the uncle-father facilitates the marriage between the ascendancy scion and his Catholic cousin.

The complex problematic of the relationship between generations and classes is treated in *When the Moon Has Set* in ways which suggest, however, that Synge was more than a little troubled by this easy absolution. The difficulty experienced by Columb in acknowledging a direct line of responsibility for the past suggests why in this play it is the uncle rather than the father who is the dying or dead paternal figura. Columb is his uncle's heir because an uncle, as Hamlet knew, is a father-usurper who is neither true father nor legitimate ruler. The uncle-father in Synge's first play rises vicariously into prominence in Act II, through the medium of his letter to his doubting heir. Communicating verbally to Columb in this highly literary drama, he inscribes himself *post-mortem* into the text of his newphew's life. Their relationship, and the accompanying sense of guilt implicit in the absolution from it, is thereby simultaneously distanced and denied *and asserted*. The uncle's letter, referred to in a notebook which is taken from his death-bed, is hidden in a portfolio sealed with the two wedding-rings of the marriage-which-never-was (or was it?). The portfolio and rings are enclosed in turn in a box which conceals the close-to-illegitimate family secrets (properties) of Mary Costello's wedding clothes, and, in later versions of the play, the infant garments of her babies who were never (or who were?) born.[7] The whole of this claustrophobic generational puzzle, stretching, like Banquo's line, to infinity, is, of course, contained within the House. Synge's society was "patriarchal, hierarchical, and, ultimately, justified by God the Father, [it] depended at every level on the supremacy and potency of the male."[8] By displacing the father-figure to the position of uncle, by giving this uncle an agnostic, radical past and by denying him marriage / potency, Synge is seeking to strike, like Christy Mahon in *The Playboy of the Western World*, a triple blow against a guilty past. The guilt shows itself interestingly in O'Neill's letter welcoming Columb's entering into his "heritage" (p. 21). "My compliments," writes O'Neill, "to the little Irish pigs that eat filth all their lives that you may prosper" (p. 21). These words, we remember, are first recorded in Synge's Aran notebooks.

In *When the Moon Has Set* a resolution of the antinomic singularity of the "one mode" of existence (p. 26) which separates "the dual puissance" (p. 27) of life exclusively into the virginal-matriarchal or the authoritarian paternal mode is attempted. "We are not right," Columb tells Sister Eileen, "to distort the dual puissance of the mind" (p. 27). This power becomes identified with the "force" of "a fertile passion that is filled with joy" (p. 27). The appeal, here, however tentative and hedged about with abstraction, is *away from* ideal form, towards content. In evolutionary-aesthetic terms, it is in part a movement towards an accommodation with the scientific naturalism which forced the poet to live "in the world of Darwin, not in the world of Plato."[9] For Synge, as for Yeats, the mechanistically interpreted post-Darwinian world undoubtedly had its horrors. Chief amongst these was the apparent denial of free will, or of any active creative role or autonomous identity to the subject and therefore to the artist. Perhaps ontogeny was merely the blind recapitulation of phylogeny, in which case, no purgatorial fires could cleanse the present from the guilt of the past other than by going out of nature. Once this aesthetic preoccupation is historicized, it suggests that for Synge, as for Yeats, the struggle for survival of the ever-and-never dying generations, the nightmare of eternal recurrence, would be all. At least a residual shudder of this fear is recorded in Synge's *Autobiography*, and the vision of a universe in which this deadly struggle seems total disturbs Columb also. In Act II, recovering from the attempt on his life, he takes up again his discussion of survival and reproduction. Despite the change from the frozen winter of Act I to the spendour of June—or rather, because of it—Columb feels his mortality. He is "haunted by that appalling sensation in which we realize the gulf of annihilation we are being whirled into," yet asserts that "through it all it is possible to find a strange impulse of joy" (p. 30). In words taken almost directly from Synge's *Autobiography* he confesses to "the envy I used to have of the wild plants that crush and strangle each other in a cold rage of growth" (p. 29).

In *When the Moon Has Set* Columb seeks in music a way of expressing and confronting these rhythms of life and death. He claims that "music is the only art that can express the first animal frenzy" (p. 30), but hesitations and reservations about this non-representational solution creep in: "In the orchestra it is a divine hymn, in literature, or painting it is horrible" (p. 30). The downgrading of the more obviously referential arts is symptomatic of the deep unease in the play about the honesty of the play's musical, or aesthetic, argument. The unease is part of Synge's struggle to recognize and come to terms with the need to confront the generational process without being overwhelmed by feelings of horrible despair, or alternatively abstracting it out of existence. In relation to the ideas of Darwin, Spencer and Huxley, Yeats and Synge set out at first towards opposite poles. Yeats turned from them to Madame Blavatsky's theosophy—with a sense of critical irony which he never abandoned—and to the temporary attractions and consolations of Celtic mysticism. He claimed to have done so in reaction against his father's post-Darwinian unbelief. Synge, however, who never knew his father, found in science, and particularly in Darwin's *On the Origin of Species*, support, albeit disturbing and even at first traumatic, for his rebellion against his mother's literalizing Christianity. It is possible to argue that he discovered the symbolic father in discovering the missing or absent historical principle of generation. In the theory of the origin of species is to be found the endorsement of the animal note, and the confirmation of the dual puissance of the body. But given this philosophical alternative, Synge was nonetheless faced with the need to forge a poetic for the creative writer and an historical identity for himself, in what still appeared to be a closed, deterministic universe. Confronted by a related historical problem, Yeats saw himself and his fellow poets pushed, at least temporarily, into linguistic abstraction by being "compelled to protect ourselves by such means against people and things we should never have heard of."[10] The censoring connotations and abstract generalizations in this statement suggest that Yeats believed that the writers of his generation had access to information which they were too young—or immature—to know about. However disturbing Synge may have found his encounter with such people and things, he did not, as an artist, regret his acquaintance. We can certainly say that in *When the Moon Has Set* the abstracting motive in the main plot is very powerful and that it underwrites certain defensive-evasive features of the dramatic strategy and style. Nevertheless, there are clear and prophetic signs of the need to bring these abstractions to the bar of symbolic action and to test them out through and against the language of the play's "peasant" characters.

The momentum of *When the Moon Has Set* is by no means exclusively in the direction of protecting the hero, the artist, his class or his society against change. Accepting, like Columb, that "the Christian synthesis . . . has fallen" (p. 32), Synge recognized the crisis of European fin-de-siecle decadence as somehow necessary. He also traced a continuity between it and the problems of his own background, seeing in the one a response to the death of an old society and in the other the problems more often caused by a refusal to recognize, accept and accommodate to change. The struggle towards a critical understanding of these problems and an attempt to relate the European to the Irish dimension, informs Columb's argument that with the breakup of the old Christian synthesis "the imagination has wandered away to grow puissant and terrible again, in lonely vigils where she sits and broods among things that have been touched by madmen, and things that have the smell of death on them and books written with the blood of horrible crimes. The intellect has peered down into the tumult of atoms and up into the stars till she has forgotten her complements in the personality, and the instinct for practical joy has taught anarchists to hate in the passion of their yearning for love" (p. 32). What is regretted here is not the acquaintance with the new scientific theories and revelations; it is, rather, the inability, as yet, of the artistic intellect and sensibility to forge a complementary creative role for the human subject. The aesthetic dis-ease is shown to be grounded in time, place and history, and in the particular actions of individuals. The death of Columb's uncle, the attempted murder of Columb by the crazed Stephen, Eileen's (Columb's) life-denying celibacy, the prevalence of mental disturbance amongst the local people, all have their roots in the Irish political and social context, not in change as such, but in a perverse and doomed resistance to it. "The old-fashioned Irish conservatism and morality," Columb writes to O'Neill, "seemed to have evolved a melancholy degeneration worse than anything in Paris" (pp. 32–3).

Columb's attitude towards change, decay and death must be distinguished from that of O'Neill and Sister Eileen. O'Neill makes of morality an obsessive aesthetic cult. Sister Eileen's particular obsession is with an outmoded religion which teaches mortification of the senses in this life in the name of spiritual life after death. For Columb, awareness of death, however horrifying, is a reminder of the need to embrace life here and now, and with it, history and change. The decay of religions and cultures, although "an immense and infinite horror" (p. 31) to him, is preferable to the compromise with death and sterility. The death of the individual, or of societies, must be seen in relation to the "cosmic faith" of Beethoven, Michelangelo, Rabelais and "the magnificent Kermesse of Rubens" which "expresses the final frenzy of existence" (p. 26). We can recognize in these statements, however strident or aesthetically inadequate, an attempt to relate artistic achievement to the artist's ability to wrestle with history and change and to accommodate the work of art to them.

The importance of the play's occasional pyrrhic victories of action over schema lies partly in the way in which they point towards Synge's future achievements. Religion, art and literature cannot absolve history by explaining it away or by imposing upon it a spurious aesthetic teleology. There are signs of a desire to reformulate the question of historical role and identity in terms of the degrees and levels of integration and separation which can be established between the two central characters and the peasant community. We can detect these forces at work, for example, in the early scene which follows Sister Eileen's initial reading from the manuscript. Bride's attempts to relight the fading fire, and her lament about the wet turf, evoke far more successfully than all of Columb's philosophizing about change, degeneration and decay, the social crisis of the Big House and the dependence of its upper class occupants on their servants. The scene also manages to convey the depression and despondency caused among the peasants themselves by the decline of the social order which reciprocally defines their own identity—but it suggests, too, their greater resilience and resourcefulness, their tenacity of life, when faced with crisis. The dying down of the fire coincides with the announcement that Columb's uncle is dead. Bride kneels before the hearth, blowing on the fading embers of the turf:

SISTER EILEEN: [*going over to the fireplace where* BRIDE *is blowing the turf with her mouth*]. You cannot light it?

BRIDE: [*talking with plaintive western intonation.*] The turf's wet, Sister Eileen, for the roof has fallen in on the turf house with the weight of the snow on it, and I haven't a bit of sticks in the whole house. I told Murphy to bring some bogwood with him out of the town—you can't find a stick here anyplace with the snow lying on the earth—but he hasn't come back, the Lord knows what's keeping him (p. 18).

Columb and Sister Eileen have lost the art of making a turf fire. Columb "throws it all about as if it was coal he had" (p. 18). They rely for keeping alive the ancestral hearth on their peasant servants who in turn find fuel difficult to come by. Columb has even "missed his way" to the Big House "at the second crossing of the roads" (p. 18). He has "got stupid about the dark" (p. 18) and has had to take directions from an old queer man—who turns out to be his would-be assassin, Stephen Costello. We have here, however briefly sustained, a much more satisfactory feeling, in theatrical terms, for the physical actuality of the world and a confidence in its capacity to carry dramatic meaning.

The contrast between the play's two styles—the abstract expository and the more substantially dramatic—emerges clearly if we compare any of the Columb-Eileen exchanges about mortality with Bride's account of the death of her father:

SISTER EILEEN: What has happened?

BRIDE: He is dead, Sister Eileen. Mrs. Brady's husband was the Moon was set [*sic*]. Then I was there a while with the old man, and a little after twelve he gave a sort of a turn, and I went over, and he was dead in the bed. Then I was afeard to be there and no one along with me, so I came up to see would Mrs. Byrne go down to keep me from being lonesome. I can't leave him altogether, and I can't stay there by myself (p. 35).

Instead of trying to *impose* an interpretation which closes in upon the complex reality of time, process and change, this passage offers—as objective correlative of the theme—the felt experience of a character acting in a particular context. Bride does not deny her sense of loss or try to translate it into an abstract philosophical gain. She responds to Columb's sympathy with words which are later spoken by Maurya in *Riders to the Sea* and which Synge first encountered in a letter written to him by his Aran friend, Martin McDonough:

BRIDE: I'm destroyed crying: but what good is in it. We must be satisfied, and what man at all can be living forever (p. 36).

These words express her personal grief; they also acknowledge the impersonal inevitability of each man's life ending with death—the "gulf of annihilation we are all being whirled into" (p. 30)—and they recognize that only by accepting this as a necessity can we begin to be satisfied. The theme of commitment to present and future emerges again in Bride's reply to Sister Eileen's polite supposition that she will remain, as before, a servant at the Big House. Bride's answer asserts a limited, yet real, personal freedom. She wishes to marry Pat Murphy; now that she has inherited the farm and cows he will accept her. Nor has she waited for her father's death or the church's benediction or approval: she already bears the future within her, in carrying Pat's child.

It is, nevertheless, only rarely in *When the Moon Has Set* that Synge manages to bring about dramatically effective interplay between the two sets of characters and their respective linguistic registers. As Declan Kiberd points out, "the rich dramatic potential inherent in the clash of character and of linguistic styles—between polite English and rustic dialect—is never developed, merely hinted."[11] The problems with which he was attempting to deal in this first play proved too *immediate*, and for this very reason at least in the main plot they are deeply repressed, and rarely achieve the dynamism of dramatic action. Synge's skills and confidence had not developed sufficiently for him to be able to control the dramatic strategy of symbolic language surely enough to use it as a shield in which to reflect and engage with the terrors of parentage and history without astonishment. Music becomes a substitute for the symbolic role which is played by language in the later works. One motive for the substitution has already been suggested: the main action is powerfully directed, on the surface, towards an attempt to stylize process and change, to admit them only as unlanguaged ultimate form.

The attempt to cope with life as language is, nevertheless, present in the metatextual devices of the manuscript and the various letters. This textualization of life is an attempt to read back into time, to transform the history of the House of Sweeny. In terms of mediation, the manuscript and its epistolary supplements emerge as the play's central *dramatis persona*. If the texts within the text are seen as palimpsests, in both the Freudian and the Nietzschean sense, then the action becomes a dramatized *explication de texte*, with the subtexts threatening, from time to time, to erupt into life. The first words of the play, which are read from the manuscript by Sister Eileen, refer to "the real effort of the artist" (p. 17) and to the relationship between this reality and biography and autobiography. As she handles and reads the manuscript, she waits for the "real" Columb, who is absently represented to her through his writings. Yet when he appears, she awkwardly avoids him, leaving the room after a brief report on the uncle's death. When she returns, meaningful conversation again becomes possible only through the letter from O'Neill. The theme of the letter is art and eros. Vicariously, it expresses Columb's desire to possess Eileen and his fear of the act of possession. O'Neill writes of how he gazed on the aesthetic archetypal image of woman, Rodin's Eve, but when a real woman came to his studio, he "could do nothing but talk" (p. 21). He became a playboy, a "Jester" (p. 21) whose words were lost gems, thrown away on girls, not women. The business with the letter leads almost immediately to the next piece of mediating *écriture*—the notebook brought by Mrs. Byrne from under the pillow of Columb's dead uncle. This notebook is a veritable treasure-house of palimpsests. It contains "a little drawing of a girl" (p. 22), again, we note, not a woman, which is variously said to resemble Bride, O'Neill, Columb's uncle, Stephen Costello and Eileen. It is "in fact" a portrait of Mary Costello. A slip of paper refers the reader to "the box between the library windows," which in turn contains "my will and a letter to be read by my heir" (p. 22). With the notebook are some keys. For the moment, Columb declines to unlock the family mystery, questioning his uncle's bid to implicate him in the past and to continue to project his patriarchal, testatory authority into the future. "I do not know," declares Columb, "that I am his heir" (p. 22).

The episode which follows anticipates, for all its awkwardness, Synge's subversive use of religious rituals and sacramental rites in his later plays. Rejecting his uncle's attempt to inscribe himself into the text of his life, Columb goes to "an old press" (p. 22). He "takes out two curiously formed wine glasses with a saucepan and decanter. Then he arranges the turf, pours some wine into the saucepan and puts it on the fire" (p. 22). He is celebrating here a communion / wedding rite, in which the wine is to be changed to mingled blood on the focal altar of the house. The fire is a *turf* fire; not, we have been reminded, made of English coal. Columb spills a little of the wine onto the embers as he stirs the flames to life. This is the cue for Sister Eileen's (equally "accidental") concelebration, as she, in turn, stains Columb's manuscript with the wine. We scarcely need to invoke Jacques Derrida's analyses to recognize the signification of this episode. Indeed, the ritual spillings are followed by a liturgical reading from the manuscript, the erotic connotations of which are barely concealed beneath the mask of the text's symphonic denotation: "After dealing with the first movement that is filled with passion and excitement I go on to the next movement—reading—'The position of the slow movement after the climax of the opening is also wonderfully suggestive. This sigh of beautiful relief, which comes as an explaination (sic) rather than a mere cessation of an excitement that is always pain, is the last utterance of man'" (p. 23). At the moment where the reading reaches the "passion of relief" and "the dissolution of the person" (p. 23) the wine obligingly boils over and Columb, pouring out two glasses, declares "My wine is ready—. . . Trinquez" (p. 23). The drinking—"C'est bien bon" (p. 23)—is followed by the highly symbolic lighting of Columb's pipe from the fire.

The metatextual action continues in Act II when Columb dictates a letter to O'Neill, using Eileen as amanuensis. This is a further example of textual mediation between Columb and his cousin. The coming of spring becomes the almost Lawrentian referent for the displaced marital theme:

> A distant cousin of mine—a nun—who had been nursing my uncle stayed on here and took care of me. It has been a curious moment. I could look out from my bed into the woods and watch the spring beginning. I had forgotten the marvelousness of the world. Soft grey days came first with quiet clouds, and the woods grew purple with sap, while a few birches that stood out before them like candle sticks with wrought silver stems, covered themselves with a dull mist of red. Then the hazels came out and hung the woods with straight earrings of gold that gave relief in their simplicity among the tangled boughs. One morning after rain spectres of pale green and yellow and pink seemed to be looking out between the trees. (p. 33)

The letter is the medium through which Columb proposes marriage to Sister Eileen. When his cousin refuses to continue writing, Columb decides that the moment has come to read his uncle's letter, thereby *substituting it for his own unwritten / rejected text*. The box containing the letter also holds the wedding rings of Columb's uncle and Mary Costello, and Mary's wedding dress, soon to be used by the couple in their own wedding ceremony. The reading of the uncle's epistle is prefaced by a further liturgical speech from Columb, deriving in theme and style from his manuscript. The episode is solemnized—and scripturalized—by the lighting of oil-lamps and the references to the oil running out. The letter makes Sister Eileen want to leave. It is only when plot and sub-plot converge, when Bride Kavanagh enacts what the letter urges Columb and Eileen to do, that the main plot breaks through into action: Eileen puts on the wedding dress and yields to Columb's will.

Commitment to life is, however, ultimately denied to the two central characters in *When the Moon Has Set*, largely because they are assigned to an alternative which is removed from history and place. They are propelled, in the last instance, towards a musical requiem, the result of which is a withdrawal from the urgent problems of history, biography and time. The price exacted by the attempted transcendence of the diseased world of habit is a renunciation of the human condition. It leads inexorably to a relinquishing of identity and loss of personal freedom. Eileen acquiesces will-lessly and wit-lessly to being caught up in "a dream that is wider than I am . . . I cannot help it" (p. 38). Synge certainly struggles against paying the price, in this play, of what he was to characterize later as utopianism. Signs of the struggle are evident even in the closing lines, which, like Martin Doul's restored vision in *The Well of the Saints*, have one eye on the church and one on the greeny bits of ferns. Payment is, nevertheless, exacted by the idealism which results from the attempt to find in an escapist aesthetic the ultimate answer to the challenge of history. In the diseased world in which the peasant characters, Bride and Pat, have to find their happiness, or not at all, Columb and Eileen would be little better than the pastoral playboys of O'Casey's *Purple Dust*, a play written partly as an affectionate parody of Synge. They become high comic equivalents of those renovators of the House of History who busk around in peasant smocks and sing pseudo-rustic songs. The most apt comment on such behaviour may be confidently left to O'Casey's First Workman: "Well, God help the poor omadhauns! It's a bad sign to see people actin' like that, an' they sober."[12]

Notes

1.   All references to the two-act version of *When the Moon Has Set* are given internally in the chapter. They follow the pagination of the critical edition of the play published in *Long Room*, Double Number 24–25, Spring–Autumn 1982, by the Friends of the Library, Trinity College Dublin. For Ann Saddlemyer's comment on the conflated version offered in the *Collected Works*, Volume III, *Plays* II, see footnote number 2, (III, 155).

2.   The entry is as follows: "Finished (?) one act Play 'When the Moon Has Set (?).'"

3.   Robin Skelton describes Florence Ross, Synge's cousin, as "the first girl to interest

him emotionally." See Robin Skelton, *The Writings of J. M. Synge* (London: Thames and Hudson, 1971), p. 9. Cherrie Matheson was a friend of the Synge family who came to stay at Castle Kevin as a companion for Florence. Synge proposed to her in 1895.

4. A similar awareness of decay permeates Synge's essay, "A Landlord's Garden in County Wicklow," in which he remarks that "if a playwright chose to go through the Irish country houses he would find material, it is likely, for many gloomy plays that would turn on the dying away of these old families, and on the lives of the one or two delicate girls that are left so often to represent a dozen hearty men who were alive a generation or two ago" (II, 231).

5. Skelton, *The Writings of J. M. Synge*, p. 19.

6. Elliot Kreiger, *A Marxist Study of Shakespeare's Comedies* (London and Basingstoke: Macmillan, 1979), p. 3.

7. See *Collected Works*, (III, 171–173).

8. W. J. McCormack, *Sheridan Le Fanu and Victorian Ireland* (Oxford: Clarendon Press, 1980), p. 244.

9. Frank Lentricchia, *The Gaiety of Language*, Perspectives in Criticism, 19 (Berkeley and Los Angeles: University of California Press, 1968), p. 38.

10. W. B. Yeats, *Essays and Introductions* (London and New York: Macmillan, 1981), p. 145.

11. Declan Kiberd, *Synge and the Irish Language* (London and Basingstoke: Macmillan, 1979), pp. 147–8.

12. Sean O'Casey, *Purple Dust*, in *Three More Plays by Sean O'Casey* (London and Basingstoke: Macmillan, 1965), p. 123.

Works Cited

Kiberd, Declan, *Synge and the Irish Language*. London and Basingstoke: Macmillan, 1979.

King, Mary C, *"When the Moon Has Set*, edited, with critical introduction". *Long Room* 24–25. Dublin: Friends of the Library, Trinity College, Dublin, 1982.

Krieger, Elliot, *A Marxist Study of Shakespeare's Comedies*. London and Basingstoke: Macmillan, 1979.

Lentricchia, Frank, *The Gaiety of Language*: Perspective in Criticism, 19. Berkeley and Los Angeles: Univ. of California Press, 1968.

McCormack, W. J., *Sheridan LeFanu and Victorian Ireland*. Oxford: Clarendon Press, 1980.

O'Casey, Sean, *Purple Dust*, in *Three More Plays by Sean O'Casey*. London and Basingstoke: Macmillan, 1965.

Skelton, Robin, *The Writings of J. M. Synge*. London: Thames and Hudson, 1971.

Yeats, W. B., *Essays and Introductions*. London and New York: Macmillan, 1981.

Yeats and Synge: "A Young Man's Ghost"*

Donna Gerstenberger

When Yeats, Lady Gregory, and Edward Martyn met to discuss their ideas for an Irish dramatic movement, John Millington Synge was not a part of their considerations, for he was a man who still considered Paris the centre of his intellectual life and criticism the work of his hand. Nevertheless, by the time of Synge's death in 1909, the young Irish playwright had become for Yeats a part of the essential trinity of the Abbey Theatre. The importance which Synge had acquired for Yeats was clearly indicated when, in Stockholm to receive his Nobel Prize in 1923, Yeats chose the Irish dramatic movement for his speech before the Swedish Royal Academy. He said: "When your King gave me medal and diploma, two forms should have stood, one at either side of me, an old woman sinking into the infirmity of age and a young man's ghost. I think when Lady Gregory's and John Synge's name [*sic*] are spoken by future generations, my name, if remembered, will come up in the talk, and that if my name is spoken first their names will come in their turn."[1] Synge's relation to Yeats, the meaning of the "young man's ghost" to the older poet, grew in part from an actual literary relationship, which is of interest in its own right, but the final importance of this slight friendship is clear only when the symbolic values that Synge acquired for Yeats are understood. Yeats transformed the actual Synge into a quasi-historical figure within a few years of Synge's death, to create a man who could take his place in Yeats's gallery of Irish heroes, and the process of transfiguration tells us, finally, more about Yeats than about Synge, for as Yeats's understanding of his own relationship to Ireland changed, his understanding of Synge's symbolic value increased.

I

Yeats's romanticized version of his discovery of the poverty-stricken Synge in a Paris "students' hotel" is vastly over-simplified, as was Yeats's general view of Synge in the early years of their acquaintance. In his Preface to Synge's *The*

*This essay first appeared in *W. B. Yeats, 1865–1965: Centenary Essays on the Art of W. B. Yeats* (Ibadan: Ibadan University Press, 1965) and is reprinted with permission of the author.

Well of the Saints, Yeats recounts his advice to the struggling young writer, advice which was to set Synge on the path to fulfilment: "Give up Paris. You will never create anything by reading Racine, and Arthur Symons will always be a better critic of French literature. Go to the Aran Islands. Live there as if you were one of the people themselves; express a life that has never found expression." Synge as Yeats saw him in Paris in 1896 was an unsuccessful young critic "full of that kind of morbidity that has its roots in too much brooding over methods of expression, and ways of looking upon life, which come, not out of life, but out of literature," and Synge became, according to further evidence from the Preface to *The Well of Saints*, a writer full of creative energies, which developed precisely because he did go "to Aran and became a part of its life, living upon salt fish and eggs," the natural genius struck to fire on those rocky islands to the west of Ireland.

The picture Yeats draws of Synge in this Preface is the famous one: it is simple, direct, and satisfying to those who like to believe that literary relationships and literary births work in this way. Yeats himself was not to remain contented with it, however, for the Synge portrayed in the Preface to *The Well of the Saints* is not the man whose name was to evoke certain qualities for Yeats in his own middle and later years. Even in this first extended evaluation of Synge, although the portrait drawn is that of a one-dimensional man, Yeats is attracted by Synge's achievement largely because it is opposite in kind to his own. Yeats's enduring admiration for Synge's ability to partake of a primitive culture, to catch the accents of peasant speech and gesture, is obvious in the Preface. Synge's closeness to the life of the people from the first linked him in Yeats's mind with Lady Gregory, who shared this quality, and it was a source of vague envy, for as critics during Yeats's lifetime and after have observed, Yeats himself was separated by some quality of mind and personality from the people of Ireland. As Maud Gonne has observed in her essay "Yeats and Ireland," Willie [was] less aware of the People than of the Land.

Although Yeats and Synge both grew up in middle-class Protestant families, the similarity of background may be deceiving rather than enlightening, for Yeats from his boyhood was exposed to the world of ideas, and an artistic, aesthetic view of life was encouraged by his unorthodox father. On the other hand, Synge's church-oriented family wholeheartedly distrusted art and the intellectual life. Yet both young men responded to a growing Irish nationalism in much the same way that many young Irishmen of the time must have: they steeped themselves in Irish history and mythology, and, for a time at least, admired the patriotic Irish poetry of *The Spirit of the Nation* school. Eventually, a growing aesthetic awareness and practical experience with Irish causes resulted for both Synge and Yeats in a rejection of nationalism in literature.

At an age at which Yeats was still dreaming with Maud Gonne of building a Castle of Heroes, Synge's instinctive avoidance of idealization and dislike of heroic abstraction had brought him to a measured view of Ireland

and Irish materials. Partly because of his years abroad and his deliberate choice of a foreign culture for his study, Synge had acquired an objectivity which was to prove invaluable when he approached Irish subjects. Synge was in this early response to Irish subjects again Yeats's opposite, for Yeats's relationship to such materials was much more conventional in his early years, to be qualified finally only by difficult and painfully-developed experience.

II

Although Yeats was six years Synge's senior, he had not entered his important phase as a playwright when Synge came to the Irish theatre movement. Yeats had not yet been able to free his own drama from Irish national involvement nor from pre-Raphaelite influence, and he found a great deal to admire in and to learn from the work of the young Irishman from Paris. Yeats's plays up to this time had been relatively slight—*Land of Heart's Desire, The Countess Cathleen, The Pot of Broth, Cathleen ni Houlihan,* and *The Hour-Glass*—plays which at best are apprentice efforts. When *Riders to the Sea* was staged in the same month as an early version of *The Shadowy Waters*, the contrast cannot have been lost on Yeats, who continued working with his dreamy play for a number of years, seeking for it more strength and a cleaner outline, until he arrived at a final version in which some critics have found the occasional influence of Synge.

It is not possible to know how much influence Synge actually had on Yeats in the drama, Synge's major area of accomplishment, but it is possible that Synge acted as a catalyst for Yeats in a general way as the older poet moved toward his mature style. Synge's plays demonstrated to Yeats what could be made of the Irish material when it was subjected to the harsh light of reality and freed of traditional romantic mists, how the world of *The Wanderings of Oisin* could be transformed in *The Death of Cuchulain.*

Ironically, it is in the area of verse that Synge's influence on Yeats has been most clearly demonstrated. This fact is ironic because Synge's poetic production was small indeed, and during his lifetime he saw none of his adult verse in print. The explanation of this irony lies, I think, not wholly in the canon of Synge's verse itself, but in what the figure of Synge had come to mean for Yeats by the time Yeats discovered to his surprise that the "solitary, undemonstrative" Synge wrote verse. The verse of Synge cannot alone explain the disproportionately large representation given it in the 1936 *Oxford Book of Modern Verse*, which Yeats edited. Nor is Yeats's claim in his Introduction that "John Synge brought back masculinity to Irish verse with his harsh disillusionment" sufficient to explain the inclusion of eight poems and four translations by Synge.

Certainly Yeats had been impressed enough by the strength, the hardness, and the masculinity of some of Synge's verses to arrange in 1908 to have an edition of poems by Synge published by the Cuala Press, and he undertook in 1909 the task of writing an introduction which would help fatten a distressingly thin volume and commemorate his friend John Synge, who had died while the poems were in the press.

The Synge whom Yeats presents in his Preface to the Cuala edition is a far more complex man than the one Yeats had drawn in his Preface to *The Well of the Saints* only four years earlier. In his introduction Yeats remembers Synge as the man who had said, "We must unite asceticism, stoicism, ecstasy; two of these have often come together but not all three," and Yeats concludes that "the strength that made him delight in setting the hard virtues by the soft, the bitter by the sweet, salt by mercury, the stone by the elixir, gave him a hunger for harsh facts, for ugly surprising things, for all that defies our hope. In 'The Passing of the Shee' he is repelled by the contemplation of a beauty too far from life to appease his mood; and in his own work, benign images ever present to his soul must have beside them malignant reality, and the greater the brightness the greater must the darkness be."[2]

The poem entitled "The Passing of the Shee" to which Yeats refers is one Synge had written in reaction to one of AE's pictures, with its romanticized treatment of mythological material, and it is a poem which summarizes the whole problem of the relationship of the Irish artist to his material:

> Adieu, sweet Angus, Maeve and Fand,
> Ye plumed yet skinny Shee,
> That poets played with hand in hand
> To learn their ecstasy.
>
> We'll search in Red Dan Sally's ditch,
> And drink in Tubber fair,
> Or poach with Red Dan Philly's bitch
> The badger and the hare.[3]

"The Passing of the Shee" trades the world of the "plumed yet skinny Shee" for that of "Red Dan Philly's bitch," anticipating the exchange Yeats was to make of the world of the Countess Cathleen for that of Crazy Jane.

Enough has been written about the influence of Synge's verse on Yeats's in diction, subject matter, images, and attitude;[4] I would only add the suggestion that Yeats's Crazy Jane probably traces her ancestry quite specifically to Mary Byrne, a character in Synge's play, *The Tinker's Wedding*, for in Yeats's Preface to the Cuala edition of the poems, he recalls Synge's dramatic creation: ". . . the drunken woman of 'The Tinker's Wedding' is but the more drunken and the more thieving because she can remember great queens. And what is it but desire of ardent life, like that of Usheen who cried 'tears down but not for God, but because Finn and the Fianna are not living'; that makes his

(Synge's) young girls of 'The Playboy of the Western World' prefer to any peaceful man their eyes have looked upon, a seeming murderer?"[5] In Synge's play, Mary Byrne, the drunken old woman of the ditch, is the symbol of the natural, the ardent life, unspoiled by the petty concerns of middle-class morality, and it would seem that in the last of the Crazy Jane poems, "Crazy Jane on the Mountain," Yeats is specifically remembering Synge's old woman in the context of his Preface to Synge's poems. Crazy Jane (like Mary Byrne), having recalled "Great-bladdered Emer," the great queen of Irish legend, and having contemplated the paltry modern situation, "lay stretched out in the dirt" and "cried *tears down*" [my italics]. The parallel situation and the invocation of the same passage in the Irish heroic legend which had occurred in the Preface discovers Mary Byrne the grandam of the ageless Crazy Jane.

The conflict between Crazy Jane and the Bishop is the conflict which is at the centre of all of Synge's art, and it is not surprising that Synge became identified for Yeats with his growing hatred of the middle class and all that represented restrictive morality as opposed to the natural, the passionate, the heroic. One of the events which came to symbolize for Yeats a crucial truth about experience in general and about Irish experience in particular was the riots at the Abbey performances of *The Playboy of the Western World*. As a public event which could serve a personal symbolic function, the riots took an imaginative place for Yeats beside the fall of Parnell and the Hugh Lane controversy. Through such events Yeats had discovered the destructive and limiting quality of the middle-class mind and felt the limitations imposed on the Irish poet and playwright who would serve the needs of a people and a nation.

Yeats had, early in his career, felt a need to explain to critics that he served the needs of Ireland in seeking an eternal as well as an Irish truth; therefore he asks in "To Ireland in the Coming Times,"

> Nor may I less be counted one
> With Davis, Mangan, Ferguson,
> Because, to him who ponders well,
> My rhymes more than their rhyming tell
> Of things discovered in the deep . . .[6]

By the date of *Responsibilities*, Yeats is no longer concerned with explaining the way that he must go, and he has only scorn for the "eunuchs" of "On Those that Hated 'The Playboy of the Western World', 1907." A remark made by Yeats in 1909 in *The Death of Synge* indicates an understanding of the inevitable conflict which Synge's work brought into focus: "At Stratford-on-Avon the *Playboy* shocked a good many people, because it was a self-improving, self-educating audience, and that means a perverted and common-place audience. If you set out to educate yourself you are compelled to have an ideal, a model of what you would be; and if you are not a man of genius, your model will be commonplace and prevent the natural impulses of the mind, its natural reverence, desire, hope, admiration, always half unconscious, almost bodily."[7] As Yeats came to understand that his own work was sacred and that what he gave to Ireland had to be separated from his role as poet, he relinquished his once-cherished idea of moulding a people into a national ideal through art. In the events of Synge's lifetime as a playwright, Yeats found support for his own decision to turn his energies away from an attempt to create a people's theatre for an unwilling audience.

III

Synge seemed to Yeats never to have hoped for anything from the Irish people; he seemed in this as in most things Yeats's opposite. Yeats speaks in *Estrangement* of having been corrupted by the "conscious patriotism" of Davis, whose "Ireland was artificial, an idea built up in a couple of generations by a few commonplace men." This is a patriotism quite different from a love for the country of one's birth, in which no attempt is made to "sum up a nation intellectually." In this matter also, Yeats feels that Synge remained free of harm, having only that instinctive love, which "left the soul free." "Synge's purity of genius comes in part from having kept this instinct and this alone."[8]

This evaluation is augmented by Yeats in his meditations on Synge in *The Death of Synge*: "1. He was one of those unmoved souls in whom there is a perpetual 'Last Day,' a perpetual trumpeting and coming up for judgment. 2. He did not speak to men and women, asking judgment, as lesser writers do; but knowing himself part of judgment he was silent."[9]

Synge has become for Yeats a much more complex figure than that man in the Preface to *The Well of the Saints* who seemed a romantic fulfilment of the dicta of *The Lyrical Ballads*, a man Yeats had sent to the Aran Islands to fulfil a need of Ireland for a rediscovery of her peasant life.

Throughout his life, Yeats returned to the figure of Synge in a number of his poems—particularly when he calls the roll of the creative men of modern Ireland: Hyde, Synge, Lady Gregory, Shawe-Taylor, and Hugh Lane. Synge was for Yeats always the meditative man, the man apart from the excitement, separated by character and will from the volatile centre of the Irish movement and in this most valuable to it. Yet Synge is, in "In Memory of Major Robert Gregory," a part of the essential Irish scene, a man who "dying chose the living world for text"; and in "The Municipal Gallery Revisited," Synge with Yeats and Lady Gregory is separated from others in "modern times" for understanding that all that would grow strong must come from contact with the soil: "We three alone in modern times had brought / Everything down to that sole test again, / Dream of the noble and the beggar-man."[10] Synge always seemed to Yeats to embody a passionate strength, a tie with the earth, which Yeats sought increasingly for his own work. Synge's emphasis on "joy" and "strength" became a part of Yeats's own tragic and poetic theory, and while Yeats most surely would have found his artistic growth without Synge, he had in the death of Synge an event which engaged him wholly, which gave imaginative substance to that which he had learned from the man living.

Synge appears in Yeats's *A Vision*, to stand beside Rembrandt as Yeats's embodiment of the Receptive Man in Phase twenty-three. Although Synge is used here to represent a general type, Yeats's comments suggest the meaning of Synge's accomplishment for him and illustrate Yeats's ability to elevate people out of his personal history into almost mythical figures, the poetic imagination at work on near-history.

The wisdom of the man of the twenty-third Phase is that of "general humanity experienced as a form of involuntary emotion and involuntary delight in the 'minute particulars' of life." The *Will* of this man is in revolt "from every intellectual summary, from all intellectual abstraction"; this man cares "only for what is human, individual and moral. To others he may seem to care for the immoral and inhuman only, for he will be hostile, or indifferent to moral as to intellectual summaries . . . if he is Synge he takes a malicious pleasure in the contrast between his hero, whom he discovers through his instinct for comedy, and any hero in men's minds."[11] The image Yeats draws of the man of this phase is one that evokes all that was antithetical to Yeats's own nature and suggests Synge's particular value to Yeats, both personal and artistic, for Yeats strove throughout his life to take to himself and his art those qualities which seemed most alien to the nature of the Yeats who discovered Synge in Paris.

It would be easy enough to over-estimate Synge's specific influence on Yeats, as Yeats himself probably over-estimated Synge's poetic abilities, but the best and safest gauge of Synge's relationship to Yeats's career is the fact that in Synge Yeats found a symbolic figure, a man who entered into his imaginative world as a very real and substantial presence for the whole extent of Yeat's life.

Notes

1. *Aut.*, p. 553.
2. Synge, J. M., *Collected Works* (ed. R. Skelton), Vol. I, London, O.U.P. 1962, p. xxxiv.
3. *Ibid.*
4. See for example, Henn, T. R., *The Lonely Tower*, London, Methuen, 1950; Jeffares, A. N., *W. B. Yeats: Man and Poet*, London, Routledge and K. Paul, 1949; and Skelton, R., "The Poetry of J. M. Synge," *Poetry Ireland*, I, Autumn 1962.
5. Synge, J. M., *op. cit.*, pp. xxxiv–xxxv.
6. *C. P.*, p. 57.

7. *Aut.*, p. 525.
8. *Ibid.*, p. 472.
9. *Ibid.*, p. 511.
10. *C. P.*, p. 369.
11. *A Vision*, p. 165.

Synge's *The Shadow of the Glen*: Repetition and Allusion*

NICHOLAS GRENE

It would be inaccurate to claim that Synge's one-act play *The Shadow of the Glen* has been neglected. Certainly by comparison with *Riders to the Sea* and *The Playboy of the Western World*, all of his other work has been relatively neglected; yet *The Shadow* has had its share of attention—a chapter or half a chapter in every full-length study of Synge, a reference in most essays and articles. Unfortunately, accounts of the play have almost always included extensive discussion of the background to its first production. Was *The Shadow* based upon the story of the Widow of Ephesus?[1] or was it an attack on Irish loveless marriages, as J. B. Yeats suggested?[2] The audience reaction to *The Shadow* is an integral part of the story of Synge's relation with the Irish nationalists, a story which has been re-told ad nauseam. It should be possible to set aside these familiar controversial issues, and to look at the dramatic effect of the play in itself. As a means to that end I want to consider particularly Synge's use of the linked features of repetition and allusion, and to show the complex structure which he thus achieves.

The folk-tale on which *The Shadow* is based contains as its central device the comic irony of the eavesdropper. The audience enjoys its superior knowledge, that the old man, supposed dead, is actually listening to the conversation of the "survivors," overhearing guilty admissions or attacks upon himself. Synge adds to the comedy of this situation by having Dan Burke repeat the conversation he has heard when he rises from his death-bed. Dan ridicules the idiotic topics which Nora and the Tramp have been discussing while he has been lying under his sheet: "It's near dead I was wanting to sneeze, and you blathering about the rain, and Darcy (*bitterly*)—the divil choke him—and the towering church" (*Plays* I p. 43).[3] There is no need to invoke Bergson's concept of the comic nature of repetition to explain why we find this funny. Even more obvious is the instance of Dan's second resurrection. Michael has just been making plans for his marriage to Nora: "We'd do right to wait now till himself will be quiet a while in the Seven Churches, and then you'll marry me in the

*This essay first appeared in *Modern Drama*, 17 (1974), and is reprinted with permission of the author.

chapel of Rathvanna, and I'll bring the sheep up on the bit of a hill you have in the back mountains, and we won't have anything we'd be afeard to let our minds on when the mist is down" (*Plays* I p. 51). Dan as he leaps from the bed brandishing his stick throws Michael's words in his teeth: "Now you'll not marry her the time I'm rotting below in the Seven Churches and you'll see the thing I'll give you will follow you on the back mountains when the wind is high" (*Plays* I p. 53). It is the eavesdropper's moment of triumph, and it is his special delight to show those overheard how completely they have been caught out.

One small but significant change, however, Dan makes in repeating Michael's words: the euphemistic "quiet" becomes the brutally coarse "rotting." This too might be interpreted as a comic touch—the stripping of shams—but, in the context of the scene that follows, it is suggestive of Dan's frame of mind. The old man's real wrath is reserved for his wife, and he turns on her and repeats words which she has spoken earlier: "There'll be an end now of your fine times and all the talk you have of young men and old men, and of the mist coming up or going down" (*Plays* I p. 53). The speeches here recalled are those in which Nora expresses her sense of the monotonous desolation of her life—"Seeing nothing but the mists rolling down the bog, and the mists again, and they rolling up the bog, and hearing nothing but the wind crying out in the bits of broken trees were left from the great storm, and the streams roaring with the rain," and her feeling of the meaningless onset of old age—"the young growing behind me and the old passing" (*Plays* I p. 49). It is apparent that Dan has completely distorted her words; these are anything but "fine times." It is the measure of Dan's obsessiveness that he can transform Nora's lament on the passing generations into evidence of a swarm of lovers. This becomes even clearer in the final instance of repetition in this scene in which Dan taunts Nora with her own picture of old age: "it's soon you'll be getting old with that life, I'm telling you; it's soon your teeth'll be falling and your head'll be the like of a bush where sheep do be leaping a gap" (*Plays* I pp. 53–55). The emphasis on "your" would bring out in speaking the fact that this is a word-for-word recollection of Nora's melancholy speech to Michael Dara: "You'll be getting old, and I'll be getting old, and in a little while, I'm telling you, you'll be sitting up in your bed—the way himself was sitting—with a shake in your face, and your teeth falling, and the white hair sticking out round you like an old bush where sheep do leaping a gap" (*Plays* I p. 51). By our sense of the difference in tone and meaning between the words when first spoken and their repeated form, we come to see the pathological character of Dan's mind, obsessed with old age and death, resentful not of his wife's infidelity, but of the very fact of her youth. He is translated from the comic stereotype of the jealous husband into a very real and terrible old man.

The atmosphere of the play's setting is established by the use of certain words and phrases which recur naturally in the dialogue. For instance, there is nothing unusual in the fact that sheep are commonly discussed among mountain shepherds. Michael Dara's lack of skill in handling "mountain ewes," Patch Darcy's expertise, these would be everyday topics of conversation. Yet Synge, by using these natural allusions to sheep, manages to create the effect of a motif through the play. Dan is particularly associated with sick or dying sheep; Nora describes his supposed death: "when the sun set on the bog beyond, he made a great lep, and let a great cry out of him, and stiffened himself out the like of a dead sheep" (*Plays* I p. 35). Towards the end of the play, as the Tramp prepares to leave with Nora, he consoles her that for the future, "there'll be no old fellow wheezing the like of a sick sheep close to your ear" (*Plays* I p. 57). This recalls and reinforces his earlier comparison where the terms were reversed: "the sheep were lying under the ditch and every one of them coughing, and choking, like an old man, with the great rain and the fog" (*Plays* I p. 39). Such references suggest obliquely an image of Dan Burke as a grotesque sheep / man—the owner grown like his animals. The animal association heightens our sense of the imminent corruption of the flesh.

Again and again in the play the mention of sheep is associated with old age and death. Nora talks of "white hair sticking out round you like an old bush where sheep do be leaping a gap" (*Plays* I p. 51). The sheep are here only indirectly connected, but with the "old bush," they make up an imaginative cluster around the idea of senility. In a passage which reveals the full power of his obsessed imagination, Dan uses the same object of comparison, as he foretells Nora's end: "It's lonesome roads she'll be going, and hiding herself away till the end will come, and they find her stretched like a dead sheep with the frost on her, or the big spiders, maybe, and they putting their webs on her, in the butt of a ditch" (*Plays* I p. 55). At no point in the play are sheep given a picturesque or pastoral appeal. This may or may not be deliberate on Synge's part, an attempt to increase his effect by the upsetting of normal literary association. In any case, the result is to heighten and intensify the desolate atmosphere of the glen.

The glen is above all dominated by the "shadow" which gives the play its title.[4] Dan "dies," appropriately enough, "the time the shadow was going up through the glen"; no doubt he chooses dusk to make it impossible for Nora to go to fetch his sister from the "big glen over the hill." More often, however, the shadow refers to the mountain mist rather than the darkness. I have already quoted Nora's famous lines about "the mists rolling down the bog, and the mists again, and they rolling up the bog," the passage which has inspired Synge's parodists, and which Denis Johnston dismisses as a "depressing weather report."[5] This is only one of a network of allusions which suggest the effect which the "shadow of the glen" has upon the lives of the people. Michael Dara is less at home in this world than any of the other three characters—he is "a kind of a farmer has come up from the sea"[6]—yet even he is aware that there are things "we'd be afeard to let our minds on when the mist is down."

Nora describes Dan to the Tramp: "He was an old man, and an odd man, stranger, and it's always up on the hill he was, thinking thoughts in the dark mist" (*Plays* I p. 35). This suggests, if not the origin of Dan's bitter obsessions, at least the condition congenial to their development, and his near-madness is made plausible by this reminder of the solitude of his daily life.

For Nora the shadow is not so much an object of fear, as a figure for boredom and loneliness. It is just that banal quality of repetition in the mists going up and down which Synge's critics have ridiculed that is typical of Nora's situation. The Tramp stands apart from the other characters although, in some ways, he is less an outsider in the glen than the "farmer," Mike Dara. He too has a healthy respect for the shadow. Though he protests his lack of fear of the hills, yet when Nora is going out to leave him alone with the corpse, he asks for a needle as talisman. His fear is not so much of natural but of supernatural forces. He was terrified by the "voice out of the dark mist," but when he learned that it had been the mad Patch Darcy, he "wasn't afeared any more" (*Plays* I p. 39). The Tramp's world is one peopled with uncanny powers which it would be foolhardy to disregard, but in so far as natural phenomena are concerned, his is the sane realism of the human being who knows his own limitations: "It's a wild night, God helps us, but it'll pass surely" (*Plays* I p. 57). It is his sanity and balance which he has to offer Nora.

The shadow of the glen can hardly be called a symbol in the play; its effect on the lives of the characters is too immediate, too direct. It suggests by turns, old age and death, boredom and loneliness, encroaching madness, because these are, so to speak, its natural associations. Just as the sea in *Riders* is a principal agent in the play, so the shadow dominates and conditions the people of the glen. Nature in both *Riders* and *The Shadow* is, at best, indifferent to man and his needs, potentially a dangerous and hostile enemy. For the shadow threatens man's reason, as the sea threatens his very life; the dread which is always with the mountain people, the fear of the "oppression of the hills," is glimpsed in Nora's phrase—"not knowing on what thing your mind might stay." The shadow is that force in nature which crushes man's consciousness and denies his being, which annihilates him with the sense of his insignificance.

By repeated references to the conditions of life in the glen, Synge evokes the atmosphere of the setting. By allusions to off-stage figures he makes us aware also of the community of the hill men who live there. Mary Brien, who is only mentioned once, is a younger contemporary of Nora's, and presumably a close neighbour. Peggy Cavanagh is an old woman who was once a prosperous farmwife, but is now homeless and reduced to begging at the crossroads. The madness and death of the herd Patch Darcy is still in some sort the local news; Patch is mentioned by Michael Dara, described at length by the Tramp and recalled admiringly by Nora. By such allusions Synge extends the dimensions of the little society presented, and gives it a familiar reality. We need not be told much about the characters whose names are mentioned; but the fact that they recur in the conversation establishes a context beyond that of the cottage room and the four people we see on stage.

Yet obviously the allusions are not merely random. Together the three off-stage figures may be seen to illustrate the plight of the play's central character, Nora Burke. Mary Brien is one of the "young growing behind" in the race of time, and Mary's life is for Nora a reminder of the meaningless passing of her own. However the fate of Peggy Cavanagh, the homeless woman of the roads, is the alternative to the monotonous career of the farmer's wife: "There she is now walking round on the roads, or sitting in a dirty old house, with no teeth in her mouth, and no sense, and no more hair than you'd see on a bit of a hill and they after burning the furze from it" (*Plays* I p. 51). This is an image of which Nora is frightened, and Dan, with an instinct for what will hurt, taunts her with it: "Let her walk round the like of Peggy Cavanagh below, and be begging money at the cross-roads, or selling songs to the man" (*Plays* I p. 53). The Tramp tries to console her with an assurance that in future she will not be "hearing a talk of getting old like Peggy Cavanagh" (*Plays* I p. 57). Nora, as she comes to see her life in the course of the play, is caught between the thought of Peggy Cavanagh and the thought of Mary Brien.

Patch Darcy's role in the play is more important and more complex. There is, of course, the suggestion that he may have been Nora's lover, though on balance this seems unlikely. His death by madness provides the most telling instance of the powers of the hills, as we can see from the first reference to him in the play. The tramp is speaking: "If myself was easy afeard, I'm telling you, it's long ago I'd have been locked into the Richmond Asylum, or maybe have run up into the back hills with nothing on me but an old shirt, and been eaten by the crows the like of Patch Darcy—the Lord have mercy on him— in the year that's gone" (*Plays* I p. 37). His death, and the manner of his death, so cows the people of the glen, that Nora expresses surprise at hearing the Tramp praise him: "isn't a grand thing when you hear a living man saying a good word of a dead man, and he mad dying?" (*Plays* I p. 47). If Nora thinks sadly of Mary Brien and Peggy Cavanagh, it is perhaps the fate of Patch Darcy which is the ultimate terror.

And yet Darcy is more than a particularly horrifying *memento mori* in the play. His name recurs in all seven times, and each of the characters express a different attitude to his memory. Nora remembers him with affection and regret: "God spare Darcy; he'd always look in here and he passing up or passing down, and it's very lonesome I was after him a long while" (*Plays* I p. 39). Dan has obviously hated him, and curses bitterly at the very mention of his name. Michael Dara, who, it must be remembered, has only recently come to live in the neighbourhood, remarks of Patch uneasily, "Is it the man went queer in his head the year that's gone?" (*Plays* I p. 47). But it is the Tramp's attitude which is most significant. He praises Patch, contrasting his skill as a shepherd with the ineptness of Mike: "That was a great man, young fellow—a great man, I'm telling you. There was never a lamb from his own ewes he wouldn't know before it was marked, and he'd run from this to the city of Dublin and never catch for his breath" (*Plays* I p. 47). This eulogy, the emphasis on the word "great," together with his spectacular death, make us think of Patch in terms of a lost heroic ideal, and it is appropriate that Nora and the Tramp should find common ground in their admiration for the dead shepherd. As Dan and Michael both in different ways reject his image, so the other two characters in their feeling for Patch Darcy seem to proclaim their identification with what is extraordinary and strange in life, their imaginative distinction.

Synge's use of language in *The Shadow* is subtle and unobtrusive. The dialogue has not the bold imaginative appeal of *The Playboy* or the high eloquence of *Deirdre*—the vivid "fully-flavoured" quality for which Synge is famous. Yet the austere simple language of the one-act play makes possible an astonishingly rich and complex dramatic structure. Synge took pains to root his folk-tale heard on Aran in the familiar setting of the Wicklow mountains. The play is, on the face of it, a naturalistic peasant drama, and Synge is careful not to infringe the conventions of naturalism. Although the Tramp's speech to Nora—"Come along with me now, lady of the house, and it's not my blather you'll be hearing only. . . ." (*Plays* I p. 57)—might seem like a set-piece of "poetry talk," this effect of artificiality would be offset on stage by Nora's movements as she gathers together her belongings. Yet if one considers briefly the different uses made of repetition and allusion, the varied levels of dramatic experience in the play become clear. The basic situation is that of farcical comedy—the comedy of the eavesdropper, with his gloating repetition of what he has overheard. This same device, however, is used to suggest the psychology of the old husband; it is at this level that we are presented with the study of the loveless marriage. By emphasising the setting of the action and the atmosphere of the glen, Synge gives to his play "a local habitation and a name." He evokes a complete community with its special way of life, its problems and its terrors. Yet the allusions and repeated words and phrases serve also to define certain universal spiritual values by which the characters are divided.

The level of dramatic response in *The Shadow* varies, therefore, from situation comedy through "problem play" and "peasant naturalism," to a drama of poetic symbolism. Such a combination would seem almost impossible to achieve without disharmony. Synge's success is partly due to the apparent homogeneity of the language and action, which allows us to respond at the various different levels without any marked sense of incongruity. When we try to define *The Shadow of the Glen* as comedy or tragicomedy, we may well find ourselves puzzled, but it is not in any obvious way an experimental mixture of the traditional genres. It is not, moreover, a progress from one form to another; it does not start as comedy and end as poetic drama, for the tiny epilogue of Dan and Michael sitting down to their drinks is as ironic and multi-faceted as any scene in the play. In the bare and uncomplicated action, in the austere and economic language, Synge presents a drama which is never simple, but constantly requires the audience to qualify one response with another, to be aware of the shifting status of the dramatic experience. Although he was to create more important works on a larger scale, in subtlety and depth Synge never surpassed this, his first stage play.

Notes

1.   The ghost of the Widow of Ephesus has, we may hope, been laid to rest by Séan O Súilleabháin in "Synge's Use of Irish Folklore," *J. M. Synge: Centenary Papers 1971*, Dublin, 1972, p. 19.

2.   An issue which is raised again in Robin Skelton's *The Writings of J. M. Synge*, London, 1971, pp. 57–58.

3.   All quotations refer to the Oxford edition of the *Collected Works, Volume III, Plays Book I*, ed. Ann Saddlemyer, London, 1968.

4.   The second title for the play, *The Shadow of the Glen*, makes this clearer than the original *In the Shadow of the Glen*.

5.   Denis Johnston, *John Millington Synge*, New York, 1965, p. 12.

6.   The distinction is between the lowland farmer of arable land and the mountain shepherd.

An Aran Requiem:
Setting in "Riders to the Sea"*

DANIEL J. CASEY

And so when all my little work is done
They'll say I came in eighteen-seventy-one,
And died in Dublin . . . what year will they write
For my poor passage to the stall of night?
    —"On an Anniversary"—J. M. Synge

The centenary of a major writer's birth frequently occasions critical reappraisal of his entire literary output. This, then, is the year to scrutinize John Millington Synge, to revive his dramas, to "discover" his poetry and translations, to pour over his prose meticulously. This is the year for John Millington Synge to step further out of the long shadow of W. B. Yeats and shed, once and for all, the opprobrium of Irish nationalist distemper and the opprobrium of certain early critics—Forrest Reid and St. John Ervine—whose myopic visions led them to spurious denials of the dramatist's creative genius.[1] And this, it seems, is the year to reconsider critically purpose and meaning in Synge's masterworks— "Riders to the Sea" and "The Playboy of the Western World"—to reconsider them as reflections of the playwright's experience and aesthetic. In 1971 John Millington Synge emerges relatively unscathed; this twelve-month re-evaluation has added measurably to his stature in Irish letters; it has, in fact, lengthened the second shadow on the Abbey stage.

But more than that, the year's criticism suggests that Synge's unique position in Irish literature is attributable to his fascination for the exotic world of the Gael and his acute awareness of his cultural distance from that world. Yeats's well-publicized counsel to the young Synge, as they stood outside the Hotel Corneille in Paris in 1896, may have spurred his intent to visit Aran, but Synge's early concern for the Wicklow peasants, his non-apostolic motive for studying Irish at Trinity, his literary involvement with Le Braz, Loti, and Renan, and his interest in Jubainville's Celtic mythology lectures at the Sorbonne also anticipated the journeys to the Islands.[2] And it is true that Synge probably would have failed in the concert halls and that Arthur Symons

*This essay first appeared in *The Antigonish Review*, No. 9 (Spring 1972), and is reprinted with permission.

was the better critic of French literature. In May, 1898, some seventeen months after Yeats's historic Paris dictum, Synge's enthusiasm lured him from the Wicklow Pale onto the western rocks to begin his literary novitiate. He turned west to experience a world he had long wondered at, a world of myth and reality that he would later express as it had never before been expressed.

In the Aran notebooks, Synge recognized the stark cultural disparity that stood between the islanders and himself: on his second visit, he entered: "In some ways these men and women seem strangely far away from me. They have the same emotions that I have, and the animals have, yet I cannot talk to them when there is much to say, more than to the dog that whines beside me in a mountain fog."[3] But with each succeeding visit to Aran the distance was narrowing, while the allurement for the Fir Bolg and their posterity increased. By October, 1902, when the text of "Riders" was complete, Synge's imagination was alive with myth, epic, and fairy and folk tales, for he had, since his first Aran visit, continued his Celtic studies at the Sorbonne, reviewed for *The Speaker* four Irish titles—*Danta Amhrain is Caointe Sheathruin Ceitinn, Cuchulain of Muirthemne, Donegal Fairy Stories,* and *Foras Feasa Ar Eirinn*—written the essay, "La Vieille Littérature Irlandaise," participated in the Breton folk revival, and compiled and edited nearly a score of notebooks in *The Aran Islands.*

The Aran sketches furnished plots for his dramas, and his reflections added an aesthetic perspective. Pat Dirane, the sgéaláí of Inishmaan, provided "He That's Dead Can Do No Hurt", and the oldest man on the island gave him the details of the infamous Lynchehaun murder story. Synge transferred Dirane's tale to the Harney cottage in the Wicklow Hills and made "In the Shadow of the Glen" of it. He removed the ancient's tale of the patricide from Achill and the Arans to a shebeen in Mayo, and there created "The Playboy of the Western World." Though he adapted the plot of "The Well of the Saints" from a medieval French farce, he also remembered Martin Coneely's miraculous Aran well at *Teampall an Ceatrair Alainn* (The Church of the Four Comely Persons), where blindness and epilepsy were cured.[4] Four of Synge's six plays might have been set in Aran, but only in "Riders to the Sea" is there the urgency of capturing the pristine qualities of the Aran requiem. "Riders to the Sea" is folk drama as no other Synge play is folk drama; it harkens back to antiquity and draws its strength from the mood of pagan fatalism that pervades the place.[5]

I. Implications of Setting

"Riders to the Sea" is an Aran requiem that opens sometime before the Celtic dawn and ends abruptly in the midst of a curious funeral in the Celtic twilight. It is a dramatic episode that depends in the end on mythical, symbolic, and allegorical interpretation, and in the beginning on John Millington Synge's Aran experience.

Understanding the implications of setting in "Riders to the Sea" contributes to an appreciation of the tragedy. Critics have indeed examined the playwright's conscious art, his use of form, ironic technique, and dialect; few have responded intuitively to *an domhain shair* (the western world) or inquired into Synge's dependence on the cottage on Inishmaan to set his dramatic elegy.[6] A cursory reading of the prose sketches, *The Aran Islands*, is unlikely to resolve the problem of response to setting in "Riders," though it will assuredly be a step in that direction. The resolution begins on a quay in Galway or aboard a turf-stacked hooker out of Carraroe. It comes of peering through a mist-laden bay for a glimpse of "a wet rock in the Atlantic." Essentially the tragedy derives its force from the interacting preternatural powers emanating from the omnipotent sea, the subterranean recesses of the defiant islands, and the mysterious psyche of the Aranmen themselves. The fuller sense of tragedy comes, of course, in the final cathartic realization of man's tenuous existence in the cosmos.

"Riders to the Sea" is, we are told, set on "An Island off the West of Ireland"; it is set on Inishmaan, the middle island in the Aran group. Conjecture as to Synge's reasons for an Inishmaan cottage setting may seem pointless. Hadn't he witnessed the aftermath of a drowning there and heard islanders' whispered versions of the tragedy? But for Synge the fisher cottage suggests more than a tragic tale; it suggests a barren windswept landscape, megalithic monuments, and the dark descendants of the Fir Bolg, a folk whose race memory is crowded with mythic allusions. Inishmaan, where more Irish is spoken, and where "the life is perhaps the most primitive that is left in Europe," provided more than an atmosphere, it provided the reason for the drama itself. The aged thatcher on Inisheer confided: "Long ago we used all to be pagans, and the saints used to be coming to teach us about God and the creation of the world. The people on the middle island were the last to keep a hold on the fire-worshipping, or whatever it was they had in those days, but in the long run a saint got in among them and they began listening to him though they would often say in the evening they believed, and then say the morning after that, they did not believe."[7] Synge sought to be witness to the most extraordinary endemic instincts and to participate, however vicariously, in the Gaelic experience. In *The Aran Islands* we have something of his observations and his reflections; in "Riders to the Sea" an aesthetic representation of those instincts and that experience.

II. THE ARAN SKETCHES AS A SOURCE

George Moore's remark that the details in "Riders to the Sea" "occasionally make the play seem little more than the contents of Synge's notebooks" has more than a hint of truth in it.[8] Among the playwright's impressions scattered through the Aran sketches are recollections of the tragic and near-tragic incidents that contribute to the dramatic episode. During his first visit to Inishmaan in May and June, 1898, Synge was intrigued by the ceremony that attended the death of an old woman in the neighboring cottage. The mournful keen at the wake and the repetitious thud of the hammer on the coffin he overheard from a distance. The following morning he recorded details of the burial—the manner in which the coffin was loosely sewn in sailcloth and borne by three cross-poles lashed to the lid; the procession of men followed by old women with red petticoats drawn over their heads; the ritual in which each old woman led an ancient recitative, bending her forehead to a stone, while the rest swayed rhythmically and intoned an incomprehensible chant; the interment, accompanied by a rumbling of thunder and a rain of hailstones; and finally the primordial recessional keen that concluded the burial. Synge was completely absorbed in the ancient lament and noted:

> The grief of the keen . . . seems to contain the whole passionate rage that lurks somewhere in every native of the island. In this cry of pain the inner consciousness of the people seems to lay itself bare for an instant and to reveal the mood of the beings who feel their isolation in the face of a universe that wars on them with wind and seas. They are usually silent, but in the presence of death all outward show of indifference or patience is forgotten, and they shriek with pitiable despair before the horror of the fate to which they are all doomed.[9]

The emphasis on aboriginal pagan ritual to the near exclusion of Catholic ritual—only the mass and an old man's simple prayer are mentioned—is evidence of what struck Synge as the most primitive of human instincts.

During his second visit to Inishmaan in September and October, 1899, he experienced what he called "the darker side of life in the islands." Gone was the vernal vitality of May and June, and in its stead came the somber grays and blacks of autumn, the unwelcome chill of the southwest wind, and the thundering waves that broke on the rock shelves to inundate the landscape. Synge's curragh passage to Aranmore was a memorable confrontation between four skilled Inishmaan rowers and an angry sea, and in his providential escape from drowning, he realized that life on the middle island held more than an aura of pagan fatalism, that the malevolent sea had a destructive force that Aranmen knew they could not reckon with. "Riders to the Sea," Synge's nature-elegy, springs, then, from the same roots as does early Irish nature poetry, and his understanding of primitive man's communion with nature and the elements is the understanding that lies beneath the "nature mystique" Ellis-Fermor has attributed to his work.[10]

During the autumns of 1900 and 1901, Synge witnessed a sequence of events that bore even more directly on his composition of "Riders." In 1900 he noted, "Now a man has been washed ashore in Donegal with one pampooty on him, and a striped shirt with a purse in one of the pockets, and a box of tobacco." The islanders trying to identify the drowned man as a fisherman from Inishere or Inishmaan, received confirmation from the man's sister, who was able to remember details about his clothes, his stockings, and his purse and tobacco. "'Ah!' she said, 'it's Mike sure enough, and please God they'll give him a decent burial.'

"Then, she began to keen slowly to herself. She had loose yellow hair plastered round her head with the rain, and as she sat by the door suckling her infant, she seemed like a type of woman's life upon the islands."[11] The visions of the dead man's disconsolate mother searching the sea, his keening sister identifying the corpse, and the suckling infant were faithfully recorded; the archetypal image of grief-stricken woman and the death-rebirth pattern were suggested to the writer. On this third Aran journey Synge again committed every vivid impression to the notebooks, including his doleful memory of the drove of pigs being transported to an English slaughterhouse by a local jobber.

During the final visit to the island in September and October, 1901, he added to his mournful impressions. One night as a hurricane was howling, Norah, a young married woman, was dying of typhus; as she was not expected to live beyond morning, coffin boards had to be borrowed from a man who had put the boards aside two years before for his aged mother. The headless body of a young man had been washed ashore after floating for several weeks in the sea, and once again keening and hammering could be heard in the vicinity of the wake cottage. The young man had taken a curragh to tow horses from a hooker to the shore of the south island. The curragh was swamped by waves and the young man was lost, but according to the lad relating the story, there were signs and prophesies preceding the drowning. Not only had the young man's dog sat beside him crying a warning, his mother had a vision of him riding a horse to the slip; she saw him catch his horse, then a second horse . . . and afterward he went out and was drowned.

Synge described the burial and funeral of the young man as "one of the strangest scenes I have met with." The mourners beat on the closed coffin; both men and women raised the keen; an old man splashed holy water on the bereaved. The gravediggers accidentally turned up the skull of the young man's maternal grandmother, and his mother seized the skull and took it aside keening and shrieking over it in wild despair. At last Synge wandered down to the shore and joined fishermen who were dragging with nets, and as he broke bread with them he reflected: ". . . I could not help feeling that I was talking with men who were under a judgment of death. I knew that every one of them would be drowned in the sea in a few years and battered naked on the rocks, or would die in his own cottage and be buried with another fearful scene in the graveyard I had just come from."[12]

Shortly afterward, the old man in the cottage where Synge lodged told a revenant tale of a mother who had been abducted by fairies but returned at night to nurse her infant. The captive spirit directed her own escape on Oidche Shamhna. She would be riding, she said, among the fairy host behind a young man on a gray horse, and her rescuers were to throw something over the two riders to release them from the fairy spell.

This sequence of connected impressions provides the episode and explains the origin of many of the playwright's "allusions." Details have been accounted for: Michael's stocking and shirt, the white boards for the coffin, the pig destined for the slaughterhouse, the vision of the rider and the two horses, the gray pony of Shamhna, and others. The wake and burial have been twice described. If Synge's tragedy succeeds, one is tempted to attribute its success to his realism, his talent for accurately representing character and situation. But, in truth, "Riders to the Sea" succeeds largely because it realized an Aran-consciousness and has a subtle awareness that character and situation are somehow subordinated to setting. Synge begins with a composite of impressions, but he manages to translate those impressions to a moving dramatic elegy.

III. THE AESTHETIC SENSE

In the aesthetic representation, Synge consciously ladens each descriptive detail, dialogue, and action with far-reaching significance, creating, as it were, continuous symbolic multiplication. The new rope that hangs by the white boards suggests deadly uses: to lash the coffin shut, to drag the pig with the black feet to slaughter, to halter the red mare that will destroy Bartley. At the same time the brevity—the playwright's restricted development of character, confinement of movement within the cottage kitchen, resistance to extended dialogue—serves to emphasize what does occur on stage. Maurya has already lost her husband and five sons; only one son remains to be buried, and his fate is symbolically sealed with his every action. His death is, in fact, anticlimactic. The focus is clear and the dramatic action is brief. The opening dialogue between Cathleen and Nora, for example, focuses immediate attention on Maurya's condition and the cause of it, and introduces the ensuing conflict between Bartley and Maurya. It is audience awareness of symbolic multiplication and response to the implications of setting that contributes to the sense of dramatic progression. In effect, the playwright has in several minutes implied that an island family will be annihilated by the sea and that supernatural forces are impotent as intercessors.

The symbols, echoes, and allusions are archetypal; they are drawn directly from a primitive folk engaged in the most elemental struggle—the struggle for survival in nature. The activity is activity of hearth—kneading bread, spinning yarn, and raking fire—and the characters are more types than *personae*; they are mother, son, and daughters before they are Maurya, Bartley,

Cathleen, and Nora. Only Maurya, in her miraculous transfiguration from petulant old woman to pagan priestess of antiquity, moves beyond type. As the tragic figure in the elegy, Maurya must elicit sympathy. Her plight, the plight of island women and women everywhere, is that she be tormented by sons who live in the face of death and by daughters who are to be subject to the same torments as she.[13] Maurya's final capitulation shows a sense of relief from death, lamentation, and uncertainty. "No man at all can be living for ever, and we must be satisfied" is natural and spontaneous, rather than profound and reflective, for it is, like most of Synge's memorable speeches, drawn from actual dialogue or correspondence.[14] "Riders to the Sea" reaches Greek-perfection, not because it is Aristotelian, but because it translates a primitive Gaelic experience which is also universal.

The playwright is obviously less concerned with character development and dramatic action than he is with effecting a pervasive fatalistic mood. Bartley's death blends with Michael's death, and the deaths of Stephen and Shawn, and Sheamus and Patch, and with the deaths of their father and grandfather before them. And Synge's color scheme—the black, white, gray, and red—suggests always death and destruction. The somber mood of the island requiem is, of course, dominated by blackness—the blackness of night, of cliffs of the north, of the knot on Michael's clothing, of "hags that do be flying on the sea." There are white rocks in the sea by which man is devoured and white boards by which he is swallowed into the earth. The spectral gray pony of Maurya's vision that carried the apparition of Michael and that knocked Bartley into the sea exists in a half-light and serves to meld the world of the dead and the world of those soon to die. In the end, though, it is the crimson of martyrdom and sacrifice that spills over the stage as old women, red petticoats drawn over their heads, file into the foreground and raise a frightful keen.

Synge's rendering of the Gaelic idiom also contributes to the ominous and mournful effect. The sea is, we are told, "middling bad" by the white rocks, but there is "a great roaring in the west" that threatens to worsen it and there is "a power of young men floating round in the sea." References to gusting winds, turning tide, and the star against the moon forebode evil. And Nora, referring to Bartley's hunger, says, "And it's destroyed he'll be . . ."; Cathleen emphasizes the ambiguous intent with "It's destroyed he'll be, surely." Dialogue is aesthetically appropriate to mood, and the episode culminates in a forceful elegiac impression rather than a dramatic resolution.

The playwright moves toward a solemn requiem for a mortal man, but mortality, the common denominator that makes all men riders to the sea, marks the ceremony a requiem for humanity. Maurya, now prophetess-priestess in an order older than that of Melchizedek, presides instinctively in the liturgy. The victim, shrouded in a bit of sailcloth, lies before her on the sacrificial table ringed in red, while the swaying, chanting mourners lend the scene an atmosphere of pagan desperation. The rubrics are curious, suggestive of a ceremony that has evolved from pagan-Christian syncretism over a millennium and a half. The celebrant kneels at the head, the two servers at the feet, the community close at hand. The ritual is deceptively complicated. Maurya rises, drops Michael's clothing across Bartley's feet, then sprinkles the body with holy water. She kneels, crosses herself, and prays silently. When she rises again, it is to spread the clothes and sprinkle them with what remains of the water. She turns the cup mouth downward on the table symbolically, and lays her hands on Bartley's feet. She kneels again. The women continue to keen inarticulately in the background as Maurya half prays half chants the *threnos*, a lament for Bartley, for Michael, for herself, and for suffering humankind. Maurice Bourgeois explains, "To Synge the Irish peasant is a latter-day Pagan on whose old-time heathendom the Christian faith has been artificially and superficially grafted."[15]

There is no young priest at this requiem; there is only the traditional priestess of the pre-Celt. Christianity cannot commune with nature, and its antecedent, a religion that lives on in dim mythology, *can* commune, even if it is powerless to contradict what has been preordained. Synge found that the islanders did not distinguish between the natural and the supernatural, that in time of crisis they reverted to ancient belief and ancient ritual, and to the race tendency to credit signs and visions and prophecies. Human opposition to the cosmic design is futile; resignation is all that is left to man. What becomes important, then, is that Michael have a clean burial, that Bartley have a fine coffin and a deep grave, and that Maurya have a great sleep after Samhain.[16]

"Riders to the Sea" is not an accurate representation of life and death on Inishmaan, nor is it meant to be. The playwright has selected from the incidents aspects of Aran life, and he has extended those aspects imaginatively. The various criticisms—that the play is too brief, that dialogue is inappropriate, that character and situation are undeveloped—are unfounded. Synge accomplished what he had set out to accomplish, a dramatic elegy that was rooted in the primitive response to death in Aran.

If art can be accepted as collaboration,[17] Synge's reasons for coming as an outsider and immersing himself in Gaeltacht traditions are apparent. His experiences, sitting huddled by a turf fire in an Inishmaan cottage listening to a wizened Gaelic storyteller, or inquiring into the vanishing vestiges of an ancient mythology, began that collaboration. Confronted with a rich trove of primary materials, he found that his imagination was overwhelmed. P. A. O'Síochaín accurately summarized Synge's aesthetic mission:

> He did pick up much of the Celtic imagery which he wrote into an exquisite word texture in English. He undoubtedly inherited some of it, but his approach to Gaelic and to the Gaelic way of life was that of a semi-foreigner with a poetic mind, a keen intelligence, and a capacity for dedication. He was attracted by the grand vision of his dreams for his own personal ambition, and in the Gaelic

and in the Aran Islands he knew that he had found something profoundly unique could he but absorb it and translate it into words of drama and literature.[18]

Synge did absorb it and translate it into the words of drama.

To return to the perhaps too obvious premise, that Synge's art begins in his fascination for the exotic world of the Gael and in his awareness of his cultural distances from that world, is to affirm the playwright's aesthetic. "If an Irishman of modern culture dwells for a while in Inishmaan or Inisheer, or, perhaps, anywhere among the mountains of Connacht, he will not find there any trace of an external at-homeness but will rather yield himself up to the entrancing newness of the old."[19] Out of Synge's representation of the Gaelic traditions that lived on Aran in his time were born the finest dramas of the Celtic Revival.

Notes

1. For a fuller treatment of Synge criticism see Alan Price's *Synge and Anglo-Irish Drama* (London, 1961), pp. 2–20.
2. Other than correcting the date of the Paris meeting, Yeats did nothing to dispel the erroneous impression that he was solely responsible for Synge's Aran journeys. See Donna Gerstenberger's "Yeats and Synge: 'A Young Man's Ghost'" in *W. B. Yeats 1865–1965: Centenary Essays on the Art of W. B. Yeats*, D. E. S. Maxwell and S. B. Bushrui (Ibadan U. P.), pp. 79–85. [Reprinted in this volume.]
3. J. M. Synge, *The Aran Islands* in *The Complete Works of John M. Synge* (New York, 1935), p. 389.
4. David H. Greene and Edward M. Stephens, *J. M. Synge 1871–1909* (New York, 1959), pp. 134–135.
5. Richard Bauman's contention that Synge's plays are not "purely" folk dramas is moot. The "Riders" episode is rooted in Aran traditions and it is representative of the folk. See Richard Bauman's "John Millington Synge and Irish Folklore," *Southern Folklore Quarterly*, XXVII (1963), pp. 267–279.
6. R. L. Collins' "The Distinction of 'Riders to the Sea,'" *University of Kansas City Review*, XIII (1947), pp. 278–284, does focus on the importance of setting.
7. *The Aran Islands*, pp. 467–468.
8. Quoted in Collins, p. 280.
9. *The Aran Islands*, p. 346.
10. Una Ellis-Fermor, *The Irish Dramatic Movement* (London, 1964), pp. 163–164.
11. *The Aran Islands*, p. 416.
12. *Ibid.*, 447.
13. Cf., Synge's oft-quoted passage in *The Aran Islands*, p. 384.
14. Synge paraphrased from a letter written to him by Martin McDonough in February, 1902. McDonough's phrasing, "But at the same time we have to be satisfied because a person cannot live always," is cited in Greene, pp. 104–105.
15. Maurice Bourgeois, *John Millington Synge and the Irish Theatre* (New York, 1965), p. 90.
16. Samhain (Shamhna), the ancient Feast of the Dead, when spirits were abroad in the land, was a night fraught with danger for mortal men.

17. In his well known "Playboy Preface" Synge claims, "All art is a collaboration; and there is little doubt that in the happy ages of literature, striking and beautiful phrases were as ready to the storyteller's or the playwright's hand, as the rich cloaks and dresses of his time." *Works*, p. 3.

18. In *Aran: Islands of Legend*, (Dublin, 1962), p. 162.

19. Quoted in Greene and Stephens, p. 65.

The Two Worlds of Synge's
*The Well of the Saints**

ANTHONY ROCHE

I

Whatever their divided effects on a parochial Dublin audience, Synge's plays stood out from the first to those concerned with the theatrical arts as the work of an original. The subsequent decades of the Abbey's history produced many plays that kept the theater full but have left no lasting imprint on literary history. There were the glorious exceptions—most notably, Sean O'Casey— but in the main the Abbey served up mediocre fare. A central irony in all this is that most of these plays focussed upon a depiction of peasant life, as Synge's had done; they were not set in O'Casey's urban slums or Yeats's timeless past. And yet the difference in quality is staggering. It does not answer the matter satisfactorily to say that these later plays pandered to their audience by presenting a complacent portrait of the humble life while Synge deliberately provoked by exposing a propensity to violence and its glorification in the peasant mind. Michael MacLiammoir was moved by such considerations to speculate on a possible source of Synge's dramatic superiority to his successors: "Can it be that these country men and women of his [Synge's] share in some mysterious way the unearthly life of those ancient figures of mythology round which Yeats built so much of his own symbolism, and that this hidden fire, glowing through the outer modern and recognisable portraits, gives to them their violent power? Certainly, the realists who followed him, and who had, it is likely, guessed nothing of the hidden blood flowing through the arteries but had observed simply the play of surface muscles under the skin, lacked, even as imitators, his essential qualities."[1]

Is there a mythological substratum in the "deep" structure of Synge's outwardly realistic plays that would help to account for their undeniable richness and complexity? One could adopt the anthropological approach and gesture toward the ways in which an Irish society which overtly shies away from the remote and exotic legendry of its past continues to nurture in its own

*This essay first appeared in *Genre*, 12 (Winter 1979), and is reprinted with permission of Oklahoma University Press and Anthony Roche.

roots the same impulses incarnated in these myths. But I would prefer to argue from the texts themselves. In the present essay, I propose to do no more than deal with one of Synge's plays, *The Well of The Saints*, and only one of its many possible mythic arteries. Considerable critical energy has already been expended in detecting general myths, such archetypal themes as death, rebirth, and the slaying of the father, operating beneath the surface of the plays. But my approach is more local and specific, its emphasis resting on the distinctive body of Irish myth and folklore which Yeats had employed so extensively and which was so much a part of the mental constitution of the people Synge was chronicling.[2]

In this inquiry into artistic sources, I do not intend overlooking the primary critical definition of the term—a pre-existent narrative which the author has reworked for his purposes as the basis of his own creation. While we may not have had direct access to Shakespeare, considerable light has been shed on his dramatic intention by a careful comparison of his source or sources for a play, where known, with the work itself—not just for what has been altered but what retained. The alterations are the most immediately striking, signifying as they do that point at which the author is most consciously making his own contribution. Among the possible sources of *The Well of The Saints* discussed by Maurice Bourgeois, who provided what is still the fullest survey in his early work *John Millington Synge and the Irish Theater* (London, Constable, 1913), he rather slights the tale told to Synge by a storyteller and transcribed in *The Aran Islands*. But the literary sources suggested by Bourgeois remain hypothetical; and the Aran folktale still appears to offer the most immediate, incontrovertible and suggestive starting-point:

> A woman of Sligo had a son who was born blind, and one night she dreamed that she saw an island with a blessed well in it that could cure her son. She told her dream in the morning, and an old man said it was of Aran she was after dreaming. She brought her son down by the coast of Galway, and came out in a curragh, and landed below where you see a bit of a cove. She walked up then to the house of my father—God rest his soul—and she told them what she was looking for. My father said that there was a well like what she had dreamed of, and that he would send a boy along with her to show her the way. "There's no need at all," said she; "Haven't I seen it all in my dream?" Then she went out with the child and walked up to this well, and she kneeled down and began saying her prayers. Then she put her hand out for the water, and put it on his eyes, and the moment it touched him he called out: "O mother, look at the pretty flowers!"[3]

What must immediately strike any reader in a comparison of this tale to Synge's finished dramatic version is the profound ironic reversal whereby the curing of Synge's protagonists, far from disclosing to them the wonders of natural creation, plunges them into a mire of disillusionment. This reversal and its implications will, of course, be dealt with. But I first wish to consider the opening sentence of the source as equally relevant to my purposes, specifically the portion which reads "one night she *dreamed* that she saw an *island* with a blessed *well* in it" (italics mine). This opening, as I hope to demonstrate, characterizes the tale which follows as belonging to one of the largest and richest bodies of Irish folk tales, the *immram* or sea-voyage to an island, which is in itself a version of that most pervasive of Irish myths, the Other World.

Although common to all cultures in one form or another, and most frequently represented in literature by the pastoral, the idea of the Other World has proved most persistently attractive to and most pervasively rooted in the Irish imagination. Yeats has claimed that this imagination "was always running off to Tir na nOg, to the Land of Promise, which is as near to the country-people of today as it was to Cuchulain and his companions"[4] and more recent studies have borne out what might at first seem chauvinistic hyperbole. Howard Rollin Patch quotes McCullough as saying that "many races . . . have imagined a happy Other World but no other race has . . . so persistently recurred to it as the Celts." He continues: "The Other World was located on this earth, often in the west, and sometimes took the form of the Isles of the Blessed, the Land-Beneath-The-Waves, the hollow hill, or the land beyond the mist, or varying combinations of these."[5] (That the islands in Synge's source should turn out to be those of Aran is therefore appropriate, located as they are off the west coast of Ireland.) Though it was also associated with fairy mounds, the most frequent location of the Other World was an island or islands which correspondingly required a sea-voyage to attain it. In its earliest manifestations, this was not to be confused with Christian notions of the Other World (though later hybrids were to occur). As the remarks by Patch make clear, the location of this elysium was on and of the earth, by no means requiring death as the means of passage, and the rewards depicted very much in terms of the natural and man-made world, a refinement but not a rejection: beautiful, fair-haired women; sumptuous food and drink; implements of finely-wrought gold and silver; flowing streams; singing birds—human life purged of the depredations of mortality:

> There is nothing rough or harsh
> But sweet music striking on the ear
> Without grief, without sorrow, without death
> Without any sickness, without debility.[6]

It is certain key details of another voyage treated by Patch, the voyage of the Hui Corra, which best attest to the kinship I have posited between the myth of the Other World and the source of Synge's play, especially with regard to the framing narrative. The description commences: "Before the journey, Lochan has a *dream* . . ."; as a result of his vision, Lochan and his brothers then "sail westwards and come upon the islands"; there, they encounter a great many of the phenomena outlined in the preceding paragraph, including "a beautiful *river* of wine (which keeps the men from perceiving wound or disease in them)."[7]

This last detail touches upon something crucial to the myth of the fortunate island in Irish Other World literature, and to my theme: the transference to an enchanted spot does not effect an actual transformation, does not actually do away with the human processes of aging and sickness; it merely gives the illusion of having done so, an illusion which persists as long as the subjects remain in that place. A return to the mainland, to the ongoing affairs of the quotidian world, is frequently accompanied by a sudden access of the accumulated aging that has been held in abeyance. But a return of some kind is usually posited, at least—in part—for a marvelous tale to be created and passed on by the survivor. The immortality a story acquires in such oral transmission provides a kind of compensation to its subject for expulsion from the paradisiacal realm.

If the son of the woman in the tale found his sight by following a vision and sailing to the Aran Islands, it is worth remarking that this is analogous to Synge's discovery of his artistic identity. Languishing in Paris, affecting the fin-de-siecle manner in both deportment and literary style, Synge encountered W. B. Yeats for the first time on 21 December, 1896. He had thus far produced little of note; but Yeats apparently sensed his potential and conspired to direct it to a more authentic and fruitful milieu. At a first or subsequent meeting, he held out to Synge a vision of the Aran Islands, exhorting him to go there and "express a life that has never found expression." Although Synge did not respond immediately, he was to visit the Aran Islands in 1898 and return every summer for the next five years. The islands, for all their ruggedness and the physical harshness of life there, enchanted him, and, even after he left them, their imprint is to be found in everything he subsequently wrote.

The preceding statement might be questioned on the grounds that only one of Synge's six subsequent plays has to do overtly with the Aran Islands. Most critics have felt that the tragedy of Maurya's progressive loss of her sons to the omnivorous Atlantic in *Riders to the Sea* provided Synge with such a definitive distillation of his experience of Aran that further dramatic treatment was unnecessary. I suggest that if we dig deeper, and bear in mind the mythological associations that cluster around islands, we will find that this judgment may have to be qualified.

II

The overt remains of the island archetype preserved in the source of *The Well of The Saints* are not made much of in the play itself. Timmy the smith recounts the story of the well and its location only as a means of drawing out the expectations of the two beggars: "Did you ever hear tell of a place across a bit of the sea, where there is an island, and the grave of the four beautiful saints? . . .[8] There's a green ferny well, I'm told, behind of that place, and if you put a drop of the water out of it on the eyes of a blind man, you'll make him see as well as any person walking in the world."[9]

But Timmy is not the one who has directly experienced the wonder; he is rather simply recounting a tale which may have travelled through many tellers ("I'm told"). Nor is the miracle to be performed on the island which is the well's source. It has been severed from its locale, its efficacy relying, not on any enchanted place, but on the divine works of a God who knows no physical bounds. Indeed, the island itself has been demythologized through its association with the grave of the four saints. Far from encouraging the Other World associations I have traced earlier, Synge seems at some pains to suppress any such reading. But just as the miraculous water has been transported from its specific locale, my contention is that the Other world perspective has likewise been imported to the inland setting of the play. The qualities which were associated with certain aspects of Synge's source are not absent, but rather displaced, displaced through the ironic reversal which is the major change he effected on his original.

There, the narrative ends with the purging of the boy's blindness at the well. The succeeding metamorphosis floods the dark vacuum he has hitherto inhabited with the splendor and beauty of natural objects. If a Christian reading of the source-tale is stressed (taking its cue from such details as the mother kneeling to pray in the conventional Christian posture), then the boy's sight is restored in order to open before him and cause him to venerate the natural world as evidencing the beneficent, variegated design of God the Creator. The boy's vocal response can then be taken as a prayer, an impassioned outburst of thanksgiving. Such an interpretation is developed by Synge in the play and placed in the Saint's mouth: "I never heard tell of any person wouldn't have great joy to be looking on the earth, and the image of the Lord is thrown upon men" (p. 166). But the narrative source can be read without any Christian associations. What we have then is the description of a voyage to a fortunate island where the voyager is subject to a vision which discloses a heightened version of the natural world in its beauty and plenitude. This tale, like so many others in Irish folklore, may well have been of pre-Christian origin, passed on orally and, though modified after the arrival of Christianity, left unaltered in its essential features since nothing in them inherently conflicted with Christian teaching. Such a process was common (especially in the Aran Islands, where the line of oral tradition was unbroken into this century); indeed, the discernible traces of the *immram* point to the earlier tradition and indicate that assimilation has most likely been at work.

But the pagan and Christian viewpoints were only seen as compatible when that was the desired result, and only by the suppression of certain key considerations—such as the emphasis in the older ethos on sensual pleasure as compared to Christianity's concern for a repudiation of the merely physical. Far from being compatible, these views were capable of achieving their fullest expression in a dialectical debate, where they emerge as inherently opposed to each other, mutually exclusive and threatening. The prime example of this from the Irish literary past, and one Synge and Yeats were certainly aware of, is the debate between Oisin and St. Patrick, where the Fenian hero returns after a three-hundred-year sojourn in Tir na nOg (the Land of the Young) to an Ireland demythologized and Christianized, with Patrick as its spokesman. The version which most sharply differentiates the protagonists and which reserves the greatest measure of its sympathy for Oisin, according to David Krause, is "recorded in *Agallamh Oisin agus Padraig*, a long poem of over 100 ballad stanzas,"[10] which was available in several late nineteenth-century translations. Oisin in it is no longer the fine physical specimen preserved in Tir na nOg; having once more come into contact with the earth, his body has all at once succumbed to three hundred years' aging; he is old, blind, feeble. But what remains as vital and undiminished as ever is his imaginative apprehension of the natural world, his unabashed celebration of the senses and delight in the particularities of a moment of existence. By comparison, Patrick emerges as an oppressive, ascetic figure, a cleric who would "murder song with barren words and flatteries of the weak" (Yeats, in his own treatment of the story).

This juxtaposition of irreconcilable values is developed in similar dialectical fashion in the *Well*. What accounts for much of the play's dramatic value is the way the opposition is not immediately apparent, but evolves in the progress of the action. Synge, in fact, charts a course which has as its starting-point the tenuous harmonizing of his source, where a joy in the beauty of nature is not inconsistent with a proper reverence for the Christian God, and has its culmination in the fully-fledged and articulated opposition of pagan and saint.

Synge's source covers barely two-thirds of the First Act, and even at that does not account for all of the dramatic elements. But the outlines are congruent: a blind person or persons await with expectation the purging of their blindness through the application of miraculous water from a well and welcome the subsequent revelation of the natural wonders of the world. Martin and Mary Doul look forward eagerly to their cure, and their initial reaction duplicates that of the boy in the tale: " 'O mother! look at the pretty flowers!' " (*Aran Islands*, p. 165). " 'Oh, glory be to God, I see now surely. . . . I see the walls of the church, and the green bits of ferns in them, and yourself, holy Father, and the great width of the sky' " (*The Well*, p. 143).

But the approach to this climax has been complicated in the play by the addition and alteration of certain salient features of the original. For a start, Synge has given us not one, but two, blind people; nor are they young, but rather considerably aged. Furthermore, the condition of their blindness, the attitudes they have evolved in their relation to each other and the external world, are delineated at quite some length. Despite its apparent limitations, they do not appear unhappy with their lot: walking the roads, telling stories, having their physical and material needs relieved by the community. Whatever their personal shortcomings (which they do not hesitate to portray graphically to each other), they favor their own society over those gifted with sight, for "the seeing is a queer lot, and you'd never know the thing they'd do" (p. 132). Since they do not have to work, their time is spent talking, to each other or whoever else will listen. Indeed, language acquires particular importance as the primary means by which their world is constituted: "If I didn't talk, I'd be destroyed in a short while" (p. 132), as Martin remarks in another context. What is most disturbing about the opening section is our awareness of how the couple have been played upon by the villagers, verbally duped into believing they possess youth and beauty. Martin's talk of Mary's yellow hair is contradicted by the audience's own organs of perception, and even the couple themselves are disturbed by the anomalous sound of their cracked, quavering voices.

But such intimations as these are insufficient to prepare them for the ironically inverted recognition scene after their sight is restored. Their gaze is painfully directed, not to the beauties of the natural world, but to the ugliness of their physical condition, which is lingered on with Swiftian savagery. Where the Saint urges them to view "the wonders of the world," Martin responds: "What was it I seen my first day, but your own bleeding feet and they cut with the stones" (p. 166). As blind people, Martin and Mary have not had to witness the visible signs of flux, change and physical decay, have not been imposed on by what Wordsworth has termed "the tyranny of the eye." Midway through the play, their cure is described as analogous to the enforced awakening of a child from a dream of grand houses, gold and horses to ride—a lost dream for which they pine and to which they willingly return in Act Three when, their sight departed once more, Martin spurns the Saint's ministrations. In his last, dignified stand and the eloquence it inspires in him, Martin most completely incarnates the spirit of Oisin:

> "Go on now, holy father, for if you're a fine Saint itself, it's more sense is in a blind man, and more power maybe than you're thinking at all. Let you walk on now with your worn feet and your welted knees, and your fasting, holy ways. . . . I'm thinking it's a good right ourselves have to be sitting blind, hearing a soft wind turning round the little leaves of the spring and feeling the sun, and we not tormenting our souls with the sight of the grey days, and the holy men, and the dirty feet is trampling the world." (p. 170)

In seeking a mythic archetype for the action of the play, several critics have suggested that of the Christian Fall:[11] the blind couple are expelled from a visionary state into a post-lapsarian world where they must labor in the sweat of their brow and where they become only too conscious of the burden of mortality. I think this theory does justice to the world into which they fall, but less so to that from which they are banished, particularly when a Christian saint is the agent of their expulsion. When Martin and Mary Doul were blind, they were given gold and silver gratis; when they can see, they must labor. When they were blind, they appeared to each other as "the finest man and finest woman," Mary in particular with her yellow hair, her white beautiful skin on her neck and on her brows (p. 132); when they can see, they behold "things that would make the heavens lonesome above, and they scaring the larks, and the crows, and the angels passing in the sky" (p. 146). When deprived of sight, their mind's eye constructed visions; their heightened other senses conveyed to them "the sound of one of them twittering yellow birds to be coming in the springtime from beyond the sea . . . and a sweetness in the air, the way it'll be a grand thing to be sitting here quiet and easy, smelling the things growing up and budding from the earth" (p. 162). The gold and silver; the vision of a beautiful, fair woman; the singing birds; the opened natural store of the earth's fecundity—all of these, as we have seen earlier, are specific elements of the Other World, a celebration of physical beauty, elegantly-wrought man-made objects and a natural world devoid of any Christian overtones. It was from just such a setting, where he had remained for three hundred years, that Oisin returned to encounter St. Patrick; and it is Oisin's Other World associations that bear on *The Well of The Saints* rather than the period preceding that, his life with Fionn and the Fianna. In the Dialogue of Oisin and St. Patrick, that aspect is represented by a plangent lament for a vanished civilization, a celebration of the pre-Christian's warrior ethic which is nowhere invoked in Synge's play. It is, rather, Oisin's enchanted sojourn with Niamh in the Land of Youth that provides the imaginative coordinates for the beggars' dream, with its memory of "grand houses of gold . . . with speckled horses to ride" (p. 153). This dream is characterised by Timmy the smith as "a wilful blindness" (p. 168) and it is this illusory, not to say delusory, nature of their world that has troubled some commentators. But it is in just this regard that Martin and Mary share their greatest affinity with the Other World—for the latter, in most of its manifestations, does not claim empirical or even spiritual authority. It makes its claims directly to the imagination, conjuring its "victims" to willingly suspend their disbelief and enter a realm where they may turn a blind eye to the ongoing onslaught of mortality. The Land of Youth, the Land-under-Wave, and all its variations, are avowedly illusionistic, places where the thousand natural shocks that flesh is heir to, "hunger, cold, ugliness, unsatisfied desire, death and decay are unknown"[12]— so long as one remains within its ambit. But parallel to that enchanted realm, the physical world continues and, if one is expelled or leaves, will renew its claims—as it does on the returned Oisin and the cured beggars in Synge's play.

III

It seems fitting to conclude with some final remarks on "sources." The context of Martin Doul's dream, which I failed to provide when quoting earlier, suggests what the continuous source of this Other World imagination may be:

MARTIN: Grand day, is it? . . . or a bad black day when I was roused up and found I was the like of the little children do be listening to the stories of an old woman, and do be dreaming after in the dark nights that it's in grand houses of gold they are, with speckled horses to ride, and do be waking again in a short while and they destroyed with the cold, and the thatch dripping, maybe, and the starved ass braying in the yard? (p. 153)

The association here between the refuge from a grimy reality provided by an illusory Other World and the power of the storyteller is one built up throughout the play. Martin's spellbinding rhetoric in Act II is almost sufficient to beguile Molly Byrne into ignoring his physical appearance: "It's queer talk you have, if it's a little old shabby stump of a man you are itself" she remarks admiringly (p. 153). Throughout the play, Martin and Mary consistently display (in their blind state) the verbal power to transfigure experience, to illuminate their darkness with the light of imagination. The knowledge they acquire of their physical decrepitude would appear to present too great an obstacle to such conversion when their sight fails once more in the third act. But the abundance of luxuriant white hair they can verbally display is finer than the actual, since unsullied by it: for "what good will our grey hairs be itself, if we have our sight, the way we'll see them falling each day, and turning dirty in the rain?" (p. 163).

In their story-telling abilities, their power of weaving verbal spells that contrasts sharply with and shines through their old, withered bodies, Martin and Mary Doul recall in this, as in so much else, the aged storytellers, the latter-day seanachies, Synge encountered on the Aran Islands:

The old dark man I had spoken to in the morning groped his way into the room. I brought him over to the fire and we talked for many hours. . . . A little after middle-age he had fallen over a cliff, and since then he had little eyesight, and a trembling of his hands and head. As we talked, he sat huddled together over the fire, shaking and blind, yet his face was indescribably pliant, lighting up with an ecstasy of humor when he told me anything that had a point of wit or malice. . . . He had great confidence in his own powers and talent, and in the superiority of his stories over all other stories in the world. (p. 189)

Synge's own voyage to these islands was fortunate in many ways, its bounty amply reflected in his subsequent dramatic creations.

Notes

1. Michael MacLiammoir, *Theatre in Ireland* (Dublin: Cultural Relations Committee, 1964), p. 15.

2. The ground-breaking essay here is David Krause's "'The Rageous Ossean': Patron-Hero of Synge and O'Casey," *Modern Drama*, 4 (1961), 268–91.

3. J. M. Synge, *Four Plays and the Aran Islands*; ed. Robin Skelton (London: Oxford University Press, 1962), p. 165. All references to *The Aran Islands* will be made in the text.

4. Preface to Lady Gregory, *Cuchulain of Muirthemne* (London: Colin Smythe, 1973), p. 14.

5. Howard Rollin Patch, *The Other World According to Descriptions in Medieval Literature* (Cambridge: Harvard University Press, 1950), p. 27.

6. All of the above details from *The Voyage of Bran*, one of the most outstandingly representative examples of the genre. Cited in Patch, p. 30. The complete translation, by Kuno Meyer, can be found in Tom Peete Cross and Clark Harris Slover's collection, *Ancient Irish Tales* (New York: Holt and Co., 1936), pp. 588–95.

7. Patch, p. 35 (italics mine).

8. Converted, significantly, from the "Four Beautiful Persons" of the Aran original, who were surely pre-Christian.

9. *The Plays and Poems of J. M. Synge*, ed. T. R. Henn (London: Methuen and Co., 1963), p. 136. All references from *The Well* will be taken from this edition.

10. Krause, p. 270.

11. See, for example, Vivian Mercier, "The Tinker's Wedding," in *Sunshine and the Moon's Delight*, ed. S. G. Bushrui (New York: Barnes and Noble, 1972), p. 82.

12. Vivian Mercier, *The Irish Comic Tradition* (London: Oxford University Press, 1969), p. 16.

Myth and the Journey in *The Well of the Saints**

KATE POWERS

In *The Well of the Saints* John Millington Synge presents a dark comic journey into vision. The opening lines of the play, "What place are we now, Martin Doul?" "Passing the gap," contain the unconscious irony of the travelers who have no awareness of the journey they have begun or the fact that they will not pass beyond the gap until they have descended into the village, tested their vision, rewritten their dreams, and returned to this very spot. Only when they have traveled the full circle of experience will they be able to pass beyond the gap into a world of liberty and risk they freely choose. Throughout the journey they are influenced by myths which they, to some degree, internalize.[1] In this essay I propose to examine the play in the context of myth and journey.

Its story is one of disarming simplicity. At the beginning the blind beggars Martin and Mary Doul, who have been habitually flattered by villagers about their good looks, discuss appearance as they wait on a mountain road leading south. They are as curious about sight as the approaching villagers are curious about a miracle. The Saint, a wandering friar carrying a can of holy water from the well of the saints, can apparently satisfy everyone by offering the couple a cure. Martin, eager for the miracle, quickly brushes aside Mary's reservations, but sight brings immediate disenchantment: he mistakes the beautiful, young Molly Byrne for his ugly, aging wife, thus exposing himself to Molly's jibes and his spurned wife's fury. Matters worsen as the unskilled Martin, now expected to support himself, labors under Timmy the smith for barest subsistence. Although described as "almost elderly," Timmy, like Martin, has an eye for Molly Byrne, and Molly has an eye for a good provider. They find a common bond in taunting Martin, who exists at the lowest level of their society. As their treatment becomes unbearable to him, Martin loses his sight and returns to Mary who is also blind again. The Douls's experiment with seeing has been disastrous: they have lost dignity, insight, and each other. Restored to their former blindness, they struggle to reach accord. When the Saint returns, offering them a second—and guaranteed permanent—miracle, Martin opposes enormous pressure from the villagers. He knocks the watering can out of the friar's hand and, warning the now hostile crowd to leave them alone, departs for the south of Ireland with Mary.

*This essay first appeared in *Colby Quarterly*, 26, 4 (December 1990), and is reprinted with permission.

* * *

What is the nature of myth in this play, and how does it function in relation to the journey? The first part of the question rejects a single answer because Synge uses three types of myth in *The Well of the Saints*: the societal myth, the racial hero myth, and the personal myth. Although the racial hero myth pervades the play in the character of the anti-hero Martin, it is the shattering of the societal myth which gets the journey underway; hence I shall address this myth before proceeding to that of the racial hero. The personal myth is realized in the culmination of the drama, and I shall save it for the place Synge reserved for it.

Of the three, it is the societal myth which is most fragile. It is myth in the leanest sense which links the Douls to the villagers: village society has offered to Mary and Martin Doul an attractive, if illusory, perspective on life, and to the extent to which the Douls accept the myth of the "beautiful dark woman of Ballinatone" and the "grand, handsome fellow Martin," they are created by society. The myth offers the dream quality of wish fulfillment, and to a large extent they do accept it.[2] The illusion which at first glance appears innocent enough contains a hidden barb. The societal myth offers them dignity from which they derive only a mock sense of independence, for as long as they accept the offered identity, the Douls's fate is controlled by the villagers, as indeed the villagers prove when they decide to change them by offering them sight. If the myth can exist with sight—and the Douls have little reason to think it will not—then the offer of a miracle is as irresistible as the myth itself.

It is Martin who expresses the greater need for the miracle; the attractiveness of the myth has such a hold on Mary that even Molly Byrne's reported jibes have had no power to assail the fortress of her belief and dignity.[3] Martin, however, has a need to learn; he is somewhat skeptical and largely curious, as he reveals in his plaintive comment to Mary: "I do be thinking in the long nights it'd be a grand thing if we could see ourselves for one hour, or a minute itself, the way we'd know surely we were the finest man and the finest woman of the seven counties of the east—(*bitterly*) and then the seeing rabble below might be destroying their souls telling bad lies, and we'd never heed a thing they'd say."[4] The journey, then, is to be Martin's journey—it is he who needs to learn that the physical sense of sight cannot identify "the finest man and the finest woman" and he who must gain the concomitant confidence to "never heed a thing they'd say." Martin is the artist, and his mythopoetic mode of consciousness cannot be conferred on him by the outside world. It is only through experiencing the paradoxical loss of vision which accompanies his restored sight that Martin can ultimately come to a realization of the value of his poetic imagination and insight and a recognition of his own identity. But Martin's search will demand time and pain. First the light of the miracle reveals the societal myth for the cold lie that it is, and the dignity based on that lie crumbles.[5] The Douls are forced to realize the harsh psychological and financial dependence which binds them to the villagers who have created and supported them.

Martin's journey is not simply a journey forward—not only does he travel in a circle before he can pass beyond the gap, but he travels backward to the church which he has passed; this regression is paralleled in the diminishing of his vision which occurs, ironically, with the regaining of his sight. Immediately, he allows sight to replace the sense which he has previously shown: he judges with his eyes rather than his mind and heart, and he is unable to recognize his lifetime companion. When he was blind, Martin separated himself both physically and imaginatively from those he referred to as "the seeing rabble below" through his road life and his intrinsically superior status. Now he separates himself from Mary: "Your hair, and your big eyes, is it? . . . I'm telling you there isn't a wisp on any gray mare on the ridge of the world isn't finer than the dirty twist on your head. There isn't two eyes in any starving sow isn't finer than the eyes you were calling blue like the sea" (139). As Martin changes, his language changes, and the animal imagery he uses to describe Mary spills over into other descriptions—the villagers are a "drove of pitiful beasts" (138) when they will not identify Mary for him. It is with the pitiful beasts, however, that he chooses to go, attempting through his descent to the village to become one of the people "below"; how well he assimilates his new life is shown in his complaint that Timmy, his new employer, will not give him enough food to "keep the life in a pig" (142)— after describing others in bestial terms, he draws attention both to the difference between himself and a pig and to his perception that socially the difference doesn't seem to matter much. Mary's reply to his assessment of her—"It's the devil cured you this day with your talking of sows; it's the devil cured you this day, I'm saying, and drove you crazy with lies" (130)—shows a degree of perception of which Martin is no longer capable. Her immediate awareness of dark vision causes her to reject it as evil. At this point in the play she shows the greater wisdom, and he has become a fool who must experience a painful journey before he can attain—and then surpass—the vision he formerly had.

The sighted Martin Doul is unacceptable to the closed society of the village. His dislike for hard physical labor, his desire for a woman who is beautiful and young, and his insistence on presenting reality as he sees it combine to make him a misfit. More importantly, he is a misfit because he is working against his intrinsic nature. At the beginning of Act II, Martin states that he is "destroying himself" through hard work; the expression as he uses it is a common enough figurative phrase in Irish usage, but it is true for Martin in an ironically literal sense. Martin cannot become one of the villagers without destroying himself because organic to Martin's personality is the myth of Oisin. Here Synge uses myth with a difference. Since the Oisin myth springs from the roots of Irish culture, the characters participate in it rather than create it. With the age of heroes dead, the only way Martin can realistically embody the mythic personage is through ironic deflation. For Oisin liberty was a *sine qua non* for life, and until Martin can realize the primary value of liberty in his own life, he will continue to destroy himself.[6]

The evidence of Martin as an Oisin figure is ample. Like Oisin who spent three hundred years of his life in Tir na nOg, the Land of Youth, Martin has been blessedly unaware of many of the effects of aging; his blindness has largely protected him from the knowledge of graying hair, withering skin, rotting teeth—the signals of human decay and approaching death. Like the Oisin who engaged in the great debates with Patrick, Martin who engages in a great argument with the Saint is old as well as blind.[7] Along with these physical traits, there are some personality traits which Martin shares with Oisin from the beginning of the play: his love of beautiful women and his ready wit are apparent early. Other traits which relate him to Oisin lie dormant until Martin becomes a self-realized character; prime among these is a conscious need for liberty and an expressed passion for nature.[8]

A brief passage from David Krause's "The Rageous Ossean" presents a thumbnail sketch of the hero in a dialogue with Saint Patrick in which Oisin defends his father Finn's right to Liberty: traces of Martin Doul are visible.

> . . . Patrick falsely declares that Finn is in bondage in hell because he committed treachery and oppression. No one was ever more generous and freedom-loving than the noble Finn, Oisin replies, and there are innumerable illustrations in the legends to support him. With characteristic fairness, as well as a naive innocence that knows no fear, Oisin insists that no God should be a tyrannical master of man. Why, he wants to know, can't Finn and God be equals like the honorable warriors; why should God want to put a hero like Finn in hell? There is a turn of comic irony in his sly innocence during the exchange; and when, after claiming that his son Oscar would easily defeat Patrick and smash his crozier, he concedes that even if God managed to bring Oscar down in a fair fight, Oisin would openly praise God for his strength. But this would simply prove that God was a brave warrior and certainly no better than his equal number, the Fenian chief Finn.[9]

The passage exhibits four basic characteristics: a desire for fairness and the personal liberty which fairness demands, a willingness to test a pagan vision against a Christian one, a sense of delight in the fight, and—most of all—an irreverent comic spirit. Martin's personality is not realized in terms of these characteristics until the final act of the play, when he is at last able to create the personal myth, or myth of self. The final myth is both a creative act and an act of recognition which together make up the will to be. Martin denies his potential while he lives in the village because he is blinded to his own identity.

After suffering the loss of the societal myth and the humiliation which his romantic dream about Molly brings, Martin experiences a terrifying ordeal when he is forced to live without illusions; it is at the same moment that he loses his sight. "Is it a storm of thunder is coming, or the last of the world?

(*He staggers toward Mary Doul, tripping slightly over a tin can.*) The heavens is closing, I'm thinking, with darkness and great trouble passing in the sky. (*He reaches Mary Doul and seizes her left arm with both his hands—with a frantic cry.*) Is it darkness of thunder is coming, Mary Doul!" (153). The world he has known since the miracle, that of the "seeing rabble below," has in this moment had its last end for him, and when he is no longer blinded by sight he turns instinctively to Mary Doul.[10] But because of the humiliation she has suffered from Martin, Mary, eager for revenge, rejects him. Humiliated, bereft of his dream and of all social support, Martin refuses to become a victim. With all joy gone, the only satisfaction left him is the perverse pleasure of invective, and at this he is highly skilled:

> Yet if I've no strength in me I've a voice left for my prayers, and may God blight them this day, and my own soul the same hour with them, the way I'll see them after. Molly Byrne and Timmy the smith, the two of them on a high bed, and they screeching in hell. . . . It'll be a grand thing that time to look on the two of them; and they twisting and roaring out, and twisting and roaring again, one day and the next day, and each day always and ever. It's not blind I'll be that time, and it won't be hell to me. I'm thinking, but the like of heaven itself; and it's fine care I'll be taking the Lord Almighty doesn't know. (156)

The passage is a blend of comedy and pain, and it is in his comic attitudes that Martin alleviates pain and hopes to transfer it to Molly and Timmy. In his agony Martin has finally learned the defense that Mary had adopted soon after the miracle: that of defiance against an unacceptable reality. But emotionally he is caught; although he can defy reality, he is still trapped by it—his is a hell of imprisonment. Martin, not yet able to follow Oisin who chose hell because it meant freedom from the tyranny of God, chooses hell because only hell can give him the revenge he wants on Molly and Timmy. His damning of Molly, Timmy, and himself is the dream which temporarily replaces the one Molly has just shattered. His projected enjoyment of the twisting, roaring, and screeching of Molly and Timmy, an illustration of the Freudian wish fulfillment principle, is great enough so he can will to reject his own pain through laughter. But the dream is a wrong one: even though it is he who has created it, it clearly shows society's control over him which negates the possibility of self-fulfillment and freedom. Even so, hope for Martin's future development is there in the emerging Oisin traits—in his stand against a society represented by Molly and Timmy and in the comic irreverence which allows him to make his prayer a curse and to hide his motives from God. Martin Doul will not be crushed.

But pain and tension still pervade Martin's being in the opening of Act III as he struggles toward a freedom which he cannot yet conceptualize. For Mary the liberating concept is that of a beautiful old woman with soft white hair.[11] She has created a new dream. Dreams—or myths—of personal identity cannot be shared, however, any more than they can be conferred. Mary can indicate the way, and Martin, no longer deceived by appearances, can learn from Mary, who, in the face of pain and disappointment, has found a palliative measure for dealing with unacceptable reality.[12] Freud in *Civilization and Its Discontents* lists three such measures: powerful deflections, substitute satisfactions, and intoxicating substances. Mary has chosen the second, a measure which Freud further elucidates by saying: "The substitute satisfactions, as offered by art, are illusions in contrast with reality, but they are none the less psychically effective, thanks to the role which phantasy has assumed in mental life."[13] Martin's earlier attempt at a "powerful deflection" hasn't functioned to make him happy; through his revenge motive he is still tied to society and controlled by it. He turns to Mary, hoping to adopt her new badge of dignity for his own; fittingly, he meets with nothing but scorn—if she did share her new identity, it would be conferred on him as the societal myth was, and it would be as worthless.

In *The Irish Dramatic Movement* Una Ellis-Fermor states, ". . . Synge sees that the genius for myth-making finds its supreme expression in creating the most satisfying myth of all, that of personality."[14] Until this point Martin has shown artistic development, but it is in the creation of self that he emerges as the true artist. There is an exuberant joy in his realization of his artistic identity: "I've this to say, Mary Doul. I'll be letting my beard grow in a short while, a beautiful, long, white, silken, streamy beard, you wouldn't see the like of in the eastern world. . . . Ah, a white beard's a grand thing on an old man, a grand thing for making the quality stop and be stretching out their hands with good silver or gold, and a beard's a thing you'll never have, so you may be holding your tongue" (161). This moment is Martin's epiphany: for the first time he realizes that working solely with his poetic imagination he can create a beauty that will color his life. The beauty of his imaginative construct, a beard which waxes long, silken, and streamy under his verbal powers, enables him to restore his confidence. He is also able to create in his imagination the economic gain which will come with his new dignity— whether in reality he will have gold and silver to sustain him is inconsequential here; for the moment, poetic imagination will sustain him, and the moment is all the time he has to deal with. To crown his triumph, he realizes that the new beauty which gives him identity is his alone—Mary can have no part in it. Martin Doul has created the myth of his own personality.

And he richly deserves the wholehearted acceptance Mary offers: "Well, we're a great pair, surely, and it's great times we'll have yet, maybe, and great talking before we die" (161). In her answer Mary cheerfully reasserts the bond between them. But she, despite the new identity her beautiful soft white hair will give, is not wholly caught up in the optimistic world of imagination as Martin is; it is he, after all, who is the poet. Her reply—with its awareness that although great times are possible, death is certain—foreshadows the darkness they will face when they cross the gap and enter the outer world.

There is only one more challenge Martin must meet before he is truly free: he has returned to the gap because society rejected him—to attain liberty, it must be he who rejects society. The villagers and the Saint provide the opportunity for him to do so almost immediately by offering a second miracle. When they hear the bell, Mary's "The Lord protect us from the saints of God!" (162) sums up a major irony of the play: the Christian society with its Patrician heritage, in a mock enactment of the Patrick-Oisin struggles, has tried so hard to save Martin that it has almost destroyed him; the only beneficial miracle for the Douls is the one they can create of themselves.

After attempting to hide, attempting to run away, and asking to be left alone, Martin enters—at first unwillingly—into the debate; the Saint rouses him by speaking of the "wonders of the world" which Martin does not see. Challenged and irritated, Martin is willing to test his pagan poet's vision against that of the Christian Saint. "Is it talking now you are of Knock and Ballavore? Ah, it's ourselves had finger sights than the like of them, I'm telling you, when we were sitting a while back hearing the birds and bees humming in every weed of the ditch, or when we'd be smelling the sweet, beautiful smell does be rising in the warm nights, when you do hear the swift flying things racing in the air, till we'd be looking up in our own minds into a grand sky, and seeing the lakes and big rivers, and fine hills for taking the plow" (167–68). In the light of his new poetic consciousness, Martin has begun drawing for the Saint a picture of ironic balance between reality and the poetic imagination. If the former held dirt and disappointment, the latter holds the magic of "swift flying things racing in the air" and the fertility of the "fine hills for the taking of the plow"—to look into their own minds is to look up; Martin and Mary see a higher world than the one available in reality, and with instinctive wisdom choose to stay in the world they can see through blindness.[15]

Martin's willingness to test his vision is one of the attitudes which reveals in him an integration of the Oisin myth and the personal myth which he has created; another of these attitudes is the passion for nature which he shows in this passage. He has given play to his attitude of comic irreverence in his damnation speech for Molly and Timmy.[16] Oisin characteristics yet unaccounted for are the desire for fair play and the personal freedom which fairness demands and a sense of delight in the fight; these traits Martin demonstrates most clearly in his two final speeches:

> Let you walk on now with your worn feet, and your welted knees, and your fasting, holy ways a thin pitiful arm. For if it's a right some of you have to be working and sweating the like of Timmy the smith, and a right some of you have to be fasting and praying and talking holy talk the like of yourself, I'm thinking it's a good right ourselves have to be sitting blind, hearing a soft wind turning around the little leaves of spring and feeling the sun, and we not tormenting our souls with the sight of the gray days, and the holy men, and the dirty feet is tramping the world. . . . Keep off now, the yelping lot of you,

or it's more than one maybe will get a bloody head on him with the pitch of my stone. Keep off now, and let you not be afeared; for we're going on the two of us to the towns of the south, where the people will have their kind voices maybe, and we won't know their bad looks or their villainy at all. (*He takes Mary Doul's hand again.*) Come along now and we'll be walking to the south, for we've seen too much of everyone in this place, and it's small joy we'd have of living near them, or hearing the lies they do be telling from the gray of dawn till the night. (171–73)

In the first passage Martin simply recognizes that freedom is a right for all and claims a share for Mary and himself. Since his view of freedom is a celebration of life in nature and since he is not willing to deny the flesh through fasting, prayer, and hard work, he stands against the mores of Patrician society and angers his listeners. Martin shows no streak of violence here—he picks up the stone only after the villagers have thrown things at him—but there is a vociferous will to defend his hard-won freedom, and there is a joyous victory of the human spirit in his ability to do so despite infirmity and age.[17] Perhaps the greatest sign of his victory lies in his new-found sense of presence which will not allow victimization: there is no stage direction for him to throw the stone. Unlike that other Synge anti-hero, Christy Mahon of *The Playboy of the Western World*, who must at the conclusion change his role of oppressed for that of oppressor, Martin—true to his Oisin heritage—has no desire to dominate even for a moment those around him. His "Keep off now, and let you not be afeared" uses the conjunction "and" to create a balance between his rights to freedom and theirs.

Finally liberated from the gray dawn and lowering skies of village life among the people of Patrick, Martin and Mary are going, not to where bad looks in reality will not exist, but where the Douls will not have to know them. This distinction is important because it separates delusion from illusion—it is in the latter they have chosen to live. Martin is a poet with a touch of madness rather than a madman with a touch of poetry. With the illusion created by poetic imagination, the Douls are able to escape much of the unhappiness which has threatened them; through it they find the strength to reject sight and society. Freud states: "We are threatened with suffering from three directions: from our own body, which is doomed to decay and dissolution and which cannot even do without pain and anxiety as warning signals; from the external world, which may rage against us with overwhelming and merciless forces of destruction; and finally from our relations to other men."[18] The Douls have removed, to the degree that it is possible, the first and third sources of suffering: in choosing blindness they will not have to watch themselves grow old and decay, and in rejecting society they escape from lies and unkindness. The second source of suffering, however, is one which cannot be removed. Mary shows a realization of this fact in her answer to Martin's final speech: "That's the truth, surely; and we'd have a right to be gone, if it's a long way itself, as I've heard them say, where you do have to be walking with a slough of wet on one side and a slough of wet on the other, and you going a stony path with a north wind blowing behind" (173).

The world into which they will now journey offers no security; instead it holds the chill of the north wind, a danger of sudden drowning, and eventual death. But death is inevitable. The world they choose is one in which they can be human, beautiful, and artistically creative—and if the prize is freedom, the risk is worth all costs to them. In choosing freedom they choose never again to be victims of a society which can create and uncreate them at will through a cruel myth; they choose to be creators of their own myth, the myth of personal identity, and to participate on a reduced scale in the heroic myth of Oisin. In the final speech of Act II when Martin has just lost his sight, he plays a mock Oisin figure in his choice to go to hell; at that time he chooses bondage. At the end of Act III the anti-hero Martin makes a truly heroic choice: the world he will go to is indeed a hell, but it is free. Unlike his body which is little, old, weather-beaten, and ugly, his spirit shows the beauty of heroic stature in this choice.

Notes

1. In this approach to the play I differ in perspective from Reed Way Dasenbrock who states that it was "Synge's peasant drama that turned the Irish dramatic movement away from mythological subjects toward the peasant drama that for a time became its signature." See "Synge's Irish Mythology," *A J. M. Synge Literary Companion*, ed. Edward A. Kopper, Jr. (Westport, Conn.: Greenwood, 1988), 136.

2. For an analysis of the psychology of wish fulfillment see *Abstracts of the Complete Works of Sigmund Freud*, ed. Carrie Lee Rothgeb (New York: Jason Aronson, 1973), 119. Alan Price in *Synge and the Anglo-Irish Drama* (London: Methuen, 1961) notes that the Douls's chief source of self-respect is that they are a distinguished couple, a belief which the villagers foster (139–40).

3. Robin Skelton, *The Writings of J. M. Synge* (London: Thames and Hudson, 1971), offers this commentary; "It may be no accident that Mary Doul calls herself the wonder of the western world, for she is, in her struggle to assert her dignity and in her fantasies of pride, kin to the playboy of the western world who also had a vision of his dignity and found it conflicting with the actual" (101–02).

4. John Millington Synge, *The Complete Plays* (New York: Random House, 1935), 123. All subsequent quotations of J. M. Synge are taken from this volume.

5. Of this passage Leslie D. Foster observes: "The symbolism is clear: The church [sic] shows man to himself as ugly and calls it a miracle." See *"The Well of the Saints," A J. M. Synge Literary Companion*, 52–53.

6. Joseph Holloway, who saw the 1905 performance, wrote of this play in *Abbey Theatre* (Carbondale: Southern Illinois Univ. Press, 1967), "To call it Irish is distinctly a libel on our race and country" (41). This observation fails to take into account not only the use of the Oisin myth but the existence as well of an analogue in Irish folklore. Sean O'Suilleabhain's "Synge's Use of Irish Folklore," *J. M. Synge Centenary Papers 1971*, ed. Maurice Harman (Dublin: Dolmen, 1972), reports that the basic theme of the blind man who, having been cured, wishes to be blind once more occurs in a folk story (21). In the story the man chooses blindness that he may

not sin; if sin is viewed at its most elemental as a betrayal of self, Martin is perhaps making the same choice for the same reason.

7. Anthony Roche, in "The Two Worlds of Synge's *The Well of the Saints*," *Genre*, 12:439–50 [reprinted in this volume], notes that the world of blindness has a parallel in Oisin's Other World: both are avowedly illusionistic.

8. Images of nature are almost nonexistent in Act I, although the rich nature imagery of Act III indicates reflections on previous blind experience. It seems reasonable to conclude that Martin has always had an appreciation of nature but that he does not begin to express it—in both its beauty and its horror—until he begins to develop as a poet through his painful experiences of Act II.

9. *Modern Drama*, 4 (1961–62): 275. In his well-known poem, "The Wanderings of Oisin," William Butler Yeats has Oisin recount his story to St. Patrick: the Fenian hero defines himself as the antithesis of the saint by expressing his delight in sensuous beauty of both the land and the gentle Niamh. Then he continues, "But now two things devour my life; / The things that most of all I hate: / Fasting and prayers" (*The Collected Poems*, New York: Macmillan, 1956).

10. Foster has difficulty understanding why for Martin and Mary sight is not a desirable solution. Martin, when he returns to Mary, tells her that he has begun to appreciate her even though she lacks physical beauty: if he can learn that, Foster feels, he can learn what he needs to be sighted (56). Part of the answer, however, lies in the experience from which he has derived this wisdom: eyes that cannot be trusted add nothing to the identity toward which he is struggling. In a larger context seers and poets, from Homer and Teiresias to Milton, have seen truth without eyes.

11. Price, after tracing Mary's revelation of her new dream, examines the significance her dream has for Martin: "Taken with this notion, and not knowing whether to prize more her new comeliness or her agility of mind, Martin cries out: 'You're a cute thinking woman, Mary Doul, and it's no lie.' His admiration is mingled with relief; he begins to see a way out of the impasse: a woman with such an appearance, and with such a facility of fancy and expression, would make an excellent partner; infinitely better than the icy, conceited Molly" (152–53).

12. M. J. Sidnell observes as a possible weakness in the play that Mary's function "becomes a passive one after the reciprocal viewing of the first act." See "*The Well of the Saints* and the Light of the World," *Sunshine and the Moon's Delight: A Centenary Tribute to John Millington Synge 1871–1909*, ed. S. B. Bushrui (Dublin: Colin Smythe, and Beirut: The American University of Beirut, 1972), 56. Mary's lead is, in fact, key to Martin's self-discovery.

13. *Civilization and Its Discontents* (New York: Norton, 1962), 22.

14. *The Irish Dramatic Movement* (London: Methuen, 1939), 176.

15. Freud, in *Civilization and Its Discontents*, discussing palliative measures for dealing with disappointments first suggests that one could become a hermit, then continues: "But one can do more than that; one can try to recreate the world, to build up in its stead another world in which its most unbearable features are eliminated and replaced by others that are in conformity with one's own wishes. But whoever, in desperate defiance, sets out upon this path to happiness will as a rule attain nothing. Reality is too strong for him. He becomes a madman, who for the most part finds no one to help him in carrying through his delusion" (28). Mary and Martin are among the fortunate "victims" of madness: not only do they belong to the society of "lovers, poets, and madmen" who have artistic vision, but they have each other to help in carrying through the "delusion" (in this case an illusion of their choosing), a task which might become too difficult for a single person faced with the overwhelming burden of reality. Martin's insistent defense of Mary's freedom when she herself has grown weak is elucidated by Freud's commentary.

16. Further evidence of Martin's comic irreverence may be found in his excited speech

to Molly, whose identity he has mistaken: ". . . for it's grand hair you have, and soft skin, and eyes would make the saints, if they were dark awhile and seeing again, fall down out of the sky" (137).

17. Yeats's lines from "The Wanderings of Oisin" might serve equally well to describe Martin's spirit at this moment: "And in a wild and sudden dance / We mocked at Time and Fate and Chance."

Works Cited

DASENBROCK, REED WAY. "Synge's Irish Mythology." *A J. M. Synge Literary Companion*. Ed. Edward A. Kopper, Jr. Westport, Conn.: Greenwood, 1988.

ELLIS-FERMOR, UNA. *The Irish Dramatic Movement*. London: Methuen, 1939.

FOSTER, LESLIE D. *"The Well of the Saints." A J. M. Synge Literary Companion*. Ed. Edward A. Kopper, Jr. Westport, Conn.: Greenwood, 1988.

FREUD, SIGMUND, *Abstracts of the Complete Works of Sigmund Freud*. Ed. Carrie Lee Rothgeb. New York: Jason Aronson, 1973.

————. *Civilization and Its Discontents*. New York: Norton, 1962.

HOLLOWAY, JOSEPH. *Abbey Theatre*. Carbondale: Southern Illinois Univ. Press, 1967.

KRAUSE, DAVID. "The Rageous Ossean." *Modern Drama*, 4 (1961–62): 268–91.

O'SUILLEABHAIN, SEAN. "Synge's Use of Irish Folklore." *J. M. Synge Centenary Papers 1971*. Ed. Maurice Harman. Dublin: Dolmen, 1972.

PRICE, ALAN. *Synge and the Anglo-Irish Drama*. London: Methuen, 1961.

ROCHE, ANTHONY. "The Two Worlds of Synge's *The Well of the Saints*." *Genre*, 12: 439–50.

SIDNELL, M. J. *"The Well of the Saints* and the Light of the World." *Sunshine and the Moon's Delight: A Centenary Tribute to John Millington Synge 1871–1909*. Ed. S. B. Bushrui, Dublin: Colin Smythe, and Beirut: The American University of Beirut, 1972.

SKELTON, ROBIN. *The Writings of J. M. Synge*. London: Thames and Hudson, 1971.

SYNGE, JOHN MILLINGTON. *The Complete Plays*. New York: Random House, 1935.

YEATS, WILLIAM BUTLER. "The Wanderings of Oisin." *The Collected Poems of W. B. Yeats: Definitive Edition, with the Author's Final Revisions*. New York: Macmillan, 1956 (twenty-first printing: 1974).

The Playboy as Poet*

JAMES F. KILROY

J. M. Synge's *The Playboy of the Western World* continues to be the most popular of his plays with both critics and the public. Recognized as a masterpiece of modern comedy, it is included in numerous anthologies and studies of drama. Its appeal is partially due to the play's dialogue: lyrical, rich in natural imagery, almost a folk dialect. But the play has also some thematic distinction, which accounts for its relevance to modern audiences and distinguishes it from the pleasant comedies of Lady Gregory and others of Synge's contemporaries. Synge admitted its serious implications: *"The Playboy of the Western World* is not a play with 'a purpose' in the modern sense of the word, but although parts of it are, or are meant to be, extravagant comedy, still a great deal that is in it, and a great deal more that is behind it, is perfectly serious when looked at in a certain light. That is often the case, I think, with comedy, and no one is quite sure today whether Shylock and Alceste should be played seriously or not. There are, it may be hinted, several sides to *The Playboy*."[1] Several interesting interpretations of the theme have been offered: T. R. Henn's discussion of the tragic nature of the plot, and its reliance on classic archetypes; Hugh H. MacLean's analysis of the scapegoat theme in the play; the political implications pointed out by David H. Greene; and Norman Podhoretz's analysis of the play as treating the rebellion of son against father.[2] Although valid, these are partial interpretations. A more central theme, the growth of the poet, is noted by Maurice Bourgeois and Alan Price, but neither critic charts its progress thoroughly to see how it directs the entire plot and how it accounts for what seem to be flaws in the play.[3] Musical and strange though certain passages of the play are, Daniel Corkery is justified in calling them excessive and uncontrolled; he proposes that the straining after unusual effects sometimes produces nothing more than "a mush of colour and sweet sound."[4] However, Synge, in this play, is portraying the gradual growth of a poet; Christy Mahon passes from an apprenticeship, in which are evident the immature poet's errors and failings—strained similes, exaggerated emotional display, and weak language—to maturity in which he achieves Synge's ideal poetry—rich and earthy, humorous but profound. Synge's playboy, then, becomes the representative of Synge's poet described in his other works. And

*This essay first appeared in *PMLA*, 83 (May 1968), and is reprinted with permission of the author.

119

Corkery, in disregarding the play's central theme, has mistaken certain purple passages as evidence of the play's weakness.

Language is a central concern of the play. Synge's preface defends the authenticity of the dialogue, a task no doubt necessary in the face of his audience's violent objections to the offensive language of the play, particularly the infamous word "shifts." But the preface recognizes the need of a union of "rich and copious" words with "the reality, which is the root of all poetry." Such a union is not always achieved in Christy's speech. Only at the end of the play has he achieved Synge's ideal: "the timber of poetry," with its "strong roots among the clay and worms."

The plot is simple and familiar: a young alleged parricide arrives in a country pub tired and afraid after running from the police. He tells the villagers of his crime and is praised as a hero. Even the arrival of his father on the next day does not diminish his self-confidence: he becomes champion of the sporting events and suitor of the publican's daughter. But when his father reappears the young hero again attacks him; such actual violence turns the villagers against him and they torture him. Fortunately, his father again enters and rescues his son; the boy leaves, the "master of all fights from now," and is lamented as "the only Playboy of the Western World."

The theme is universal: into an isolated and lonesome setting comes the alien poet, whose strange character makes him immediately attractive to the deprived society which hears him. Their adulation, in turn, encourages the poet in ambitious feats of verbal display, accompanied by a marked change of personality. Even contradictions of fact cannot discourage the poet as long as he is encouraged by his audience. But when he is turned on and branded a liar, he is, paradoxically, graced with the last requisite of the true poet: strength and a firm grasp of reality, without which his poetry would remain ethereal and weak.

Christy's first comments are terse and prosaic; even when he describes his great crime he does so simply: "I just riz the loy and let fall the edge of it on the ridge of his skull, and he went down at my feet like an empty sack, and never let a grunt or groan from him at all."[5] The sentence structure in which a series of phrases are loosely linked, and the single uninspired simile contrast sharply with his later speeches.

He hardly comprehends Pegeen's praise of his small, aristocratic feet and noble brow, and asks "with a flash of delighted surprise": "Is it me?" Truly this is the beginning of Christy's discovery of himself; he has met the proper audience and now the neighbors he has left behind seem "bloody liars." The confidence of his approaching manhood brings more daring and colorful speech: "I've seen none the like of you the eleven long days I am walking the world, looking over a low ditch or a high ditch on my north or south, into stony, scattered fields, or scribes of bog, where you'd see young, limber girls, and fine, prancing women making laughter with the men" (pp. 29–30). Pegeen notes the power of that speech: poetry like Synge's own, with effects resulting from the counterpoint of hyperbole ("walking the world") with limiting details ("eleven long days"), musical repetitions ("low ditch or high ditch on my north or south"), and concrete, frank references ("fine, prancing women"). She likens him to Owen Roe O'Sullivan, an apt comparison, for the eighteenth-century Irish poet provides a model for both Christy and Synge. He was one of the "fine, fiery fellows with great rages when their temper's roused," and he is also, like Christy, an alienated poet, forced constantly to wander, lonely but glorious in his poetic mastery.[6]

Christy's life has been unhappy, restricted by a tyrannical father. His only joy was found in nature, the proper school for a poet: "I'd be as happy as the sunshine of St. Martin's Day, watching the light passing the north or the patches of fog, till I'd hear a rabbit starting to screech and I'd go running in the furze" (p. 32). His father later describes Christy as "a liar on walls, a talker of folly, a man you'd see stretched the half of the day in the brown ferns with his belly to the sun." The description is arresting, almost a definition of a poet.

By the end of the evening, Christy has persuaded even himself that he is a daring and handsome hero. Once believing this, he thinks he can rise above "the clumsy young fellows do be ploughing all times in the earth and dung," and forsake life in nature for an easy life working in the pub. But doing so he would discard one of the most fruitful sources of his poetic inspiration.

The second time he tells his story, he embroiders it considerably, making it almost epic in imagery and exalted language. The story concludes: "With that the sun came out between the cloud and the hill, and it shining green in my face. 'God have mercy on your soul,' says he, lifting a scythe. 'Or on your own,' says I, raising the loy.

"He gave a drive with the scythe, and I gave a lep to the east. Then I turned around with my back to the north, and I hit a blow on the ridge of his skull, laid him stretched out, and he split to the knob of his gullet" (pp. 50–51). Once more the girls comment on his poetic powers: "That's a grand story . . . He tells it lovely." The progress of his poetic skill can be gauged by this speech. The dramatic phrasing ("says he . . . says I") and the visual details are most evident. But just as important is Christy's deliberate exaggeration for dramatic effects ("split to the knob of his gullet"). Such grotesque effects have increased in the speech of all the characters, as Pegeen's accusations of Widow Quin rearing a black lamb at her breast indicate; but they seem to be the stock of the poet particularly. His description of the woman he has escaped from marrying inspires him to eloquence: "she did suckle me for six weeks when I came into the world, and she a hag this day with a tongue on her has the crows and seabirds scattered, the way they wouldn't cast a shadow on her garden with the dread of her curse." Describing his loneliness, Christy employs strong visual details and commanding dramatic phrasing through the use of the present tense: "It's well you know it's a lonesome thing to be passing small towns with the lights shining sideways when the night is down, or going in strange places with a dog noising before you and a dog noising behind, or drawn to the cities where you'd hear a voice kissing and talking deep love in every shadow of the ditch, and you passing on with an empty, hungry stomach failing from your heart" (p. 56). Such is Christy's poetry at its best. However, when he learns that his father is not dead, a distinct change in the quality of his talk is evident. He does not fall apart, nor does he revert to shyness and silence. Rather his poetry becomes self-conscious and hollow. Immediately following his father's conversation with the Widow Quin, Christy is enraged: "To be letting on he was dead, and coming back to his life, and following after me like an old weasel tracing a rat, and coming in here laying desolation between my own self and the fine women of Ireland, and he a kind of carcase that you'd fling upon the sea." His mastery of curses and violence is still sure; but he falters on delicate subjects. In Pegeen he sees "the love-light of the star of knowledge shining from her brow," and hears "words would put you thinking on the holy Brigid speaking to the infant saints." Poetic though such phrases may be, they defy explication. Christy is trying out his role as a poet, and the Widow Quin recognizes his failure: "There's poetry talk for a girl you'd see itching and scratching, and she with a stale stink of poteen on her from selling in the shop." Momentarily unhinged by the news of his father's arrival, Christy's mastery of language has failed; he answers the Widow Quin impatiently: "It's her like is fitted to be handling merchandise in the heavens above, and what'll I be doing now, I ask you, and I a kind of wonder was jilted by the heavens when a day was by" (pp. 71–72). There is a certain appeal to such naïveté of metaphor, but it is patently unlike Christy's confident speeches both before and after this scene. He has fallen back upon conventional poetic imagery and techniques, and remains crippled for the rest of the act.

Fortunately, the failure of Christy's verbal skills is only temporary. When he reenters the scene in the last act, after proving himself a champion in the races, he is again the master of language. Appropriately enough, his prizes are bagpipes, a blackthorn, and "a fiddle was played by a poet in the years gone by." The love duet between Christy and Pegeen includes the most elevated sentiment and a wealth of natural imagery: "When the airs is warming, in four months or five, it's then yourself and me should be pacing Neifin in the dews of night, the times sweet smells do be rising, and you'd see a little, shiny new moon, maybe, sinking on the hills . . . you'll feel my two hands stretched around you, and I squeezing kisses on your puckered lips, till I'd feel a kind of pity for the Lord God is all ages sitting lonesome in His golden chair" (p. 90). She compliments him on his eloquence, which encourages him to even more poetic speech, climaxed by his most rapturous proclamation: "If the mitred bishops seen you that time, they'd be the like of the holy prophets, I'm thinking, do be straining the bars of Paradise to lay eyes on the Lady Helen of Troy, and she abroad, pacing back and forward, with a nosegay in her golden shawl" (p. 91). Pegeen makes it clear what attracts her in Christy:

his "savagery" and "fine words." Apparently both are requisites of a poet in her eyes.

When Pegeen learns that Old Mahon is not dead, she accuses Christy of lying, lacking in savagery, and covering it up with his display of verbal skill. He is surprised, being still intoxicated by his newly acquired poetic powers: "hearing my voice this day saying words would raise the topknot on a poet in a merchant's town." The power he possesses seems an independent entity, not under his own control.

Christy again assaults his father for the sake of Pegeen. He feels he must regain his reputation for savagery in order to win her. But again she turns on him: "I'll say, a strange man is a marvel, with his mighty talk; but what's a squabble in your back-yard, and the blow of a loy, have taught me that there's a great gap between a gallous story and a dirty deed. Take him on from this, or the lot of us will be likely put on trial for his deed to-day" (p. 108). He is betrayed by Pegeen and the villagers, but his poetic strength does not diminish; he now sees himself as a popular hero, mourned by beautiful ladies and immortalized in ballads.

When his father returns and he is released, Christy finally becomes master: he now has both the verbal and the physical powers of a hero. His growth was accomplished by his experiences with the people of Mayo: "Ten thousand blessings upon all that's here, for you've turned me a likely gaffer in the end of all, the way I'll go romancing through a romping lifetime from this hour to the dawning of the judgment day" (p. 112).

What has evolved reveals the growth of a poet. Different from other men in his sensitivity to nature, the poet suffers from loneliness. He is inspired to eloquence by the adulation of his audience and particularly by the love of a woman. As a result of his greater confidence, he becomes a true poet, and, concurrently, achieves physical mastery of his own life. The nonrealistic nature of his subject matter momentarily threatens his mastery and his poetry suffers; but finally he achieves maturity to the point that he can do without the praise of an audience. In this reading Pegeen represents the true lover of the poet's art, but one unable to accept its primacy over fact; she is the one who suffers most as a result.

It is not inappropriate to relate this theme to Synge's own life, especially because Synge conceived of art as "the gradual and conscious expression of his personality in literature."[7] The Irish public was scandalized by his earlier play, *In the Shadow of the Glen*, because it was not sufficiently realistic. They argued that Nora was far worse than the typical Irish woman, without recognizing in her a sensitive poetic soul who chooses art over the mundane by going off with a tramp who has a poet's nature. Synge, like Christy, profited from the public's rejection, although his obvious sympathy for Pegeen indicates that he never simply despised the audience which could not reconcile art with actuality.

The mature speech of Christy represents Synge's ideal of poetry as described in the preface to his volume of poems: "the strong things of life are needed in poetry also, to show that what is exalted, or tender, is not made by feeble blood. It may also be said that before verse can be human again it must learn to be brutal."[8] His own success in meeting that ideal is revealed in the volume of poems. In fact, the pronounced change in his poetic style parallels that of Christy: the natural imagery and delicacy of "Glencullen," his earliest published poem, develops into the stark vigor of "A Question" and other late poems. In his recently published *Autobiography*, further evidence of the application of Christy's experience to Synge's life may be seen. Synge describes himself as a lonely youth, who found solace and joy in nature, and later in music.[9]

The intention of Synge's mature drama and poetry was best expressed as a common goal by Yeats in "The Municipal Gallery Revisited":

> John Synge, I and Augusta Gregory, thought
> All that we did, all that we said or sang
> Must come from contact with the soil, from that
> Contact everything Antaeus-like grew strong.[10]

The soil referred to is not only nature, but actuality in all its facets. Contact, and not conflict, between fact and imagination is the achievement of Christy and Synge. Christy grew to maturity even after attaining the knowledge that his tale of parricide was a fiction.

The Playboy of the Western World dramatizes the gradual development of the poet's craft from its first uncertain expression to the full display of mature art, uniting rich language with a clear view of facts, "the root of all poetry." In realizing himself and his abilities, the poet grows from insecurity to manhood and self-assurance. And in his relations to society he moves from initial reliance on an audience for encouragement to the necessary breaking away from a public that does not understand his art.

Notes

1. Letter to *Irish Times*, dated 30 Jan. 1907, quoted in David H. Greene and Edward M. Stephens, *J. M. Synge, 1871–1909* (New York, 1959), p. 244.
2. T. R. Henn, *The Harvest of Tragedy* (London, 1956), p. 204; Hugh H. MacLean, "The Hero as Playboy," *UR*, XXI (Autumn 1954), 9–19; David H. Greene, "The Playboy and Irish Nationalism," *JEGP*, XLVI (April 1947), 199–204; Norman Podhoretz, "Synge's Playboy: Morality and the Hero," *EIC*, III (July 1953), 337–344.
3. Maurice Bourgeois, *John Millington Synge and the Irish Theatre* (London, 1913), p. 205; and Alan Price, *Synge and Anglo-Irish Drama* (London, 1961), pp. 161–180.
4. Daniel Corkery, *Synge and Anglo-Irish Literature* (Cork, 1931), p. 197.
5. *The Playboy of the Western World*, in *The Works of John M. Synge* (Dublin, 1910), II, 23. Subsequent references to this work are incorporated into the text.
6. Daniel Corkery, *The Hidden Ireland* (Dublin, 1925), pp. 193–246.

7. From an unpublished draft of a preface to the poems, in *Collected Works, Vol. II: Prose* (London, 1966), p. x.

8. *Collected Works, Vol. I: Poems* (London, 1962), p. xxxvi.

9. *The Autobiography of J. M. Synge*, ed. Alan Price (Dublin, 1965).

10. In *Collected Poems* (New York, 1956), p. 318.

A Carnival Christy and a Playboy
for All Ages*

GEORGE BRETHERTON

The Playboy of the Western World is John Millington Synge's best known, by most accounts his best, play and certainly his most controversial one. The controversy surrounding the play is, and has been for some time, passé. During its first production and subsequent early revivals many people associated with the Abbey and the world of theater and art thought the controversy in most of its aspects pathetic and ludicrous. "Audiences broke up in disorder at the word shift," was Lady Gregory's explanation of the vigorous reaction to the play's premiere (Gregory 67). Her verdict has set the tone for most accounts of these early audiences and their reception of the play ever since, spirited attacks on prudish, lower middle-class philistinism giving way in recent years to bemused tolerance for a sort of low comedy from the audience (Kenner 34–61).

With a passing smile most critics today move on from the controversy to the play itself. This essay will look once again at that controversy, its background and origin in "the minds of the beholder," the audience, and in the play itself. After all, Synge, if he did not write his play with a particular audience in mind, chose to present it before a group of Dubliners, most of them Catholic, most of them lower middle-class, whose prejudices and opinions were bound to clash with those of the author, an upper middle-class Protestant and scion of the landed gentry and Evangelical clergy.

The unfavorable reception given the play by those early audiences was on account, it is usually claimed, of its antinational, antipopular bias. The play made fun of Irish people, specifically Irish countrymen and women. Why, then, should an urban audience take exception to that aspect of the play?[1] In any event, Synge's reply, seconded by his defenders, that he was taking aesthetic liberties in order to create "an extravagance" contradicts his prior claim to be merely eavesdropping on his subjects.

A number of contradictions and confusions exist so far as play, audience, and reception are concerned. What sort of statement did Synge intend? Is *The*

*This essay first appeared in *Twentieth Century Literature*, 37, 3 (Fall 1991), copyright *Twentieth Century Literature*. Reprinted by permission.

Playboy to be read as symbolist or realistic drama, or some combination of the two? Is it extravagance, fantasy, or a faithful dramatic rendering drawn from Synge's country sketches such as *The Aran Islands*? What does the reaction of Synge and his friends at the Abbey—Yeats's impassioned defense of the play and its author comes quickly to mind—tell us about the Abbey and its audience as well as the theater and its uses in a time of change? After all, the Abbey was christened by its founders "The Irish National Theatre," and those who patronized it naturally expected it to live up to its name.

To begin with the play itself: two issues need to be addressed; the first is a point that has been discussed a number of times, the Christology of the main character and its meaning for the play; the second matter, which seems to have gone unnoticed, has to do with intergenerational differences and conflict.

As to the Playboy, Christy Mahon, there can be little doubt that he is meant to represent and remind us of some aspects of Christ, that his entry into a community, apotheoses, and rejection by that community followed by his own leave-taking, an ascendancy of sorts, echoes the progress of Christ on earth. Whether we accept all this in a serious vein and regard the play as an analogue "of the ministry and crucifixion of Jesus," or emphasize the comedic elements of the play, treating Christy as a "mock Christ" is of some consequence and has given rise to argument.

The serious as opposed to the mock Christy is seen as "one example of many in an Anglo-Irish tradition of rejected and betrayed would-be delivery from political or even spiritual oppression . . . a messiah-like figure bearing a new dispensation" (Sultan 54). The figure who would have come to mind most vividly at the time of the *Playboy*'s premiere was Parnell. Those who see in Christy "a parody of Christ rather than a reflection of him," such as Robin Skelton, maintain that societies get the leaders they deserve, and this particular Mayo village wanted and got someone who could be compared with "Daneen Sullivan [who] knocked the eye from a peeler" and "Marcus Quin who told stories of holy Ireland till he'd have the old women shedding down tears about their feet" (Skelton 60).

We can learn more about what sort of a Christ Christy becomes if we consider how he assumed the role, which occurs in the course of the play and not before it. The scared, rabbit-like fugitive that creeps into Michael James's pub is transformed in the course of the play into someone quite different. How does this transformation occur? Patricia Meyer Spacks believes that Christy changes himself. In an essay entitled "The Making of the Playboy," she writes: "Certainly there is no question that Christy grows before our very eyes in 'The Playboy.'" The play "presents essentially the vision of a man constructing himself" (Spacks 316).

We may wonder if Christy's transformation is so completely of his own making. In the scene in which we learn that he has killed his father the information is gradually obtained from him by Pegeen, Michael James, and his friends but not without effort. "Were you never slapped in school, young fellow, that you don't know the name of your deed? . . . Did you strike golden guineas out of sodder, young fellow, or shilling coins itself? . . . Did you marry three wives maybe? . . ." and so on (*Playboy* 15–16). When Christy finally tells his interlocutors that he killed his father, Philly Cullen remarks: "There's a daring fellow," and a few lines later Jimmy Farrell chimes in: "Bravery's a treasure in a lonesome place, and a lad would kill his father, I'm thinking, would face a foxy divil with a pitchpike on the flags of hell," an endorsement that leads to Christy's employment as potboy (*Playboy* 18–19).

In other words, Christy's evaluation accompanies his acceptance, indeed is a necessary part of his entry into this little community. For the people who make up this community Christy is first an object of great curiosity, but he becomes far more than that, and it is arguable that it is the people in his newfound world who play a major part in making him over. And what is this new self? It is compounded of bravery, strength, and a certain lightheartedness and ease. Christy's new personality, the antithesis of his old, is that of a playboy. Yet, a pun is intended here, for the boy Christy is playing a part, has been cast in a novel role by his new friends, and that role is a royal one. Christy becomes the most royal potboy and playboy in all Mayo. He is the churl who "rose happy as a King" (Bakhtin 197). His realm though is a carnival with most of the features and consequences that Mikhail Bakhtin has discovered in his study of popular festival forms.

First, it is the community that creates the carnival; it is "the only feast the people offer to themselves" (Bakhtin 246). Carnival, then, has elements of democracy and liberality, libertinism, in fact; the rules are fewer and simpler than in the everyday world. An "atmosphere of equality, freedom and familiarity" prevails, and "each and everyone may play the fool and madman as he pleases" (Bakhtin 246, 254). For the people in Michael James's pub, their carnival madness is a release from the heavy hand of the English law, the magistrates and police that lurk in the background, an ominous offstage presence that threatens in the form of the peelers to burst into the pub at any moment and end the Carnival and the magic spell it has cast on its participants. The same thing may be said of that other great pillar of the real world and foundation of the people's lives, the Church, exemplified in phrases like "the holy bishops and the Court of Rome," but personified in the play by the all-knowing Father Reilly who like the peelers threatens an entrance at any moment and the destruction of the grand illusion that the people have made for themselves (*Playboy* 8).

In this carnivalesque world, hierarchy is simplified. All are equal save Christy, their King. But, then, in keeping with the traditions of Carnival, it is they who have crowned him, and they have chosen someone who fills them with wonder and admiration, someone who has answered their innermost hopes and aspirations. Yet, their yearning and admiration can only exist so long as the Carnival does, and it and Christy's reign must inevitably end.

It is, again, the people who determine when his reign and the Carnival shall end, though they do so in reaction to the "second murder" of his father, which will be discussed in more detail below. Nonetheless, this sudden and unanimous termination of Christy's kingdom and the decision to turn him over to the peelers is in keeping with the carnivalesque tradition. "The King is crowned, only to be uncrowned, abused and scourged as was the King of the Jews" (Bakhtin 198).

It would seem then that Christy is a mere mock Christ and not a heroic one, and that Skelton's appraisal is nearer the mark than Sultan's. Two points can still be made to support a somewhat modified version of Sultan's analysis, however. The people of the play who join together to end Christy's reign— they are never so united in their object as at this moment, Pegeen Mike, Shawn Keogh, Michael James, and the rest who have been at odds until then—not only want to put an end to Christy's reign, they want to kill him. If they succeed in taking him to the peelers, he will be tried for murder and surely hang, they believe. The scorching of Christy's shins, rather like the scourging of Christ before his crucifixion, is emblematic of death and Carnival's end. The Roman Carnival that Goethe described concluded on its last night with a Fire Festival or *moccoli*, which means candle stump. "Death to anyone not carrying a candle" is the cry of these strange revelers along the Corso, and so "fire is combined with the threat of death" (Bakhtin 248). The King must die in his prime, he cannot grow old or his people will perish, is a belief shared by many traditional societies.

So it is with Christy when his people turn on him after he has achieved what he believes to be his greatest triumph, the second killing of his father. For that act follows his humiliation at his father's hands in the previous scene; the second murder should have restored the people's faith in him and Pegeen Mike's love. Attempts to explain his people's unexpected reaction in terms of the difference "between a gallous story and a dirty deed" being the equivalent of the difference between fantasy and reality are strengthened when we realize that the Carnival spell is being cast off, and Christy has become its sacrificial victim. For an instant he achieves a tragic stature that quickly alters with the return, the second coming of his father. In that moment, though, he can bear comparison with Parnell and all the other lost leaders rejected and betrayed by their people (Sultan 49).

If Christy is cast in the role of Carnival's King, mock Christ, and manages a moment of tragic greatness, it is not clear that he welcomes either role, and, indeed, he struggles very hard to avoid the consequences of the second. The point has already been made that it is the other people in the play who make Christy their Christ and King, but how aware and accepting is Christy? He delights in being the Playboy of the Western World, in the love and admiration of Pegeen Mike and the other girls who Magi-like come bearing presents. He welcomes the adulation of the crowds at the games on the strand, and comes to have a sense of confidence and self-worth quite unlike his former self. All well and good, but what does it mean to Christy? Throughout the play Christy's two chief concerns are escape and acceptance: escape from the tyranny of his father and acceptance into his newfound community, especially acceptance by Pegeen Mike. His preoccupation with these issues precludes much understanding of the role in which the community has cast him, at least until the penultimate moment when he is betrayed. That experience changes him again; it is his second conversion. In the first part of the play he goes from a frightened child, "an ugly young streeler," to a dashing young man, filled with a sense of his new powers; but at the end he acquires a better understanding of life and maturity (*Playboy* 47). At last, he comes into his own, as he goes off with his father, their roles now reversed and Christy "a gallant captain with his heathen slave" (*Playboy* 80).

We come now to that other theme, intergenerational conflict and its various related issues—growth, maturation, youth, age, life, and death—with which the play abounds. It may seem ingenious to introduce this theme in connection with *The Playboy*. After all, it is a play in which a son tries to kill his father on two occasions and each time believes himself to be successful, or does he? Yeats insisted that neither Christy, nor his interlocutors, nor the audiences ever thought there had been a murder, it was from the beginning merely "a gallous story" (Gerstenberger 50). Yet the play derives much of its tension and fascination, not to mention its comedy, from the "did he or didn't he" doubt that stays with us and the great enthusiasm for the deed among the other characters. Would they have shown such enthusiasm for a mere story, a lie?

Of course, their reaction is disturbing but nonetheless not that atypical of Irish country life, where questions of generational succession and inheritance occur, for these issues give rise to concerns that confuse and pull apart one's sense of familial and generational loyalty. The quarrel between Christy and his father was one that existed in virtually every Irish farming family—as the young heir comes of age and makes demands on the older generation that will send them into the west room; naturally, the elders will resist rather than go willingly.[2]

Here the quarrel is starker than in the plays of Synge's fellow Abbey playwright, Padraic Colum, for whom the rights of succession and the meaning of mastership are major preoccupations though expressed in a realistic mode rather than a carnivalesque one.[3] The confrontation between the two is certainly less involved than in either Colum's plays or in the struggle that actually went on within most Irish families. Christy has neither siblings nor a mother to complicate the issue, a fact that adds a touch of poignancy to his situation and further enhances both our sympathy for him and our condemnation of his father's tyrannical behavior.

That last point should be restated for the sake of clarity: though Synge reduces his dramatic conflict to a straightforward encounter between father and son, other characters and concerns are near enough to hand to muddy the waters. The issue that pushes Christy to the point of raising the loy against his father is the latter's insistence that he wed the Widow Casey, who, Christy tells us, "did suckle me for six weeks when I came into the world" (*Playboy* 36). Christy is profoundly shocked at the suggestion that he should marry his surrogate mother, "two score and five years, and two hundred weights and five pounds in the weighing scales" (*Playboy* 35).

The horror of incest pushes Christy to the murder of his father, or perhaps mock or pretended murder, a nice reversal of the oedipal pattern. He then must flee the scene of his crime. Interestingly enough, this flight has helped us to lose sight of the original source of the bitterness between father and son, which, as we have seen, originated in a dispute over land and rights of succession. Yet Christy never forgets his patrimony, which with characteristic hyperbole he enlarges into "wide and windy acres of rich Munster land" (*Playboy* 22). Exile, then, is added to Christy's sufferings, which end, temporarily at least, with his welcome into the little community of Michael James's pub. Though his initial period of wandering is relatively short-lived, its devastating impact on Christy and all those who sympathized with him in both the play and the audience should not be underestimated, for exile in the minds of most Irish people was equated with death. Among the furnishings of the west room, associated with *Tir na nÓg*, the land of beyond, into which the elder generation retires upon surrendering control of the farm to the young, were kept "pictures of the dead and emigrated members of the family" (Arensberg 19, Miller 556–68). Synge's own account of the "true story" behind the play, which he inserted in *The Aran Islands* and frequently cited in reaction to the criticism that his plot was preposterous and libel against the Irish people, has the young parricide emigrating to America once the police have stopped looking for him, and he is able to get away (*The Aran Islands* 369–70). His escape, then, is not the end, only the beginning of his torment.

Christy is saved from this fate by the people who welcome him to Michael James's pub, and his wanderings are over in less than a fortnight. Considering the nature of his deed we might expect the older people to be less sympathetic than the younger ones when he reports that he has killed his father. But in this carnival world the reverse is true. Michael James and both of his friends, Philly and Jimmy, are quick to approve what Christy has done and commend him for it. As Philly puts it: "The peelers is fearing him, and if you'd that lad in the house there isn't one of them would come smelling around if the dogs itself was lapping poteen from the dung-pit of the yard" (*Playboy* 19).

Pegeen Mike is more circumspect. Of course, this would be in keeping with a maidenly demeanor. Shawn is, on the other hand, actively suspicious and hostile toward the Playboy, which fits with his position as her suitor. Still, this example of generational misalliance stands as one of several instances when members of one generation oppose one or more of their own, while people from another generation take their side. Throughout the play, Shawn's place is with the older generation and especially with its authority figures, beginning with Father Reilly, whom he is forever invoking. His character is a compound of craftiness and cowardice. His personality could be described as old-womanish. The older generation respects his wealth, which gives him position in the community; for Michael James he is a prospective son-in-law, but no one respects his timid ways or fastidiousness.

Several aspects of this sort of generational misalliance and other people's reaction to it, together with what might be called generational displacement (that is, the exhibition by a character of traits or behavior more appropriate to another generation than his own) can be seen in the scene just before Christy's arrival. Michael James and his friends want to go to Kate Cassidy's wake. Pegeen Mike wants her father to stay home. She probably wants company more than anything, but she appeals to her father's paternal sense as her protector: "It's a queer father'd be leaving me lonesome these twelve hours of dark . . . and my own teeth rattling with the fear" (*Playboy* 11). Michael James's solution to the problem is to ask Shawn to stay with his daughter. Any young suitor would welcome the opportunity to spend the night unchaperoned under the same roof with his intended, one would think. "Let Shawn Keogh stop along with you," he says, and we can almost see him wink when he speaks his next line: "It's the will of God, I'm thinking, himself should be seeing to you now."

These sentiments would have seemed inappropriate at most times in most places but our own. For a people who supposedly found the mention of the word "shift" scandalous they must have been outrageous. Michael James and his friends are acting like young people who are off to a party.

There is another sort of displacement here, and it involves a greater span of time than a generation. The behavior of Michael James, Philly, and Jimmy is distinctly old-fashioned; it was much more typical of pre-famine than post-famine Ireland. The sort of wake where heavy drinking and revelry were thought of as proper respect paid to the dead, where "five men, aye, and six men, [were] stretched out retching speechless on the holy stones," was largely a thing of the past (Bretherton 161–62). Where it continued to exist at the beginning of the twentieth century, as in parts of the west, more people thought it deplorable than amusing.

Shawn, in his objection to Michael James's behavior and in his steadfast refusal to defy propriety and spend the night with Pegeen, represents modernity, albeit a Catholic and Victorian one. "Leave me go, you old Pagan," he cries to Michael James as he fights his way out of the house, leaving Michael James holding "the coat of a Christian man" (*Playboy* 13). The gulf between these two generations in the persons of these two particular men takes on the dimensions of the gulf between pagan and Christian Ireland.

Michael James and his friends do not, however, regard Shawn as representative of the younger generation, but as someone old beyond his years, old beyond theirs for that matter. "Lock him in the west room," Philly says with contempt as Shawn struggles to get away; "He'll stay then and have no sins to be telling the priest" (*Playboy* 12). More than locks and doors would have separated Shawn from Pegeen, for the west room was, of course, where the old generation retired once its active life was over, the room associated with exile and death.

Christy's arrival moves us along to another scene. When he first enters he seems nearly as timid as Shawn: the one is a poor wanderer, the other a prosperous farmer—wealth marks the difference between the two. Yet as the scene continues, Christy appears as Shawn's antithesis in other ways. Just as the company in the pub makes Christy over into their King and Christ, so they begin a process of differentiation that distinguishes Christy from Shawn, his contemporary, and from the nameless, nebulous tramp he at first appears to be, "that queer dying fellow" moaning in the ditch. In the course of their examination of Christy, which occupies a little more than seven pages of text before they learn Christy's name, they call him or refer to him, for the most part, as "young fellow" or "lad." These terms are used in these seven pages no less than nine times, a reiteration that has the effect of helping us to see Christy as a young man, of helping him to shed the weariness and misery that has brought him to the pub. Christy comes back to life in response to this sort of encouragement as his story is drawn out of him; he takes on a new vitality.

On the other hand, Michael James and his contemporaries abandon for a moment the tipsy antics that led to the roughhousing with Shawn. The arrival of their savior and King has redressed the generational imbalance. They may well have Kate Cassidy's wake at the back of their minds, but for the moment Christy has their attention, and they are on their best behavior. They are sober, respectable people acting their age. Christy's inquiry about the likelihood of the police appearing provokes from Michael James an indignant reply: "If you'd come in better hours, you'd have seen 'Licensed for the Sale of Beer and Spirits, to be consumed on the premises,' written in white letters above the door, and what would the polis want spying on me" (*Playboy* 14).

What might be called our first episode of generational displacement is brought to an end. Michael James acts the part of the responsible publican and father seeing to it that all is well before going off to the wake, and when he and his friends depart Christy and Pegeen are left alone. Their solitude is ended by the arrival of the Widow Quin and so too the hiatus in the generational contretemps. The widow appears in the sort of parental role that Michael James slipped in and out of so easily. She represents the older generation; she comes, indeed, at the request of its most proper and punctilious representatives, Shawn and Father Reilly.

We soon are given reason to believe that she is poorly suited to this role. To begin with it is readily apparent that she is nothing if not scheming and manipulative. Second, we learn that she killed her husband and "buried her children" (*Playboy* 25). These accusations, freely confirmed by the widow, are lumped together and we cannot be sure that she does not bear some direct responsibility for the children's deaths as well as her husband's (*Playboy* 27). Third, and most important, she soon embarks on the seduction of Christy.

Seduction may be too simple and strong a term to describe behavior that begins, at least, in an ambivalent manner. The Widow Quin's treatment of Christy initially is parental; in the one obvious sense, it is downright maternal. Christy, who has just grown to manhood before our eyes while telling of killing his father and beginning his first fumbling courtship of Pegeen, is reduced to childhood by the Widow. "Well, aren't you a little smiling fellow," she says on finding him with his supper. "It'd soften my heart to see you sitting so simple with your cup and cake, and you fitter to be saying your catechism than slaying your da." Though her attitude toward Christy soon starts to change—in her next speech, she says, "It's of the like of you and me you'd hear the penny poets singing in an August Fair" (37). Echoes of her maternal feelings toward Christy persist throughout the play. In the scene in which the three girls with their gifts appear followed by Widow Quin, Susan Blake speaks of Christy as a sort of prospective child-husband to the Widow: "and she with a great yearning to be wedded, though all dread her here. Lift him on her knee, Sara Tansey" (37).

As for Christy, he seems so nearly oblivious as he can be to the Widow's intentions, and with a straight face describes to her his flight from that other widow with whom his father would have had him wedded; "and she a woman of noted behavior with the old and young" (37). This reminder of generational misalliance is followed by her question, and she asks Christy why his father would have done that. Christy replies: "He was letting on I was wanting a protector from the harshness of the world," and the Widow Quin responds. "There's maybe worse than a dry hearth and a widow woman and your glass at night" (*Playboy* 35–36).

Christy's childlike innocence is matched by the Widow's cunning and her offer of constant parental attention, all carrot and no stick. She is a grotesque combination of Mary Magdalene and the Virgin. It is in that later and intercessory role, not her favorite part, that she most appeals to the Playboy. "Aid me for to wed Pegeen," he pleads, and she complies, going so far as to spend a good part of the last two acts placating Christy's father in the bargain (*Playboy* 53).

While the Widow has some notion of the ultimate impossibility of fulfilling her fondest desire, romance with Christy—"Well, it's an error to be aged a score," she says at her first exit—the elder Mahon has no such notion of his limitations (29). From his first entrance he is an Old Testament God, filled with jealousy and rage (jealousy of his son's youth and triumph, rage at his own injury) and spouting recriminating fire and brimstone. A patriarch beyond the possibility of parody superficially, he is in essence a spoiled child grown to monstrous proportions. Obstinacy and vindictiveness carried to the level of brutality plus a good measure of self-pity sum up Christy's father, and he will have his revenge. "And I after holding out with the patience of a martyred saint till there's nothing but destruction on, and I driven out in my old age with none to aid me," he says in answer to one of the Widow's taunts; conveniently forgetting that it is his son who has fled with him in pursuit (*Playboy* 48).

It is with a touch of satisfaction that we hear of his second murder. It is with a sense of regret that we witness his resurrection. The regret is allayed by relief, for in the interim, Michael James, Pegeen, and the others have done their Judas turn on Christy. When Christy leads his father off in submission we feel it only right.

Age is finally put in its place, but youth has hardly been well served in the play. "And isn't it a great shame when the old and hardened do torment the young?" the Widow Quin remarks. Her words are apt in several ways. The economics of post-famine Irish agriculture that made little gods of the paterfamilias, allowing their offspring the options of escape into emigration or a grim lifetime of celibate obedience until their fathers died or went into the west room, was one sort of torment that every Irishman from a rural background would have understood. Christy's escape was of a somewhat different and much more dramatic kind. It was an escape into fantasy, an extravagance as Synge put it, and not one entirely of his own making. Christy has been cast in a role, seemingly great but actually limited and circumscribed, that he can play for only a time. This too is a torment of sorts and one imposed on him by his newfound friends. He is the King who must in time be sacrificed, and he can reign only so long as Father Reilly, the law, and Christy's own father are held at bay. The fantasy reaches its most idyllic moment just before the return of reality as Pegeen's father gives his blessing to their marriage. Pegeen, too, is a victim to the illusion that she can marry a penniless parricide, that her father or any Irish father of means would consent to a marriage without lengthy discussions with the groom's father concerning dowry and exchange of property (Arensberg 76–98). The elder Mahon gets his "destruction on" with his penultimate entrance, and it is a destruction to abort this final episode of Carnival, the marriage of King and Queen.

At this moment, the Widow Quin returns in her intercessory role. There is "none to pity him but a widow woman, the like of me, has buried her children and destroyed her man," an indication that she has escaped the tyrannical cycle of life and inheritance in the Irish countryside, but at the expense of her reputation (*Playboy* 54). While the Playboy asks: "And I must go back into my torment is it, or run off like a vagabond straying through the Unions with the dusts of August making mudstains in the gullet of my throat" (*Playboy* 73).

It is the second alternative that Christy pursues with his father in tow. They will not go back to their "windy corner of high, distant hills," but like trampers follow the roads of Ireland, which in his life and work John Millington Synge much preferred (*Playboy* 19).

Notes

1. Sultan's article is an instance of the first position, while the second may be found in Skelton's.
2. The west room is the one into which members of the older generation move after relinquishing control of the farm to their children.
3. "The Land" deals with succession and "Thomas Muskerry" with the loss of mastery.

Works Cited

Arensberg, Conrad. *The Irish Countryman.* Garden City. NY: Natural History Press, 1968.
Bakhtin, Mikhail. *Rabelais and His World.* Bloomington: Indiana UP, 1985.
Bretherton, George. "Against the Flowing Tide: Whiskey and Temperance in the Making of Modern Ireland." Eds. Susanna Barrows and Robin Room. *Drinking: Behavior and Belief in Modern History.* Berkeley: U of California P, 1991. 147–64.
Colum, Padraic. *Three Plays.* Dublin: Brown and Nolan, 1963.
Gerstenberger, Donna. "A Hard Birth." Ed. Harold Bloom. *J. M. Synge's* The Playboy of the Western World: *Modern Critical Interpretations.* New York: Chelsea House, 1988. 41–59.
Gregory, Isabella Augustus. *Our Irish Theatre.* New York: Oxford UP, 1972.
Kenner, Hugh. *A Colder Eye.* New York: Knopf, 1983.
Miller, Kerby A. *Emigrants and Exiles: Ireland and the Irish Exodus to North America.* New York: Oxford UP, 1985.
Skelton, Robin. *The Writings of J. M. Synge.* Philadelphia: Bobbs, 1971.
Spacks, Patricia Meyer. "The Making of the Playboy." *Modern Drama* 4 (1961), 314–33.
Sultan, Stanley. "A Joycean Look at *The Playboy of the Western World.*" Ed. Maurice Harman. *The Celtic Masters.* Dublin: Dolmen Press, 1967. 49–67.
Synge, J. M. *The Complete Works of J. M. Synge.* New York: Random, 1935.

Synge's Ideas on Life and Art: Design and Theory in *The Playboy of the Western World**

WILLIAM HART

It is customary for artists to theorize for a time, explaining themselves to themselves, and then fortunately to begin to put theory into practice. Such was the case with Richard Wagner, such was the case with J. M. Synge. The comparison, however, is even closer, for just as Wagner was musician, playwright and poet, so too was J. M. Synge. Nor is one forgetting that some months before leaving Ireland to study music in Germany the twenty-two-year-old Synge recorded in his diary: "Started words and music of an opera on Eileen Aruin."[1] Also it would seem that Synge's own eclectic thinking on art and drama derives in part from Wagner. The German tone poet, however, was more fortunate than the Irish student of music and languages. Wagner at least was able to give his theorizing that organic character which brought it into print. Synge never got that far yet as sometimes happens with artists, Synge's art, especially his *Playboy* art, both realizes and completes his theorizing. In fact it may be said that Synge's *Playboy* provides both the key and the master link which holds together in organic fashion the seemingly disparate and disjointed articles of his artistic creed. It is impossible to prove so large an assertion within the limits of this paper. Nevertheless, because the subject bears so much upon an appreciation of Synge and his play, it seems of some value to investigate one essential aspect of that large assertion, namely, how the formal design of the *Playboy* derives ultimately from a general philosophy of life and art which shaped Synge's theory of poetry and drama. I am arguing, therefore, that Synge's ideas on life and art generated a theory of poetry and drama which determined the formal design of his play. Hence the tripartite subject matter of this paper: the play's design, the playwright's philosophy of life and art, and his ideas on poetry and drama.

The design of the *Playboy* has two formal characteristics: an essential dualism and a cyclical movement. The play's parallel currents of what Synge calls the "poetical" and the "Rabelaisian" constitute the dualism. These currents may be considered analogous to the major and minor chords of a musical

---

*This essay first appeared in *Yeats Studies*, No. 2 (Dublin: Irish University Press, 1972).

composition; so too may the cyclical movement of these currents, the design's second characteristic, be likened to symphonic arrangement. The "poetical," or minor current, which Synge variously refers to as the romantic or lyric note, is the love interest and its attendant moods of loneliness and melancholy. The "Rabelaisian," or major current, is the wild, joyous gusto of imagination which is rich in Dionysian humour and half-savage grotesqueries. Although one may regard these currents in terms of plot and subplot, it is more rewarding to see them in terms of their predominant dual notes of the romantic and Rabelaisian. A glance at an extant scenario for Act I, dating probably from the autumn of 1906, readily shows the essential dualism.[2]

Act 1	1	Pegeen and Shawn current her loneliness crescendo	comedy and locality
	2	Ditto and 3 men current keeping of Shawn climax	Molièrean climax of farce
	3	Ditto and Christy current (a) to find out his crime (b) to keep him exists climaxed by Shawn's	savoury dialogue
	4	Pegeen and Christy current (sub)—growing love interest	to be poetical—very strong
	5	Ditto and Widow Quin current taking off of Christy	to be Rabelaisian—very strong
	6	Pegeen and Christy short finale	diminuendo ironical

The playwright conceives the act in six scenes of varying currents working toward a "poetical" climax followed by a "Rabelaisian" climax that gradually gives way to an ironic curtain line not unlike the "Picardy third" in musical composition where the piece ends in the minor mode on a major chord. In addition each scene has its own inner conflict and serves a dramatic purpose whose general nature is characterized in the right-hand column. A closer look at the structure shows an almost symphonic cyclic arrangement of action and feeling from lesser to greater crescendos. Each scene has its own small cycle of arsis and thesis leading into the next larger cycle so that the movement of a scene is in fact the patterned movement of the whole, the mirror or microcosm of the full dramatic action. The light comedy of the opening scene rolls into the heavy comedy of the second, whose climactic laughter then leads into the serious quiet of suspense and attention to finding out the stranger's crime which builds then to the full chorus of acceptance.

PEGEEN: That'd be a lad with the sense of Solomon . . .

PHILLY: The peelers is fearing him . . .

JIMMY: Bravery's a treasure in a lonesome place . . .

PEGEEN: It's the truth they're saying, and if I'd that lad in the house, I wouldn't be fearing the loosèd khaki cut-throats, or the walking dead.

CHRISTY: (*swelling with surprise and triumph*) Well, glory be to God!

The movement ends, the men leave, an easy transition of fun with Shawn leads into the current of love interest whose crescendo of poetry and action finds a timely interruption with the Widow Quin's arrival. Conflict for possession of Christy swells the action to the rhythm of the two women's biting quarrel until the Widow's disclosure of Pegeen's coming marriage to Shawn quiets the action. This gives Christy a fleeting fear which Pegeen dispells as she prepares his bed: "I've put a quilt upon you I'm after quilting a while since with my own two hands, and you'd best stretch out now for your sleep, and may God give you a good rest till I call you in the morning when the cocks will crow." Faithful to the ritual, Christy returns Pegeen's antiphonal blessing in the sincere yet exaggerated tones of a tinker, but once she has shut the door behind her, Christy ends on the major chord of the Rabelaisian: "Well it's . . . great luck and company I've won me in the end of time—two fine women fighting for the likes of me—, till I'm thinking this night wasn't I a foolish fellow not to kill my father in the years gone by."

Acts II and III continue the same design. The bright atmosphere of the opening scene presents a new-born Christy polishing Pegeen's shoes, sizing up the pub and picturing himself in the days to come drinking in the lazy grandeur of it all; a comic Narcissus at the looking-glass, startled into brief hiding by the sudden arrival of the romance-starved village girls. The action dialogue of Sara taking up Christy's boots quickly engages Susan and Honor, widens to engulf Christy, is then counter-balanced by the Widow Quin's commandeering entry, and climaxes perfectly in Sara's toast to "the wonders of the western world." Pegeen enters, gaiety halts abruptly. From the act's opening curtain, the contrasting notes of the lyrical and the grotesque, the romantic and the Rabelaisian, have been sounding continuously. Now begins a duet between Pegeen and Christy, Pegeen on the major chord sharply taunting Christy with a grotesque account of a hanging and the treachery of men, while Christy, miserable and frightened, moves on the minor chord toward his rhapsody of loneliness: "It's well you know it's a lonesome thing to be passing small towns with the lights shining sideways when the night is down, or going in strange places with a dog noising before you and a dog noising behind, or drawn to the cities where you'd hear a voice kissing and talking deep love in every shadow of the ditch, and you passing on with an empty hungry stomach falling from your heart." Pegeen softens into wanting Christy to stay. Christy *"with rapture"* envisions his days filled with "that look is coming upon you meeting my two eyes, and I watching you loafing around in the warm sun, or rinsing your ankles when the night is come." Pegeen ends the scene on the Rabelaisian note confessing, "I wouldn't give a thraneen for a lad hadn't a mighty spirit in him and a gamey heart." This scene is also a clear example of the recurring cycle of Christy's emotions, from joy to grief and back to joy.

The emotional cycle repeats itself in the following scene: Christy *"still in high spirits,"* arrogant and pugnacious with Shawn, is *"very natty"* in Shawn's new clothes and *"as proud as a peacock,"* until *"he swaggers to the door, tightening his belt . . . then staggers back"*: "Saints of glory! Holy angels from the throne of light! . . . It's the walking spirit of my murdered da!" Christy's mood remains down until, at Old Mahon's exit, the Widow's lashing comment "Well, you're the walking playboy of the western world" stings him into grotesque curses on his father and lyric blessings on Pegeen. Christy returns to his high spirits once the Widow Quin gives up her "poetical" but futile effort to capture him for herself and agrees instead to help him to win Pegeen. Christy's wildly poetical, prayerful entreaties to the Widow recall his Act I curtain blessing on Pegeen just as here the Widow's tag ending "if the worst comes in the end of all . . . none to pity him but a widow woman, the like of me . . . has destroyed her man" ironically contrasts with Christy's Act I curtain line: "Well it's . . . great luck and company . . .—two fine women fighting for the likes of me—. . . wasn't I a foolish fellow not to kill my father in the years gone by."

The analysis of the formal characteristics of essential dualism and cyclic movement in Act II confirms how closely Synge keeps to his deliberate design, as set forth in the scenarios for Act II.[3] A study both of the play's growth through numerous versions and of the agonizing difficulty Synge has in containing the Widow Quin in the creative process reveals those same formal characteristics controlling the play's design. Throughout Act II Synge is working a cycle of romantic suspense alongside a building cycle of Rabelaisian surprise, and in that creative process his guiding rule seems to be to reject anything in character or action that threatens the orchestral balance and symphonic movement of the poetic and Rabelaisian currents, the dual notes of the lyric and grotesque. Two suggestions in Notebook 34 for Act II developments which were eventually rejected illustrate those same characteristics in design. "Make scene with and after fight with father as harrowing as possible to be relieved by farce at end" and "strong *grotesque* climax leading to lyric climax immediately of Pegeen and Christy."[4]

In Act III, as Synge himself said, both notes have to climax "no matter who may be shocked." In reply to an Irish-American critic's charge that the play was "unduly grotesque" and "superfluously coarse" Synge explained:

"When he blames the 'coarseness,' however, I don't think he sees that the romantic note and a Rabelaisian note are working to a climax through a great part of the play, and that the Rabelaisian note, the 'gross' note, if you will, *must* have its climax no matter who may be shocked."[5] Nowhere in the play is the orchestral design so evident as it is in the deliberate balance of savage action and fiery poetic speech in the play's closing scenes. Marginal notes to the last drafts bear such directions as: "Give Christy big speeches while he is on the ground" and "give Christy an outburst that has majesty and poetry."[6] "Work up Romantic note in Christy's speeches in this scene broken speech by speech of the others. Vivify crowd."[7] The point need not be laboured much further. The *Playboy's* essential dualism and cyclic movement as seen in its characteristic contrasting and climaxing of romantic and Rabelaisian notes, moods and movements constitute the play's formal design. That design, which is in effect the play's "rationalized concatenation of events," is clearly in imitation of the play's soul or form—Christy's cycle of psychic rise and fall— what Francis Fergusson calls the plot "as the first actualization of the directly perceived action."[8] An examination of the other characters and their language would disclose how they too imitate that same cyclic action.[9] Needless to say, such organic homogeneity in art is often the invisible signature of genius. That, however, is another matter. What remains now is to see how the play's design relates to Synge's theory of life and art which together shaped his ideas on poetry and drama.

In this matter one may proceed in either of two ways. One may begin with an analysis of the quintessential article of Synge's creed, namely, "All art is a collaboration" and on having examined that dictum in the context of the *Playboy's* preface and the play's genesis, see how it relates to the rest of his thinking on life and art. The second way, the one this paper elects to follow, is to return to the Synge of the 1890s and trace the genetics of his theorizing both before and after Yeats invited him to give up criticism and become an Irish artist.

During the middle and late nineties Synge devoted much time to working out his ideas on life and art. His manuscripts from those years suggest that he may have been attempting a semi-fictional portrait of the artist and his art: first in prose composition, later in a mixture of prose and poetry, and finally in dramatic form in his first complete play, *When the Moon Has Set*. All these efforts failed. The morbidity and melancholy in some of the early manuscripts caused Yeats to suggest that Synge go to Aran.[10] And Synge's own experience with those early compositions may have caused him to conclude: "All theorizing is bad for the artist, because it makes him live in the intelligence instead of in the half sub-conscious faculties by which all real creation is performed."[11] At any rate, Synge's view of life as expressed in those early writings is emotive, pantheistic, evolutionary and tragically joyous. Asserted in *Flowers and Footsteps* and in the *Autobiography*, echoed in the *Vita Vecchia* and in the *Étude Morbide*, his composite view of life and art is given almost philosophic exposition through the convention of a fragmentary manuscript on aesthetics in *When the Moon Has Set*. There he writes: "Every life is a symphony and the translation of this sequence into music and from music again, for those who are not musicians, into literature, or painting or sculpture, is the real effort of the artist."[12] The analogy with music is intrinsic. Life is a sequence of emotions which are in themselves eternal, cosmic and divine. "The emotions which pass through us have neither end nor beginning, are a part of eternal sensations, and it is this almost cosmic element in the person which gives all personal art a share in the dignity of the world."[13] The emotions are divine because: "The world is a mode of the Divine exaltation and every sane fragment of force ends in a fertile passion that is filled with joy. It is the infertile excitements that are filled with death. That is the whole moral and aesthetic of the world."[14] "Neglect nothing, for God is in the earth and not above it. In the wet elm leaves trailing in the lane in autumn, in the deserted currents of the streams, and in the breaking out of the sap, there are joys that collect all the joy that is in religion and art."[15] Humanity is evolutionary in a world of blind force, doomed to annihilation but not without some joy. "Humanity has evolved from the conditions of the world, and will return to the nothing it has come from."[16] "[H]umanity itself may die out but a turmoil of life is within us. It has come from eternity, and I suppose will go on for eternity."[17] "We are at an ultimate climax of desolation, yet . . . through it all it is possible to find a strange impulse of joy."[18] Synge's view of man's life and emotions is tragically joyous. The cosmic emotions, divine and eternal in themselves, in man derive from and centre about the poles of life and death.[19] "All the solemnity of art is begotten by the obsession of death. All power and mirth are associated with the thought of the unconscious will of reproduction. That is the symphony. The utterance of passion is the only sincere utterance of life. . . . I say it again, the two poles of existence from which all our emotions are derived lead at last to the joy where we begin or to the horrible corpse where we end."[20] This view of life recalls Northrop Frye's idea that "tragedy is really implicit or uncompleted comedy" and "that comedy contains a potential tragedy within itself."[21] An example may clarify that observation. In the *Autobiography* Synge recalls an experience he had on the occasion of his aunt's death. "The sense of death seems to have been only strong enough to evoke the full luxury of the woods. I had never been so happy."[22]

Everywhere there is an imperious reaction from the weight of death. . . . Even now my gaiety is rising. . . . The scherzo has its place in the symphony even after a dead march.[23] Death should pass us like the dead march in a symphony, where a turn of the hand can wake a new movement of life.[24]

The gaiety of life is the friction of the animal and the divine. A life given to the search of gaiety is restrained by the sorrow that exists with it on the same plane and creates the opposite ecstasy of pity. . . . Gaiety and pity are essentially in coexistent conflict. A man who lives in amusement reminds me of a man lighting a fire in the rain.[25]

For Synge life is the symphony. It is the cycle of sorrow and turmoil creating their opposites joy and tranquility "by which they are themselves created." "No one has understood motion therefore no man has understood the condition of life, for life is motion and sorrow and turmoil are the condition of life as are joy and tranquility their opposites whom they create and by which they are themselves created."[26] "A cycle of experience is the only definite unity, and when all has been passed through, and every joy and pain has been resolved in one passion of relief, the only rest that can follow is in the dissolution of the person."[27] Death, however, must not be taken as a denial of life's beauty but rather must be regarded as an affirmation of its glory which centres on the fact that man shares in the dignity of nature through that very cosmic element in him which relates him to joy and sorrow, to turmoil and tranquility, to the eternal and divine. By reason of that cosmic element "his soul and the soul of nature are of the same organisation."[28] Consequently, "[t]he moods of nature do not differ much from those of men."[29] As nature is cyclic in its motion so is man in his emotion. Around the poles of existence, birth and death, gather man's emotions of mirth and melancholy, and since life is a self-renewing cycle, so too are the emotions. Thus may it be said: "The two subjects on which all our glory is constructed are the facts of love and death."[30] Or, as Synge wrote much earlier in his discussion novel *Flowers and Footsteps*: "The human joys and human pities are the two feet of the human being on which he moves in the limited human life."[31] Finally, just as the cosmic element of emotion in man is the ontological basis for his share "in the dignity of nature," so too is that cosmic element of emotion or mood the ontological basis for personal art and for art's own "share in the dignity of the world." "Things have always a character and characters have always a mood. These moods are as perpetually new as the sunsets. Profound insight finds the inner and essential mood of the things it treats of and hence gives us art that is absolutely distinct and inimitable,—a thing never done before and never to be done again."[32] "The emotions which pass through us . . . are a part of eternal sensations, and it is this almost cosmic element in the person which gives all personal art a share in the dignity of the world."[33] Thus for Synge Art is because Nature is because Man is because God is.

In short, Synge's view of life is emotive, pantheistic, evolutionary and tragically joyous. It is also fundamentally dualistic and cyclical. The fundamental dualism is clear: nature with its moods of turmoil and tranquility, man with his emotions of joy and sorrow as they focus on life and death. Motion is sequential, symphonic, evolutionary and cyclical. The "cycle of experience is the only definite unity" and although death is a finality, a joyful perspective is there in the sense that life must go on. "Gaiety and pity are essentially in coexistent conflict" and the "scherzo has its place in the symphony even after a dead march." That is Synge's view of life. Standing firmly upon it is his view of art. Art is essentially expression, the expression of mood. "Real art is always a suggestion, an intangible emotion lurks behind the things that we produce as life lurks within the body. . . ."[34] "Real art is the expression of an emotion which cannot be confined."[35] "Every life is a symphony and the translation of this sequence into music and from music again . . . into literature, or painting or sculpture, is the real effort of the artist."[36] Among Synge's papers is a full schema of what art is for the artist. It reads in part: "Art (for the artist) [is the] (1) Expression of joy or sorrow, (2) Expression and by means of the expression satisfaction of the craving for joy—Objectively by the forming of works that appease this craving or express it—Subjectively by the forming and considering of certain ideas and the culture of the characters accordingly."[37] According to his schema the "germ of drama" is found under the first heading, art as the expression of joy or sorrow, whereas "higher poetry and drama" are directly classified under the second heading, art as the expression and by means of the expression the satisfaction of the craving for joy. That latter distinction recalls a statement Synge made in an article prepared for the *Manchester Guardian* on "Irish Plays, Players, and the Dramatic Movement." In it he wrote of the "eternal" problem "in all the greater arts, the problem that is to say of finding a universal expression for the particular emotions and ideas of the personality of the artist himself."[38] Ideas themselves are born of moods. "Art is but the expression of a mood and in each mood a thought is also given birth. . . ."[39] Mood is everywhere, in man and in nature; the artist's task is to find "the inner and essential mood." "Profound insight" finds the mood but if the artist's soul is not in harmony with the mood of the earth, his art is without value. Nature, showing forth the art of God or recalling to us the art of men, suggests great emotions in us and in these is art rooted. "[A]ll art that is not conceived by a soul in harmony with a mood of the Earth is without value."[40] "In nature is the art of God and unless our souls are godly enough to produce an art more beautiful than nature . . . it is better to be silent."[41] "I believe that the art we feel and recall among the greater moods of nature is the only art which is begotten of a mood that is healthy."[42] Art is, therefore, a modality, the expression of a mood, of the emotions of joy or sorrow, of turmoil and tranquillity, which are a part of the world's sequence of eternal sensations. Art is in man and nature's moods. Through sympathetic observation, the artist distills the essence of a mood and expresses it in the medium of his art form along with the ideas that the mood engenders in the creative process. "This then is the task of all who labour [to] create, to light with transcendental imagination the data no sane instructed being may deny."[43] None can deny that joy and sorrow are the condition of life. Just as birth and death are "the two poles of existence from which all our emotions are derived" so it follows that "tragedy and humour . . . are the two poles of art."[44]

The artist in his work must take a full view of the entire reality of life.

Life is many-sided but the aesthete's work is one-sided, proceeding from a "one-sided exaggeration of the personality." "Beauty is an attribute of art . . . but not the end or essence of it."[45] For the same reason may one reject the extremes of naturalism. The tramp's life has "a certain wildness that gives it romance" and is of value to the artist intent on a full view of life, but "the maniac in real life, and Des Esseintes and all his ugly crew in the arts, are freaks only."[46] As Synge wrote in two of his letters to his friend Stephen MacKenna: "no drama can grow out of anything other than the fundamental realities of life" and "Ireland will gain if Irish writers deal manfully, directly and *decently* with the entire reality of life."[47] In a draft of his preface to *The Tinker's Wedding* he asserted: "The value of good literature is measured by its uniqueness, and in works that are not purely subjective by its richness also. But when a work is rich and unique it must be taken freshly and directly from life, and it must be many-sided, so that it has a universal quality, and is therefore sane, as all insanity is due to a one-sided exaggeration of the personality."[48] Finally, a work of art will be unique and of value if to the artist's distinction of personal originality there is added a great distinction of time and place. "No personal originality is enough to make a rich work unique, unless it has also the characteristic of a particular [time] and locality and the life that is in it."[49] Art for the artist as Synge describes it is very much the work of collaboration.

Anyone familiar with Synge's method of composition knows how thoroughly he practised collaboration. His notebooks are filled with jottings and materials taken "freshly and directly from life." Entire passages in his topographical essays on Wicklow, Kerry and Connaught can be justly described as lyrical sight-sound pictures suggesting the "inner and essential mood" of men and places. So too is his *Aran Islands* filled with observations on the sympathy between man and nature. "I cannot say it too often, the supreme interest of the island lies in the strange concord that exists between the people and the . . . powerful impulses of the nature that is round them."[50] Atmosphere is of the essence in all these works, just as it is of the essence of all his plays. Nor is one forgetting Synge's defence of his *Playboy* in a letter to MacKenna: "The story—in its *essence*—is probable given the psychic state of the locality."[51] Synge himself said that the full view of reality was his aim. "In my plays and topographical books I have tried to give humanity and this mysterious external world."[52]

The emotive, dualistic and cyclical view which Synge took of humanity and the world, along with his conviction that the artist's real effort is to translate that reality in its fullness, conditioned his ideas on poetry and drama. Poetry is of two kinds, the poetry of exaltation which is highest and the poetry of ordinary life, the vital verse of wide interest "occupied with the whole of life—as it was with Villon and Shakespeare's songs, and with Herrick and Burns."[53] Vital verse, the poetry of real life, has "strong roots among the clay and worms."[54] Exalted poetry needs its influence. To Yeats he wrote: "That if verse, even great verse is to be alive it must be occupied with the whole of life. . . . For although exalted verse is the highest, it cannot keep its power unless there is more essentially vital verse at the side of it as ecclesiastical architecture cannot remain fine when domestic architecture is debased. Victor Hugo and Browning tried in a way to get life into verse but they were without humour which is the essentially poetic quality in what I call vital verse."[55] Those same ideas he expressed in more polished form in his preface to his *Poems and Translations*. In Notebook 47, however, which dates from the same year as his preface, 1908, there are some rough notes expressing the same distinction, "the poetry of real life" and "the poetry of the land of the fancy," after which Synge adds: "That is obvious enough, but what is highest in poetry is always reached where the dreamer is leaning out to reality or where the man of real life is lifted out of it, and in all the poets the greatest have both these elements that is they are supremely engrossed with life and yet with the wildness of their fancy they are always passing out of what is simple and plain."[56] Synge's distinction between the kinds of poetry which is very much what Yeats calls the two ways open to literature—"the way of the bird" and that of "the market carts"[57]—would seem to derive from that same dualistic view of life which Synge feels the artist must translate. Certainly the violent juxtaposition of the lyrical and grotesque in language and mood is characteristic of Synge's poetry. The last eight lines from "Queens" is a typical example of that style.

> Queens who cut the bogs of Glanna
> Judith of Scripture, and Gloriana,
> Queens who wasted the East by proxy,
> Or drove the ass-cart, a tinker's doxy,
> Yet these are rotten—I ask their pardon—
> And we've the sun on rock and garden,
> These are rotten, so you're the Queen
> Of all are living, or have been.[58]

That same technique, the juxtaposition of the lyric and the grotesque, of the sigh of ecstasy and the cry of rage, is the hallmark of Synge's work. Yeats was the first to remark it when he wrote in his preface to Synge's poems: ". . . the strength that made him delight in setting the hard virtues by the soft, the bitter by the sweet, salt by mercury, the stone by the elixir, gave him a hunger for harsh facts, for ugly surprising things, for all that defies our hope."[59] Nevertheless, while it may be true that Synge had "a hunger . . . for all that defies our hope," it is his humour, or more precisely his irony that gives lasting strength to his work. His essentially ironic temperament yoked "the market carts" to "the way of the bird" to give us "what is highest in poetry" and attained "where the dreamer is leaning out to reality or where the man of real life is lifted out of it." That is the style of the great love passage in the *Playboy*.

CHRISTY: It's little you'll think if my love's a poacher's or an earl's itself when you'll feel my two hands stretched around you, and I squeezing kisses on your puckered lips till I'd feel a kind of pity for the Lord God is all ages sitting lonesome in his golden chair.

CHRISTY: (*with rapture*) If the mitred bishops seen you that time, they'd be the like of the holy prophets, I'm thinking, do be straining the bars of Paradise to lay eyes on the Lady Helen of Troy, and she abroad pacing back and forward with a nosegay in her golden shawl.

The saving irony in that style is the humour, "the nourishment, not very easy to define, on which our imaginations live."[60] That is the humour he described to Yeats as "the essentially poetic quality . . . in vital verse." As he said in his preface to *The Tinker's Wedding*: "Of the things which nourish the imagination humour is one of the most needful, and it is dangerous to limit or destroy it."[61] This is the special quality of "joy" one must have on the stage, as he asserts in his *Playboy* preface. It is what he designates in his scenarios as "Rabelaisian" and what in that same preface he describes as being "found only in what is superb and wild in reality."[62] Just as that "humour" is vital to health of imagination, so too is it a necessary part of drama. Without it, neither the artist nor the spectator can safely take the full view of life which art requires. "Certain portions of life, wild and coarse in a sense, that we can never get away from can only be looked at safely when they are seen with the humour which makes them human. . . ."[63]

Synge's humour eventually becomes the principle by which he triumphs over nature and the limitation of form to fashion the complexity of his comedic design. Nevertheless, that humour or irony can become, as Hegel said, the "perversion and overthrow of all that is objectively solid in reality."[64] This is one of the principal reasons some critics cannot abide Synge. The action of men reaching for drinks at the end of his comedies suggests an ironic impulse that says it is all going to happen again. The dramatic rhythm implies it and some critics will not have it. Yeats seems to explain their objection when he writes to John Quinn: "The truth is that the objection to Synge is not mainly that he makes the country people unpleasant or immoral but that he has got a standard of morals and intellect. . . . they shrink from Synge's harsh, independent, heroical, clean, wind-swept view of things. They want their clerical observatory where the air is warm and damp."[65] It was necessary to write at some length on Synge's idea of "joy" not only because of its importance to the present argument but also because an understanding of the canonical dicta in the *Playboy* preface requires it. Synge's preface is more than a tribute to the people and imagination of rural Ireland. It is more than a defence of his language and subject. It is a compact statement both of his creative method and of the dramatic language and literature the stage must have. Collaboration is his method because it is his philosophy of art, and, as Daniel Corkery observed, Synge's "practice of collaboration was more comprehensive than his statement of it."[66] By collaboration Synge means directly his practice of going to the Irish country people for the subject matter, the living speech and living imagination, the psychic moods and emotions of a particular time and place for the creation of his drama. Because their language and imagination is "rich and living" it is possible for the dramatist's language to be both "exalted" and "vital" ("rich and copious") and so communicate "the reality, which is the root of all poetry, in a comprehensive and natural form." Yet what is that reality and the reality one must have on the stage?

In the light of Synge's theatre reality means the whole of life, the tinker and the tramp, the queen and the publican's daughter, the wonder and the misery, the flowers and the worms. Reality in each of his plays involves some form of love and death that either exits with gypsy laughter in an imaginative escape or else is itself transformed into that tragic instant of exaltation wherein the spirit slips the bonds of time and chants in Maurya and Deirdre the canticle of the artist's vision in which "stoicism, asceticism and ecstasy" are at last united.[67] Reality in the context of the *Playboy* preface means "the profound and common interests of life." Reality in the composite of his theatre and theorizing are those same interests of love and death with the emotions of joy and sorrow centring about them in the cyclic condition of tumult and tranquillity. Recall that for Synge reality is cosmic motion and human emotion, the ever returning cycle, "the sequence of existence," the full view of which cannot be taken without humour. The technique of ironic contrast communicates the wonder and misery of life with a "joy" or humour that nourishes the imagination and keeps art healthy and free from one-sided exaggerations. Thus does the artist, by juxtaposing the lyrical and grotesque, the romantic and the Rabelaisian, "give the reality, which is the root of all poetry, in a comprehensive and natural form."[68] In that way the artist combines the "reality" character of naturalism with the "rich" character of symbolism and, if he joins to his own personal originality the "characteristic of a particular [time] and locality and the life that is in it," he "gives us art that is absolutely distinct and inimitable— a thing never done before and never to be done again." He gives us the romance of reality, *The Playboy of the Western World*.

Synge's mind is in his art. Taken both separately and together, Synge's theory and practice suggest that his view of life, its essential dualism and cyclical movement, predicated in poetry a duality and juxtaposition of the lyrical and grotesque in language and mood; and that some composite view of life and art generated in the creative process of the *Playboy* design an essential dualism and symphonic arrangement of the romantic and Rabelaisian.

Notes

1. J. M. Synge, *Plays*, Book 1, in *Collected Works*, vol. III, ed. Ann Saddlemyer (London: Oxford University Press 1968), p. xiv. All quotations from Synge's published work are taken from the *Collected Works*.

2. *Plays*, Book 2, p. 296.

3. Ibid., p. 297.

4. Ibid., p. 352.

5. Ibid., p. xxv.

6. Ibid., p. 170 note 4.

7. Ibid., p. 164 note 3.

8. Francis Fergusson, *The Idea of a Theatre* (Princeton: Princeton University Press 1949), p. 49; see also pp. 36–37.

9. In Notebook 28 Synge wrote: "work out relations of outside types so as to make play in a sort [of circle]." After "sort" Synge drew a straight line ending in a circle. See *Plays*, Book 2, p. 362.

10. W. B. Yeats, *A Vision* (London: Macmillan & Co. 1962), p. 167. See also W. B. Yeats, *Autobiographies* (London: Macmillan & Co. 1956), p. 344.

11. *Prose*, p. 347.

12. *Plays*, Book 1, pp. 174 note 3, 279.

13. Ibid., p. 174.

14. Ibid., p. 168 note 2.

15. Ibid., p. 164 note 2.

16. *Étude Morbide* in *Prose*, p. 29.

17. *Plays*, Book 1, p. 168 note 2.

18. Ibid., p. 164 note 1.

19. Ibid., p. 168 note 2.

20. From an unpublished dialogue in *When the Moon Has Set*.

21. Northrop Frye, "The Argument of Comedy," *Modern Essays in Criticism*, ed. Leonard Dean (New York: Oxford University Press 1967), p. 84.

22. *Prose*, p. 7.

23. From an unpublished passage in *When the Moon Has Set*.

24. *Plays*, Book 1, p. 176.

25. *A Rabelaisian Rhapsody, Plays*, Book 1, p. 186.

26. Ibid., p. 185.

27. Ibid., p. 176.

28. Notebook 17, c. 1899, Synge Estate Papers.

29. Clipbinder 18, c. 1899, Synge Estate Papers.

30. *Plays*, Book 1, p. 176.

31. Ibid., p. 278.

32. Notebook 20, c. 1898, Synge Estate Papers.

33. *Plays*, Book 1, p. 174.

34. Ibid., p. 278.

35. "Flowers and Footsteps," Notebook 15, c. 1896, Synge Estate Papers.

36. *Plays*, Book 1, p. 174 note 3.

37. Item 50, containing materials from 1893–1905, Synge Estate Papers.

38. The original nine-page holograph of this unpublished article is in the Berg Collection of the New York Public Library. See *Plays*, Book 1, pp. xxvii–xxviii.

39. Clipbinder 22, c. 1896–1898, Synge Estate Papers.

40. Ibid.

41. Notebook 15, c. 1896. For a variant reading in *Étude Morbide*, see *Prose*, p. 35.

42. Item 50, c. 1896, Synge Estate Papers.
43. Item 50, c. 1903, Synge Estate Papers.
44. *Prose*, p. 350.
45. Notebook 30. c. 1903, Synge Estate Papers.
46. *Plays*, Book 2, p. 363.
47. Ann Saddlemyer, "Synge to MacKenna: The Mature Years," *Irish Renaissance*, ed. Robin Skelton and David R. Clark (Dublin: Dolmen Press 1966), pp. 67–68.
48. *Plays*, Book 1, p. 291.
49. *Prose*, p. 350.
50. Ibid., p. 75 note 1; see also p. 143.
51. Skelton and Clark, *Irish Renaissance*, p. 75.
52. *Prose*, p. 351.
53. From Synge's letter of 1908 to Yeats, *Poems*, p. xv.
54. Synge's preface to his *Poems and Translations, Poems*, p. xxxvi.
55. *Poems*, pp. xv–xvi.
56. Ibid., pp. xiv–xv.
57. W. B. Yeats, "Personality and Intellectual Essences," *Essays and Introductions* (New York: Macmillan Co. 1961), pp. 266–67.
58. *Poems*, p. 34.
59. Ibid., p. xxxiv.
60. Preface to *The Tinker's Wedding, Plays*, Book 2, p. 3.
61. Ibid., p. 3.
62. Ibid., p. 54.
63. From a draft of the preface of *The Tinker's Wedding, Plays*, Book 2, p. 291.
64. William K. Wimsatt, Jr., and Cleanth Brooke, *Literary Criticism: A Short History* (New York: Alfred A. Knopf 1959), p. 380.
65. From Yeats's letter to John Quinn, 4 October 1907: see Allan Wade, ed., *The Letters of W. B. Yeats* (New York: Macmillan Co. 1955), p. 495.
66. Daniel Corkery, *Synge and Anglo-Irish Literature* (Cork: Cork University Press 1931), p. 85.
67. *Poems*, p. 34 note 1.
68. Preface to *The Playboy of the Western World, Plays*, Book 2, p. 53.

"Too Immoral For Dublin": Synge's "The Tinker's Wedding"*

Denis Donoghue

Commentators on Synge's plays have had surprisingly little to say about *The Tinker's Wedding*, and there seems to be general agreement that the play has little or no merit. Professor Corkery's resentment culminates in a statement that "the play is scarcely worth considering either as a piece of stagecraft or as a piece of literature."[1] Another critic regards it as "dramatic wild oats sown in moments of relaxation. . . ."[2] Professor Green, borrowing a phrase applied by a greater critic to a greater play, describes "this unruly little farce" as "an artistic failure" and comments: ". . . a fair estimate of 'The Tinker's Wedding' is that it contains a crude farcical element which is typical of Synge, little or no deftness of characterization, perhaps one good scene at the end where the tinkers rush off in confusion."[3] While I have no desire to exaggerate the merits of the play, I think it is possible and necessary to point out certain aspects of significance within the text which seem to have escaped notice. It may also be possible to show that the lack of "deftness of characterization" is not in this instance a damaging criticism, that the comedy derives from another source.

The Tinker's Wedding is based on a story which Synge recounted in his Wicklow sketches:

Then a woman came up and spoke to the tinker, and they went down the road together into the village. "That man is a great villian," said the herd, when he was out of hearing. "One time he and his woman went up to a priest in the hills and asked him would he wed them for half a sovereign, I think it was. The priest said it was a poor price, but he'd wed them surely if they'd make him a tin can along with it. 'I will, faith,' said the tinker, 'and I'll come back when it's done.' They went off then, and in three weeks they came back, and they asked the priest a second time would he wed them. 'Have you the tin can?,' said the priest. 'We have not,' said the tinker; we had it made at the fall of night, but the ass gave it a kick this morning the way it wasn't fit for you at all. 'Go on now,' said the priest. 'It's a pair of rogues and schemers you are,

*This essay first appeared in *Irish Writing*, 30 (1955) and is reprinted by permission.

and I won't wed you at all.' They went off then, and they were never married to this day."[4]

A comparison of this yarn with *The Tinker's Wedding* shows that Synge's most significant addition to the story is the "action," the roughness. The priest is manhandled; Sarah threatens Mary with a hammer; Mary, who does not appear in the story at all, is drunk and rowdy. Indeed, this is one of the plays in which Synge, the man of ill-health, most clearly reveals a Keatsian delight in roughness, wildness and violence. W. B. Yeats records that in Ireland Synge "loved only what was wild in its people:"[5] this view is supported by Jack B. Yeats: "He loved mad scenes. He told me how once at the fair of Tralee he saw an old tinker-women taken by the police, and she was struggling with them in the centre of the fair when suddenly, as if her garments were held together with one cord, she hurled every shred of clothing from her, ran down the street and screamed. 'Let this be the barrack-yard'. . . . But all wild sights appealed to Synge."[6] It seems clear that this feeling of Synge's for wildness in conduct became identified with (or inseparable from) the cult of individuality which appears in the Wicklow sketches. It determines the whole comic structure of *The Tinker's Wedding*: in emphasising the earthiness of the comic situation, it sets the play in scornful opposition to that "morbidity of mind" which Synge attacked in the Preface:—". . . the infancy and decay of the drama tend to be didactic . . . in these days the playhouse is too often stocked with the drugs of many seedy problems . . . Of the things which nourish the imagination humour is one of the most needful, and it is dangerous to limit or destroy it. Baudelaire calls laughter the greatest sign of the Satanic element in man; and where a country loses its humour, as some towns in Ireland are doing, there will be morbidity of mind as Baudelaire's mind was morbid."[7] It is, I think, a serious error to regard *The Tinker's Wedding* as sheer farce: for one thing, the play is solidly grounded on an important social premise, namely, that the life of a tinker in Ireland is religion-less. This point is significant because it determines so many attitudes within the play. Throughout, the attitude of the tinkers to the world of religious reference is quite explicit: they do not deny the existence of "Almighty God" (quite the contrary), but He with His priest, His prayers, His sacraments and His Church, is on one side of the fence: the tinkers are on the other, not in opposition, but simply in a different field. In Act 1, Mary says to the priest:—"If it's prayers I want, you'd have a right to say one yourself, holy father; for we don't have them at all, and I've heard tell a power of times it's that you're for." Again, in Act 2, she says to the same victim:—

It's sick and sorry we are to tease you; but what did you want meddling with the like of us, when it's a long time we are going our own way—father and son, and his son after him, or mother and daughter, and her own daughter again; and it's a little need we ever had of going up into a church and swearing—

I'm told there's swearing with it—a word no man would believe, or with drawing rings on our fingers, would be cutting our skins maybe when we'd be taking the ass from the shafts, and pulling the straps the time they'd be slippy with going around beneath the heavens in rain falling.

When they have caught the priest, Mary suggests that they might let him go if he agreed to swear an oath that he would not inform against them: Michael comments:—

MICHAEL: What would he care for an oath?

MARY: Don't you know his like do live in terror of the wrath of God?

Finally, it is again Mary who makes the existence of the fence quite clear in her last speech to the priest:—". . . and it's little need we ever had of the like of you to get us our bit to eat, and our bit to drink, and our time of love when we were young men and women, and were fine to look at." This last speech contains the whole world as far as the tinkers are concerned: within the tribe, the tinker governs his life, not by ethics, but by "the pure-action norms of manners."[8]

To recover the metaphor, if God has His companions on one side of the fence, the tinkers are not quite alone on the other, for like all Synge's "sympathetic" characters, they relate themselves sensuously to the world of nature, to "dark ditch . . . spring is coming in the trees . . . when the night's fine and there's a dry moon in the sky . . . hearing the dogs barking, and the bats squeaking. . . ." This relationship is particularly emphasised in a passage which Synge discarded from the early drafts of The Tinker's Wedding:—"What is it the Almighty God would care of the like of us? You'd never see the Almighty God doing a thing to the larks or to the swallows or to the swift birds do be crying out when the sun is set, or to the hares do be racing above in the fine spring and what what would he be following us in the dark nights when it's quiet and easy we are, and we never asking him a thing at all."[9] With the omission of this passage, the tinker-Nature relationship in The Tinker's Wedding is not underlined as heavily as the Tramp-Nature kinship in The Shadow of the Glen, but we are sufficiently aware of it within the play to appreciate why the tinkers do not regard themselves as "outsiders." The tinkers, as a tribe, with their "natural" life, form a self-reliant world, complete in itself, which offers no incentive to feelings of resentment, reaction, or divergency from a higher, more respectable norm. In fact, the whole action of the play derives from the "unnatural" hankering of Sarah, one of the tribe, after such respectability. This "unnatural" desire causes all sorts of disturbances on both sides of the fence, disturbances which determine the shape of the play and likewise its formulation in terms of comic and ironic reversal.

The first reversal is fundamental, the irony of the situation itself. Sarah's marriage-notion, which would be conventionally be regarded as "the proper thing," is here interpreted, within the conventions of her own class, as a highly irregular, foolish and improper suggestion. Her desire to make an honest woman of herself has no moral value whatever in the eyes of her associates. The same applies, of course, to Michael: when he has agreed to do what society would call "the right thing" by Sarah, he finds it necessary to make a sheepish apology to his mother; not only that, he speaks as if the intention itself were immoral:—

MARY: *(turning to Michael)* And it's yourself is wedding her, Michael Byrne?

MICHAEL: *(gloomily)* It is, God spare us.

A further point of ironic reversal derives from the season in which the action takes place: the Spring. At the beginning of the play Michael says angrily:—"Can't you speak a word when I'm asking you what is it ails you since the moon did change?" and Sarah musingly answers:—"I'm thinking there isn't anything ails me. Michael Byrne; but the springtime is a queer time, and it's queer thoughts maybe I do think at whiles." The same time-location is continuously underlined throughout the play in association with the moon: Spring and the moon, conventionally associated with romance and young love, are here the background against which Sarah gets the dull notion of bringing her relationship with Michael into line with the staid morality of that convention. It is significant that the first draft of the play was entitled "Movements of May."

This reversal is extended to the presentation, within the play, of marriage itself. Conventionally related to romance, marriage here has no such implications. Within the tribe the romantic principle is irrelevant, it does not arise: but its repudiation is not shown immediately. At the beginning, it looks as if it has some place:

MICHAEL: . . . but what will you gain dragging me to the priest this night, I'm saying, when it's new thoughts you'll be thinking at the dawn of day?

SARAH: *(teasingly)* It's at the dawn of day I do be thinking I'd have a right to be going off to the rich tinkers do be travelling from Tibradden to the Tara Hill; for it'd be a fine life to be driving with young Jaunting Jim, where there wouldn't be any big hills to break the back of you, with walking up and walking down.

MICHAEL: *(with dismay)* It's the like of that you do be thinking!

Later, however, the romantic myth is shown in all its irrelevance when Michael says:—"If I didn't marry her, she'd be walking off to Jaunting Jim maybe at the fall of night; and it's well yourself knows there isn't the like of her for getting money and selling songs to the men."

Many of the comic reversals in the play are associated with Mary: the real villian of the piece, the old drunkard is the one to say:—"Ah, it's a bad, wicked way the world is this night, if there's a fine air in it itself." The mock-moral comments are intensified in the passage in which she sets herself to defend the Lord against the flightiness of the young:

SARAH: (*in a low voice*) And what time will you do the thing I'm asking, holy father?, for I'm thinking you'll do it surely, and not have me growing into an old, wicked heathen like herself.

MARY: (*calling out shrilly*) Let you be walking back here, Sarah Casey, and not be talking whisper-talk with the like of him in the face of the Almighty God.

Here, all "real" roles are reversed: Sarah, indefatigably pursuing the good life with benefit of clergy, is treated as if she were about to be indecent: Mary of the permanent thirst is the mock-Defender of the Right: the priest, she suggests, is far below her in virtue. Indeed, the implications of her phrase "the likes of him" are made explicit and brought into the open almost immediately when Mary follows up her holier-than-thou attitude:—"You'd never have seen me, and I a young woman, making whisper-talk with the like of him, and he the fearfullest old fellow you'd see any place walking the world." Here it becomes clear that, in Mary's eyes, Sarah's alleged flirting is wrong, not because its object is a priest but because that priest is "the fearfullest old fellow . . .": the crime is simply bad taste.

The final reversal arises from the true-or-false "clannishness" of the tinker tribe: blood being thicker than water or mere justice, Mary's offence is forgotten, and the three tinkers come together to beat up the priest. The moment Michael takes off his coat to fight the priest, all disunity among the tinkers disappears.

As I have suggested, the comedy of *The Tinker's Wedding* depends on the mock-conflict between certain attitudes in the tinkers themselves and all those other conventions which are covered by the word "orthodoxy." In fact, an examination of any of the "funny bits" in the play will show that the humour in each case arises from some basic incongruity (or attitude, pose, or moral orthodoxy) within the particular speech itself: two examples will be enough to make the point. At the beginning of the play, Michael is upbraiding Sarah for her marriage-idea, and says:—". . . and isn't it a mad thing I'm saying again that you'd be asking marriage of me, or making a talk of going away from me, and you thriving and getting your good health by the grace of the Almighty God?" This speech is funny because, in pressing together ideas drawn from the *natural* and from the *religious* lives, it conveys the shocking notion that the satisfactoriness of the present Michael-Sarah relationship is not only *condoned*, but in some way was actually *blessed*, by "the grace of the Almighty God." Ironic reversal can go no further. The same kind of humour is active in the opening words of the play:—

SARAH: (*coming in on right, eagerly*) We'll see his reverence this place, Michael Byrne, and he passing backward to his house tonight.

MICHAEL: (*grimly*) That'll be a sacred and a sainted joy.

The multiple suggestions contained in Michael's statement include at least (a) a personal criticism of the priest, (b) a parody, broadened by the alliteration "sacred . . . sainted," of the word "reverence" as applied to the priest, (c) a sneer conveyed through the blatant exaggeration of the word "joy," and (d) by implication and extension, an expression of Michael's resentment at the intrusion of "religion" on his happy-go-easy life. And here we may return briefly to that "deftness of characterization" the lack of which is lamented by Professor Greene. If "characterization" means the presentation of a character with photographic clarity and detail and with a feeling of completeness, then I agree that this is indeed absent from the four characters in *The Tinker's Wedding*. It might reasonably be maintained that Synge has made available in the text sufficiently clear sketches of these characters for his comic purpose; but that argument may be allowed to pass. What is more to the point is that in this play Synge has contrived his comic effects from the sheer interplay of attitudes on certain questions of morality and social living. "Characterization" is not the only source of dramatic interest.

In 1906 Synge wrote of *The Tinker's Wedding* to Max Meyerfeld: "We have never played it here as they say it is too immoral for Dublin."[10] It is clear that Synge regarded himself as fully justified in manipulating character, speech, and attitudes to any extent necessary for maximum comic effect, irrespective of the known tendency of audiences to extract from a play a crude, generalised "moral." *The Tinker's Wedding* is not meant to prove anything, or to effect any reforms; it is meant to be funny. In any piece of literature, it is necessary to reduce a poetic or dramatic entity to a conceptually analytic statement; the form itself, the poetic or dramatic enactment of a role within that form, can provide a pretext for the entry of motives and ideas which, if not thus complicated, would be inadmissible. *The Tinker's Wedding* does not mean that all, or even most, priests are mercenary: for the comic purposes of the play, a mercenary priest was necessary: a devout, saintly priest in the same circumstances would have called out from Synge's audience a totally different set of responses, alien to the particular comic organization the dramatist wanted. For these reasons, a mercenary priest was necessary, likewise a drunken female tinker. The comic pattern needed them.

Notes

1. Daniel Corkery: *Synge and Anglo-Irish Literature* (1931), p. 149.

2. Owen Quinn: "No Garland for John Synge" in *Envoy*, October, 1950.

3. David H. Greene: "The Tinker's Wedding, a Revaluation"; *Publications of the Modern Language Association*, September, 1947.

4. Synge: *Works*, Vol. 4. P. 47.

5. W. B. Yeats; Synge and the Ireland of his Time (1911), p. 12.

6. *ibid.*, p. 42

7. Synge: Preface to *The Tinker's Wedding*, 1907.

8. Albert Cook: *The Dark Voyage and the Golden Mean: a Philosophy of Comedy*. 1949, p. 39.

9. Quoted by Greene, *supra*.

10. "Letters of John Millington Synge from material supplied by Max Meyerfeld"; *Yale Review*, Vol. 13, 1924.

The Tinker's Wedding*

WELDON THORNTON

In Synge's first two plays, we have seen him presenting his audiences with challenges to the received or stereotyped ways that their "aesthetic set" predisposed them toward the works. In *The Shadow of the Glen* he did this by evoking a familiar plot-character stereotype and then allowing the true lineaments of the situation to emerge. In *Riders to the Sea* he did it by presenting faithfully a milieu that does not conform to our Western conceptualizations. While it is true that *The Tinker's Wedding* was thought to be potentially offensive to Irish audiences and it was refused production by the Abbey for fear it would provoke trouble, the offending element was hardly so subtle or complex as to deserve description as a challenged aesthetic disposition. The only stereotype Synge might be said to be challenging here is that of the sanctity of the priest. It was feared that the Irish audiences would not tolerate seeing a man of God beaten and sacked by a bunch of tinkers. But if the audience had rioted at the priest's being abused by the tinkers, they would have misdirected their anger. Whatever meaningful challenge the play offers to the priestly image comes not from his being beaten—the poor man cannot be held responsible for that—but from the worldliness he has displayed in his dealings with the tinkers earlier in the play. Our interest in this play lies, however, not in its repetition of a device we have seen in the earlier plays, but in certain situations and themes developed within the play.

If we look within the play we find the theme of abstraction and reality dramatized in the experience of the young tinker woman, Sarah, who in the course of the play learns a great deal about "cultural relativism" and the intangibility of ideals. Whether she could articulate what she has learned is not the point—probably she could not—but she has learned the speciousness of mere abstractions and the difficulty of transferring them from one culture to another. For the dramatic and psychological interest of the play grows largely out of the interplay of two cultures poised against one another: that of the itinerant tinkers who seem to have no culture, or who define themselves by contrast with that other, orthodox culture, here represented by the priest. The foiling of these two is set up in the opening scene: "*In the background, on*

*This essay first appeared as "First Fruits" in *J. M. Synge and the Western Mind*, Irish Literary Studies 4 (New York: Barnes and Noble, 1979), and is reprinted by permission of Colin Smythe Ltd.

the left, a sort of tent and ragged clothes drying on the hedge. On the right a chapel-gate."[1] The implicit contrast pervades the play.

The dramatic situation focuses upon one important contrast between the two cultures—their attitudes toward the institution and ceremonies of marriage. The play is set in motion by Sarah's idea that she wants to do as the ladies do and marry her man, complete with ring (of sorts), priest, and ceremony. The progress of this idea in Sarah's mind is the main basis of the play's psychological interest and thematic continuity. We note that neither of the other tinkers thinks much of Sarah's idea. Michael sees it as trivial and bothersome and goes along with it only to keep peace in the family. Mary, the older woman, grasps more fully what is going on in Sarah's mind, but she too regards it as foolish. Michael sees this new idea of Sarah's as a whim, related to recent changes of the moon, that will as quickly pass away, and Mary suggests the same.[2] There is, however, more to it than that, and perhaps more than Michael is capable of seeing until some life-crisis grips him. For Sarah is in a life-crisis, and her turning to the possibly magical effects of the ceremony of marriage reflects that. This is suggested by several of her statements about what she hopes for from being married, and it comes into the open in the play's thematic climax. Note Sarah's appeal to the priest: "And what time will you do the thing I'm asking, holy father? for I'm thinking you'll do it surely, and not have me growing into an old, wicked heathen like herself." (*Coll. Works*, IV, 21). The priest assumes that Sarah's emphasis falls on her hopes that the ceremony will redeem her from being a "wicked heathen," and he replies, "I'll marry you for [ten shillings and a can], though it's a pitiful small sum; for I wouldn't be easy in my soul if I left you growing into an old wicked heathen the like of her." (*Coll. Works*, IV, 23). But it is not heathendom Sarah is concerned to escape, and the adjective *old* is more than simply an intensive. Sarah admits that "spring-time is a queer time, and it's queer thoughts maybe I do think at whiles" (*Coll. Works*, IV, 7), and the queer thoughts going through her head now turn on her own beauty and how quickly she will lose it. In Mary she has constantly before her the image of what she will all too soon become, an old woman wandering on the roads. Her life with Michael and Mary has begun to seem dull and ordinary, and she feels herself moving quickly toward old age. As a result, she turns in her dissatisfaction to that other world the tinkers have always lived beside—the world of ladies, of houses, of stability, of ceremonies—and she endows one of its ceremonies with almost magical powers. She decides that *marriage* will give her life some quality it now lacks.

Whether this is what Sarah really wants is doubtful, for she is a tinker by nature and by choice, and she is probably largely satisfied with that life. As D. H. Lawrence points out, we are continually subject to both trivial desires and profound desires, and it is not easy, especially in times of crisis, to distinguish them.[3] Sarah looks at Mary and sees her own life rushing toward age and the hardship of a hand-to-mouth existence. We can hardly expect her to see at this time what a strong, even admirable, woman Mary is. For Mary is aware of ageing and hardship, and she has in all likelihood gone through crises of dissatisfaction and fear similar to Sarah's. But Mary has reconciled herself to life as the tinkers know it, and she accepts it fully. She too is curious about the ways of settled society and the orthodox church—she would like to hear a "real priest saying a prayer" (Coll. Works, IV, 21)—but she attributes to the rites of that society none of the special, almost magical quality that Sarah invests them with. She knows that the settled society has its ways and the tinkers have theirs, but that they are worlds apart, and there is little point trying to make the ways of the one fit the other. She knows too that beneath the trappings of the societies, human nature is fairly constant, and the problems people face do not vary nearly so much as the devices they use to palliate them. It is amusing how easily Mary's appeal to the priest to share a drink with her touches the man beneath the cassock and brings out his own complaints about his hard life, what with running back and forth to say Mass and trying to satisfy the bishop. Mary must know, too, that the ceremonies and institutions of society and the church are not magical or absolutely true, but are their own devices for dealing with the perennial problems of temporality and death. The song she sings tells us this:

> And when we asked him what way he'd die,
> And he hanging unrepented,
> "Begob," says Larry, "that's all in my eye,
> By the clergy first invented."
> —(Coll. Works, IV, 17)

Orthodox folk may have the consolations of the church to ease them through old age and death; the tinkers find their own ways of coping with them.

These issues are brought together in the crisis of the play. Michael shows signs of being infected by Sarah's fantasies about society's rituals, expressing fear that she may leave him if he does not marry her, but Mary begins to set both of them straight:

MARY: And you're thinking it's paying gold to his reverence would make a woman stop when she's a mind to go?

SARAH: [angrily]. Let you not be destroying us with your talk when I've as good a right to a decent marriage as any speckled female does be sleeping in the black hovels above, would choke a mule.

MARY: [soothingly]. It's as good a right you have surely, Sarah Casey, but what good will it do? Is it putting that ring on your finger will keep you from getting an aged woman and losing the fine face you have, or be easing your pains, when it's the grand ladies do be married in silk dresses, with rings of gold, that do pass any woman with their share of torment in the hour of birth, and do be paying the doctors in the city of

Dublin a great price at that time, the like of what you'd pay for a good ass and a cart? [*She sits down.*].

SARAH: [*puzzled*]. Is that the truth?   (*Coll. Works*, IV, 35, 37)

Sarah is taken aback by Mary's forthright statement, for she had expected something special from her ceremony. Though it takes her some time to accept what Mary has said, the process of her seeing society's rituals for what they are has been set into motion, and it soon works itself out. Sarah tries to maintain her belief in the special efficacy of the priest and the marriage ceremony, but when the father wrongly accuses her of having tried to trick him, all of her misgivings are precipitated. Her attack on him expresses more than anger at being accused of duplicity. It expresses also her disappointment and frustration at her inability to find what she had hoped for in his rituals. She realizes that she is a tinker, and that her only defenses against life are those of the tinkers—a direct and willing acceptance of each day as it comes, in full awareness of its transiency and of the approach of old age and death. She must take Mary as her model, and not a bad one at that. The older woman becomes their spokesman when she says to the sacked priest:

That's a good boy you are now, your reverence, and let you not be uneasy, for we wouldn't hurt you at all. It's sick and sorry we are to tease you; but what did you want meddling with the like of us, when its a long time we are going our own ways—father and son, and his son after him, or mother and daughter, and her own daughter again—and it's little need we ever had of going up into a church and swearing—I'm told there's swearing with it—a word no man would believe, or with drawing rings on our fingers, would be cutting our skins maybe when we'd be taking the ass from the shafts, and pulling the straps the time they'd be slippy with going around beneath the heavens in rains falling. (*Coll. Works*, IV, 47).

Mary's comment shows that the tinkers do indeed have their own society and their own kinds of tradition.

As the play draws to an end, a clearer-eyed Sarah puts her ring onto the priest's finger and says, "There's the ring, holy father, to keep you minding of your oath until the end of time; for my heart's scalded with your fooling; and it'll be a long day till I go making talk of marriage or the like of that" (*Coll. Works*, IV, 49). And Mary again is the one who sets them right about their own mode of life when she says, "She's vexed now, your reverence; and let you not mind her at all, for she's right surely, and it's little need we ever had of the like of you to get us our bit to eat, and our bit to drink, and our time of love when we were young men and women, and were fine to look at" (*Coll. Works*, IV, 49).

Along with this rounding out of the psychology and theme we have been tracing, there is an amusing, almost capricious, twist at the play's end. Mary half-seriously suggests, "Maybe he'd swear a mighty oath he wouldn't harm us, and then we'd safer loose him" (*Coll. Works*, IV, 47). Though she has earlier expressed curiosity about hearing a real priest say a prayer, she has consistently been sceptical about the priest's modes of power. All along we have seen Sarah as duped by the supposed power of the marriage oath and Mary as shrewdly sceptical of it. Now Mary is the one who suggests that the father vow not to harm them. Does she, then, believe in the priest's vows and in his power to harm them? The play is delightfully subtle and true to life on this count, for it shows that clear-eyed scepticism about the ceremonies and abstractions of another culture is not an either/or matter. Mary can see the foolishness of Sarah's ideas about marriage, but not be at all clear whether her own feelings about the priest's mysterious oaths and curses are foolishness or not. When the tinkers scatter before the priest's Latin malediction, they do so in fear of the possible power of this dark language. It is not exactly that they believe in these powers—certainly they do not in any orthodox sense—but there is some question in their minds, and it is better not to take any chances!

Notes

1.   Quotations from *The Tinker's Wedding* are from the *Collected Works*, IV (1968). The passage quoted here is from IV, 7. Subsequent page references are given parenthetically.

2.   Robin Skelton takes an opposite approach to this, arguing that the association of Sarah's desire with the changes of the moon suggests that it grows out of deep, pagan sources (*The Writings of J. M. Synge*, pp. 75–76). But the play bears out what Michael implies—that it is a mere whim, as changeable as the moon. Doubtless some of Sarah's feelings spring from deep sources but this desire for orthodox marriage is not one of those. It makes more sense to see this desire as abstract and superficial, an attempt on Sarah's part to adapt to her own situation ideas from another milieu.

3.   See "Apropos of Lady Chatterley's Lover," in *Lady Chatterley's Lover* (London, 1961), esp. pp. 26ff.

Deirdre of the Sorrows
Literature First . . . Drama Afterwards*

ANN SADDLEMYER

"My next play must be quite different from the *P. Boy*. I want to do something quiet and stately and restrained and I want you to act in it." When Synge wrote these words to his fiancée Molly Allgood early in December 1906 he was ill, on the verge of disillusionment with the Abbey Theatre, and thoroughly fed up with Christy Mahon and the myth-making Mayoites. He was just recovering from his bitterest quarrel with Molly and was facing an even greater crisis with his mother, to whom, from a safe distance in England, he was at last breaking the news of his engagement. Opening night of *The Playboy of the Western World*, already postponed once, was less than two months away, but he was still dissatisfied with the third act and uncertain of the players' ability to fulfil his wishes. He was worried about his poverty and his ill-health, the two greatest obstacles to his marriage. No wonder he longed for peace, security and a change of pace, if only in his art.

But Synge was to face greater turbulence still. The shattering history of *The Playboy's* reception is well-known: on the first night actors were hooted from the stage, controversy raged in public and the press for months, his fellow-directors (one of whom disliked the play intensely) and the theatre suffered a serious loss of support for several years to come. Never a fighter, Synge retired to Kingstown with a bad cold, developed influenza and was not seen at the theatre for almost six weeks. However, he was not unduly depressed by the reaction to his comedy. "I feel like old Maurya today," he wrote to Molly after the first performance, " 'It's four fine plays I have, though it was a hard birth I had with every one of them and they coming to the world.' It is better any day to have the row we had last night, than to have your play fizzling out in half-hearted applause. Now we'll be talked about. We're an event in the history of the Irish stage." He tended to blame part of the trouble on the actors' lack of preparation and inability to express the "subtleties" his play required; he rejected well-meaning friends' criticisms of structure and mood, insisting that it was "certainly a much stronger *stageplay*" than any of

*This essay first appeared in *J. M. Synge: Centenary Papers*, (Dublin: Dolmen, 1971) and is reprinted with permission.

his other work; and he justified the offending "Rabelaisian" note as an essential counterpoint to the romantic element in the play. As far as he was concerned *The Playboy* was an artistic success, if not yet one in performance; he was confident that he had achieved the sound comic structure, the precise patterning of characters and motifs, that he had worked for so painstakingly and so long. "The story—in its *essence*—" he affirmed, "is probable given the psychic state of the locality," and in the preface to the published text he unashamedly compared himself to the greatest of Elizabethan dramatists.[1]

Now, confined to bed, he had time to recollect past experience and to dream of future plans. With *The Aran Islands* finally published, he planned two more travel books out of his raw material on Wicklow and Kerry; he made arrangements for *The Playboy* to be translated and produced in the continental theatres that had already seen *The Shadow of the Glen* and *The Well of the Saints*. He dug out old poems, re-worked them, and wrote new ones for Molly. In search of reading material for her, he rediscovered old favourites— R. L. Stevenson, George Meredith, Tolstoi, Walter Scott, the *Mabinogion*, the Arthurian tales. He delved further into his own past and re-examined portions of an old autobiography; he may even have attempted yet another revision of his first completed play, *When the Moon Has Set*, for notebook jottings of this period bear a close resemblance to some of the later drafts. Later that year he revised the unpublished, unproduced *Tinker's Wedding* and theorized further still about comedy, drama and literature. Then, during the summer months, he spent an idyllic convalescence in the Wicklow mountains with Molly.

It is impossible to say with any certainty when he decided to turn to ancient saga material for his next play, although it is apparent from his notebooks and published writings that he had been interested especially in the Deirdre story for at least five years. Even before he enrolled in de Jubainville's course in Old Irish at the Sorbonne in the spring of 1902 he had attempted his own translation of "The Sons of Usnach" during a visit to Aran. When he reviewed Lady Gregory's book *Cuchulain of Muirthemne* Deirdre's lament was cited as one of its finest passages, and he may well have had this story in mind when he wrote to Lady Gregory herself, "What puny pallid stuff most of our modern writing seems beside it!"[2] A few years later he again singled out passages from the Deirdre story when reviewing A. H. Leahy's *Heroic Romances of Ireland*; but this time the translation was criticized as a "deplorable misrepresentation of the spirit of these old verses" and the author was sternly advised to study Andrew Lang's translation of the medieval French *cante-fable, Aucassin and Nicolette*, a book he also recommended to Molly as "filled with the very essence of literature and romance."[3]

Following Lady Gregory's lead, other Abbey Theatre dramatists were exploring Ireland's past for fresh material. Æ's only play, *Deirdre*, was well-known and frequently revived by amateur companies throughout the country. In November 1906 Synge and Molly observed with some misgivings Yeats's one-act *Deirdre*; the same month he sent her *Aucassin and Nicolette* (which became their favourite book) and also recommended Lady Gregory's "charming" translation of "The Sons of Usnach." Now, in March 1907 after the *Playboy* fracas, Yeats's earlier "Cuchulanoid drama"[4] *On Baile's Strand* was revived, with Molly playing one of the musicians, followed two weeks later by Yeats's revised *Deirdre*, Molly again in the cast. At the same time, she was rehearsing the title role of W. S. Blunt's *Fand*, based on "The Only Jealousy of Emer," another story from Lady Gregory's *Cuchulain*. Spurred by this renewal of interest in saga material, and encouraged no doubt by his reading of Walter Scott, Synge revised an early poem, "Queens," and drafted an essay entitled "Historical or Peasant Drama." The poem ended with the questions,

> And are these ladies, I ask your pardon
> As dead as the doornail of Jim McCarden,
> Are all these queens of love and laughter
> As dry as Mahony's chimney rafter?[5]

The essay concluded that historical fiction was now impossible and insincere, that modern poetry apart from a few lyrics was a failure, and again ended with a question: "Is the drama—as a beautiful thing a lost art? . . . For the present the only possible beauty in drama is peasant drama, for the future we must await the making of life beautiful again before we can have beautiful drama."[6]

But if Synge was not yet ready to accept "the drama of swords," he could not deny the magnificence and tenderness of Ireland's popular imagination, which he had eloquently praised in the preface to *The Playboy* and out of which the saga material had grown. Other aspects of theory had also matured, for by now, too, he had reconciled the role of the artist with an earlier role, the lonely sensitive observer of nature's moods. Despite a reluctance to theorize, he found himself formulating an aesthetic creed and observing it in his prose works. The individual, he believed, could not achieve wholeness in himself until he was in harmony with nature and had attempted a wholeness within the entire cycle of experience. Just as the natural and the supernatural as he observed them on Aran are all part of the same spectrum of experience, so man must sound all the chords and moods of his own nature before he can hope to recognize and sympathize with the various moods and aspects of the universe of which he is a part. Life and nature at their most intense provide a sharpness to experience and hence greater joy in being and becoming; life at its most primitive provides the greatest opportunity for experiencing this sympathy between man and the natural world; therefore the hunter, the tramp and the poet, who are most free to roam and are constantly testing themselves are most receptive and sensitive to all of nature's moods. This is especially true of the artist, whose privileged position requires him to be not only sensitive but objective, openly sympathetic but inevitably alone. Loneliness became for

Synge a necessary experience, balanced by a heightened exultation in the richness of "what is superb and wild in reality," and an inevitable part of the fully developed personality.[7]

But beyond this spectrum available to the "prepared personality" is the evolutionary pattern of the universe itself, of which man's total experience is but one small part. For Synge had recognised in the twilights of Wicklow and the grey mists of Aran that nature too has a psychic memory, that time and place in turn range beyond the hours and seasons to include incidents from the distant past and hints of the future. His one-act tragedy *Riders to the Sea* had revealed this layering of events within the story of one family through the experiences of old Maurya, whose grief became at the same time personal and universal, encompassing the loss of three generations while centering on the last of six strong sons. Her final lament is for all mothers, everywhere, and for all who mourn, have mourned and will mourn the coming of death: "No man at all can be living forever, and we must be satisfied." Now he delved deeper into Ireland's past in an effort to identify and capture what is richest and most lasting in life, nature and time, and came at last to that meeting-place where man's story becomes part of the universal experience, to the fountainhead of all literature—folk history and primitive knowledge. In *The Well of the Saints* Synge had examined man's need for a myth out of which to carve the reality of his dreams; in *The Playboy of the Western World* he had explored the process of myth-making and celebrated its dangers and glories; now he turned to his most difficult task yet, the re-creation, in terms significant to modern man, of the myth itself. It was to lead him back through the unsophisticated peasant of Wicklow, Aran, and Kerry into the Irish folk spirit of legend, to the mingling of the immediacy of passion with those unyielding constants, Death and Time.

The starting-point on this journey must be the artist's personality and individual experience. For the first time the joy of a love returned matched Synge's exultation over beauty in the natural world, and his letters to Molly illustrate a fresh awareness of the sharp pain of intense emotion:

> All that we feel for each other is so much connected with this divine world, that our particular affection, in a real sense, must be divine also.
>
> You feel as fully as anyone can feel all the poetry and mystery of the nights we are out in—like that night a week ago when we came down from Rockbrook with the pale light of Dublin shining behind the naked trees till we seemed almost to come out of ourselves with the wonder and beauty of it all. Divine moments like that are infinitely precious to both of us as people and as artists . . . I think people who feel these things—people like us—have a profound joy in love, that the ordinary run of people do not easily reach. They love with all their hearts—as we do—but their hearts perhaps, have not all the stops that you and I have found in ours. The worst of it is that we have the same openness to profound pain—of mind I mean—as we have to profound joy, but please

Heaven we shall have a few years of divine love and life together and that is all
I suppose any one need expect.

Illness and exile had forced him also to a profound awareness of the
brevity of man's span within the universal cycle:

There is nearly a half moon, and I have been picturing in my mind how all our
nooks and glens and rivers would look, if we were out among them as we should
be! Do you ever think of them? Ever think of them I mean not as places that
you've been to, but as places that are there still, with the little moon shining,
and the rivers running, and the thrushes singing, while you and I, God help
us, are far away from them. I used to sit over my sparks of fire long ago in Paris
picturing glen after glen in my mind, and river after river—there are rivers like
the Annamoe that I fished in till I knew every stone and eddy—and then one
goes on to see a time when the rivers will be there and the thrushes, and we'll
be dead surely.

Long before he had begun to write, Deirdre's lament at leaving Alban was
part of his own experience.

But it would be a mistake to suggest that morbidity led Synge to the
story of Deirdre. His first fears in tackling the theme were that "the 'Saga'
people might loosen my grip on reality." Diffidently, he expressed doubts as
to his ability to write a satisfactory play. "These saga people, when one comes
to deal with them, seem very remote," he complained to John Quinn; "one
does not know what they thought or what they ate or where they went to
sleep, so one is apt to fall into rhetoric." But he admitted it was an interesting
and challenging experiment, "full of new difficulties, and I shall be the better,
I think, for the change."

Many of those difficulties were inherent in the material itself, for the tale
of Deirdre and the Sons of Usnach was the most familiar of all legends of the
heroic cycle of Cuchulain and the Red Branch. Although manuscripts might
differ in details, the general outline, the beginning and the end, were well
known and the facts with which Synge worked were common to most versions.
Even before Deirdre was born it was prophesied, so the story goes, that she
would grow to be of great beauty and thereby cause the ruin of Ulster, the
downfall of the House of Usna, and the death of many men. Hearing this, the
High King Conchubor took her for his ward and placed her in a secluded place
in the charge of a nurse and a tutor; but before he could claim Deirdre as his
bride, she met Naisi and persuaded him to elope with her. The lovers,
accompanied by Naisi's brothers Ainnle and Ardan, fled to Scotland where
they took service with the King and won great honour by their feats of valour.
Eventually they were found by Fergus, who as Conchubor's emissary brought
pledges of forgiveness and a safe return to their beloved Ireland. Naisi, despite
Deirdre's dreams foretelling disaster, agreed to return, but Conchubor had

arranged to separate Fergus from his charges. With the help of magic, Naisi and his brothers were killed; Fergus sought revenge by pillaging and burning Emain, the seat of kings for many generations; and Deirdre, having fulfilled her unhappy prophecy, killed herself.[8]

But the problem remained: how to express the reality of this well-used myth "in a comprehensive and natural form"? Yeats had chosen to concentrate on the last scene of the drama, using a chorus of musicians to explain events of the past and illuminate Conchubor's treachery. His two proud lovers remain frozen in their eagle-like passion until released by death. Synge followed Æ's earlier example and wrote his play in three acts, but with none of Æ's mysticism or unconscious bathos ("Thou art the light of the Ultonians, Naisi," intones the druidess Lavarcham, "but thou art not the star of knowledge.") From the beginning, although their story is foretold, Synge's characters remain true to their own natures; the action is the result of strong personalities clashing because they cannot do otherwise and still be themselves. Although he retained a hint of mysticism until very late drafts, eventually he rejected all dependence on prophecy or premonition; similarly the Sons of Usna meet their death not through druidic incantations but because they are tricked and outnumbered. But Synge's greatest originality remains the blending of theme and character, the shifting of emphasis and climax, in keeping with his developed theory of art and drama. He would not be satisfied until all was strengthened, "made personal," simple, intense, charged with his own vision of the world. In this experiment "chiefly to change [his] hand," he moves from the bright sunlit world of comedy and the melodramatic exaggeration necessary for the vividness of the amoral, to the moonlit world of tragedy and the patient anatomization of passion against a stark background of death and time. He wrote in his notebook, "Sudden in the romance writer a real voice seems to speak out of their golden and burning moods, it is then they are greatest."[9] He sought this same greatness in his dramatization of the saga of Deirdre of the Sorrows.

Synge completed his first draft of the play in November 1907. The ninth and final draft of Act I was completed four months later; but Act III, which ran to eleven drafts, was not in a finished state until mid-January 1909, and the second act was still unsatisfactory in its fifteenth draft, when Synge entered Elpis Nursing Home for the last time. During the fifteen months he was at work on the play there were many interruptions, but all contributed to his development of the story: theatre responsibilities—directing, managing, and coaching—made him more aware of heightened dramatic effect; publication of his poetry forced him to clarify further his thoughts on language and the artist; bouts of illness sharpened his sense of the beauty of this world and the urgent need to "play all the stops"; comradeship with Molly intensified his belief in the purity of the passions; his mother's final illness served to remind him of the untidiness of a lingering old age and the reality of death. It is always intriguing to contemplate what might have been, but even in its unfinished state, with additional help from the notebook drafts, it is possible to see how closely Synge wove themes developed out of his personal view of the world through the framework of the established myth and, beyond the established text, to glimpse the shadowy pattern of the planned masterpiece. Had he lived to complete the play I believe it would have retained the same shape, but colour and theme would have been infinitely enriched through character and mood, the lyrical romanticism balanced by a tough fibre of the grotesque.

As it now stands, *Deirdre of the Sorrows* is a twilight play, beginning in the darkness of storm clouds and ending in the stillness of death.[10] Twilight for Synge, especially in Ireland, was a time filled with "vague but passionate anguish," when "moments of supreme beauty and distinction" are possible, tinged with suggestions of death and loneliness. On such a night an ageing king will feel conscious of empty days and time passing, a young princess will become aware of her destiny, joyous young princes of their moment of triumph. It is the romantic hero Naisi who voices the tension already evoked by the forces of nature: "At your age you should know there are nights when a king like Conchubor would spit upon his arm ring and queens will stick their tongues out at the rising moon. We're that way this night, and it's not wine we're asking only. . . ." Distant thunder and threat of the worst storm in years are an appropriate background to the rare moment when the young child of nature sheds the duns and greys of her peasant world, lays aside nuts and twigs from the hillside, to don the jewels and robes and destiny of a queen. For Deirdre will be no ordinary queen, one rather who will be "a master, taking her own choice and making a stir to the edges of the seas." A woman of her like cannot deny the natural impulses within her, must in fact reach out and grasp what is hers, "the way if there were no warnings told about her you'd see troubles coming." She dreads Emain, the Dun of an ageing High King, because it is an unnatural resting place for one who has learned to be at one with the woods, the birds, the rivers, sun and moon. The threat of death holds less fear, being a natural part of nature's law; "All men have age coming and great ruin in the end." Just as nature has schooled Deirdre in the wisdom of time, so nature unites the two lovers: "By the sun and moon and the whole earth, I wed Deirdre to Naisi . . . May the air bless you, and water and the wind, the sea, and all the hours of the sun and moon." It is significant that Lavarcham, learned wise woman that she is, cannot wed them; she is committed to the rule of the High King, who is at war with time, careless of nature, and ambiguous in his feelings towards Deirdre. It is Ainnle, "who has been with wise men and knows their ways," yet is fellow huntsman and comrade-in-arms to Naisi, who performs the ceremony and thus initiates the Fate of the Children of Usna.

Seven years in Alban are happy and bright, with love as pleasing as "the same sun throwing light across the branches at the dawn of day." But it is at the beginning of the darkness of winter that the lovers choose to leave, "the

time the sun has a low place, and the moon has her mastery in a dark sky."
Twilight now is the foreshadowing of death and the end of love: "It's this hour
we're between the daytime and a night where there is sleep forever." Earlier
the woods promised fulfillment of love; now they deny hope of safety, for
independently both lovers confess their awareness that in the course of nature
nothing can stand still. "There are as many ways to wither love as there are
stars in a night of Samhain, but there is no way to keep life or love with it a
short space only." The quiet woods below Emain Macha hide the promised
grave, open to receive them "on a dark night." When Deirdre at last mourns
the death of Naisi and prepares for her own death, she bequeaths the strange
dignity of her loneliness to the little moon of Alban, left "pacing the woods
beyond Glen Laid, looking every place for Deirdre and Naisi, the two lovers
who slept so sweetly with each other." Lavarcham's final speech underscores
this sympathy with the natural world, but at the same time assures the
permanence of a universe in which their story can be told forever: "Deirdre is
dead, and Naisi is dead, and if the oaks and stars could die for sorrow it's a
dark sky and a hard and naked earth we'd have this night in Emain."

Against this background of the natural passage of time, Deirdre and
Naisi's decision to return to Emain becomes much more significant and
meaningful. Just as they had earlier chosen life in the woods and exile from
Ireland, now they choose to accept the harsh facts of nature and go gladly
forward to meet fate in an effort to retain the fullness and freshness of their
love. "Isn't it a better thing to be following on to a near death, than to be
bending the head down, and dragging with the feet, and seeing one day a
blight showing upon love where it is sweet and tender?" For seven years they
have had perfection of love and comradeship; but the dread of the natural
course of life and love, heretofore unspoken, has now fallen like a shadow
across that perfection of passion. Unlike Lavarcham, who speaks for the
unfolding of the full course of nature, they prefer to cut their time short. Nor
do they wish to fight off or distort the true course of nature like Conchubor,
who sees Deirdre as surety against old age and death, or Owen, who attempts
to seduce Deirdre from her natural mate. But their decision has far-reaching
implications, for Ainnle and Ardan, who have been satisfied with comradeship
and fraternal loyalty, are pulled along with them; "four white bodies" will
share the grave chosen by Deirdre and opened by Conchubor.

But if the lovers' decision prepares the way for joy and triumph in myth,
where love reigns supreme over death, it introduces a contrasting leitmotif,
the pain of love in the real world, with the ultimate irony of the grave's victory.
As the moment of nature's perfection can never be isolated, so the dream of
perfect love in this life proves impossible. The climax of their story occurs not
in Act II, at the decision to return to Emain—that is a continuation of their
acknowledgment of the inexorable laws of nature—, but here in Act III at
the edge of the grave prepared for Naisi by Conchubor. Panicking at the

realization of what they must lose to retain their place in the saga, Deirdre reneges on that pact in the woods and seeks an unnatural compromise with Conchubor. She pleads for the very right to age and withering mortality that she had earlier rejected: "I'll say so near that grave we seem three lonesome people, and by a new made grave there's no man will keep brooding on a woman's lips, or on the man he hates. It's not long till your own grave will be dug in Emain and you'd go down to it more easy if you'd let call Ainnle and Ardan, the way we'd have a supper all together, and fill that grave, and you'll be well pleased from this out having four new friends the like of us in Emain." But it is too late, for Conchubor is helpless to break the chain of events earlier forged by the two lovers; Ainnle and Ardan are attacked. Now Deirdre, for the first time, forces Naisi to choose between his brothers in battle and complete absorption in her love. Because he can no longer follow his whole nature (foreshadowed in the brothers' quarrel at the end of Act II), Naisi breaks under the strain and bitterness erupts, cracking the perfection he and Deirdre had risked everything to attain. Hurt by the threat of loss, the lovers quarrel and in a stroke of painful irony lose the safety of the grave.

But Naisi's death in the shadow of Deirdre's mockery heightens his role at the end of the play; Deirdre's grief is intensified by the memory of their quarrel: "It was my words without pity gave Naisi a death will have no match until the ends of life and time." The story told forever threatens to be one of pain, not comfort; not only have they lost their love—their own choice—but they have lost their triumph as well, and Deirdre is left truly desolate. The only way to retain the fullness of their story and thus preserve their love is for Deirdre to grow even further in stature, until Conchubor becomes "an old man and a fool only," and a greater High King, Death, marks her for his own. To regain a sense of her own strength and retrieve the dignity of her loss, she must turn her thoughts back from this night "that's pitiful for want of pity" to the splendour of their life in the woods. Her lament must embrace not only the glory of the past but also the future, where palaces fit for queens and armies become again the haunts of weasels and wild cats, crying on a lonely wall below a careless moon. Finally, sorrow itself must be cast aside to make room for the cold pity of prophecy and the impersonal triumph of the myth. Only then, by giving up all claims to this world, can Deirdre be assured of her joy with Naisi forever. Exulting in her loneliness, she stands imperious and triumphant over the grave of the Sons of Usna, free at last of all demands both of man and time itself:

I have put away sorrow like a shoe that is worn out and muddy, for it is I have had a life that will be envied by great companies. It was not by a low birth I made kings uneasy, and they sitting in the halls of Emain. It was not a low thing to be chosen by Conchubor, who was wise, and Naisi had no match for bravery . . . It is not a small thing to be rid of grey hairs and the loosening of the teeth . . . It was the choice of lives we had in the clear woods, and in the grave we're safe surely.

Not only do the characters represent various stages on the spectrum of choice and reaction to time, they also indicate the full range of the passions of love and loneliness. While on Aran Synge had observed the simplicity of primitive man's judgment, "that a man will not do wrong unless he is under the influence of a passion which is as irresponsible as a storm on the sea." Now, using material "filled with the oldest passions of the world," he set out to construct through his various characters a chord which would sound all the notes of love and longing, ranging from Naisi's romantic defiance of destiny to Lavarcham's wise acceptance of the passing of love. In contrast to the character development of his comedies, here he must start with persons already fully developed, infinitely themselves, "types" in a special sense. It might not be too fanciful, in fact, to trace this simplification of character and emphasis on individual ruling passions back to his earlier studies of music and French literature. The currents or leitmotifs of destiny (as well as the consuming fire at the conclusion) are expressed in a grand Wagnerian manner, while the starkness and grandeur of passion and the inevitability of its consequence are reminiscent of French classical theatre, in particular the dramas of Racine.[11]

When he reviewed Lady Gregory's *Cuchulain of Muirthemne*, Synge remarked, "Everywhere wildness and vigour are blended in a strange way with impetuous tenderness, and with the vague misgivings that are peculiar to primitive men. Most of the moods and actions that are met with are more archaic than anything in the Homeric poems, yet a few features, such as the imperiousness and freedom of the women, seem to imply an intellectual advance beyond the period of Ulysses."[12] Now in the character of Deirdre, written especially for Molly, he sought to convey the same imperious freedom, strength of will, and maturity of passion. The full responsibility of action rests finally on Deirdre alone; the intensity and purity of her love must be above question, and matched by greatness of soul in both herself and her lover. But Deirdre must also be sufficiently realistic to be "probable," perhaps like the young girl he admired on Aran: "At one moment she is a simple peasant, at another she seems to be looking out at the world with a sense of prehistoric disillusion."[13] By using nature not as atmospheric background only but as the living standard by which Deirdre determines her actions, Synge attempted to combine the present with the past and emphasize the inevitability of her decisions. The framework and scope of her personality are fully developed in the first act: although caught in the web of prophecy, she is eminently herself. Wild with the wildness of nature, she has spent her days on the hillside or alone in the woods, "gathering new life . . . and taking her will." It is "wilfuller she's growing these two months or three," Lavarcham complains to Conchubor, and Deirdre echoes the warning: "I'm too long watching the days getting a great speed passing me by, I'm too long taking my will, and it's that way I'll be living always." The "like of her" is not for Conchubor, blind to the ways of nature, and careless of Deirdre's schooling in freedom, greedy for a comrade to ease the weight and terror of time. In place of nuts, twigs, birds and flowers, he offers her dogs with silver chains, white hounds, grey horses, symbols of the constraints of his role. However, Deirdre seeks not her opposite, but "a mate who'd be her likeness," whose high spirits will match her wildness, and who in the violence of youth will wrench love from its hiding place and taste "what is best and richest if it's for a short space only."

Like Deirdre, Naisi has been a long time in the woods and dreads neither death nor "the troubles are foretold." Challenged by Deirdre, he accepts his destiny, "and it earned with richness would make the sun red with envy and he going up the heavens, and the moon pale and lonesome and she wasting away." Perhaps he has more to lose, for he and his brothers have "a short space only to be triumphant and brave." A warrior as well as a hunter, he knows long before Deirdre the untidiness of death, "a tale of blood, and broken bodies and the filth of the grave." And in Act II, although Deirdre first voices her dread of the passing of love, "wondering all times is it a game worth playing," it is Naisi who acknowledges responsibility for that dread and tries to protect Deirdre from the advance of time. But after seven years the safety he offers in the woods is as ineffective as the security of Conchubor's High Chambers; reluctantly he must acknowledge the justness of Deirdre's decision to return. Just as Naisi had more to lose in their flight to Alban, now he has greater troubles to bear: the prophecy foretells the ruin of the Sons of Usna, while Deirdre's fate is left undetermined. He must carry with him the memory of their love and the bitter possibility of being superseded by another; and he stands to lose not only Deirdre's love but the perfect comradeship of his warrior brothers, a double loneliness in the grave.

On either side of the two young lovers stand Conchubor and Lavarcham, representing two aspects of love tempered by age. Again their characteristics are clearly identified in the first act. Lavarcham, wise in the ways both of man and the natural world, combines the function of chorus (in the Elizabethan sense) and the tolerance of age. She has taught Deirdre nature's lore and recognizes her pupil's affinity with the life of the woods: "Birds go mating in the spring of the year, and ewes at the leaves' falling, but a young girl must have her lover in all the courses of the sun and moon." Reminding us constantly of the troubles foretold, she recognizes also that Deirdre too has the right to a life of her own choosing. And it is she who counsels Conchubor, in vain, not to meddle where he has no natural right: "Fools and kings and scholars are all one in a story with her like." But in spite of her role as wise teacher, Lavarcham is vulnerable in her love for Deirdre: anxiety gives way to insolence and bitter anger when the sons of Usna discover Deirdre's hiding-place in Act I; grief at the prospect of Deirdre's sorrow in Act II forces her again to defy fate in a desperate attempt to keep the lovers in Alban. Owen tells us that Lavarcham too has had her share of love and happiness, but in contrast to

Deirdre, she has chosen to accept the limitations of old age. "There's little hurt getting old, saving when you're looking back, the way I'm looking this day, and seeing the young you have a love for breaking up their hearts with folly." Yet there is room in her pity for Conchubor as well; it is she who remains at the end to mourn the deaths of Deirdre and Naisi, and to offer comfort to the broken, desolate old king.

Conchubor on the other hand refuses to accept age and its consequences. Defying the course of nature, he claims Deirdre for his bride although his role in her upbringing makes him more father than lover. In Act III he remains stubbornly tied to the remnants of passion, asserting again his unnatural right: "It's little I care if she's white and worn, for it's I did rear her from a child should have a good right to meet and see her always." Bewildered, he at last recognises he will never deserve the grief Deirdre holds for Naisi, and having lost the right to both love and kingship in his last desperate fight against time, he is led away by Deirdre's old nurse, a pathetic, broken old man. "There's things a king can't have. . . ."

Where Ainnle and Ardan give support to Naisi's role as hunter and warrior and through Naisi's desertion of them highlight the relationship between the two lovers, Fergus gives support to Conchubor's cause and shares in Conchubor's blindness. In Act II he too speaks from the vantage point of age and serves to underline one other aspect of the natural world—love of one's country. But his early arguments originate in the alien society of Conchubor's world as opposed to the universe of the lovers: he emphasises the loneliness of the exile's lot, especially with encroaching old age and separation from their children; he mocks the warrior brothers for paying heed to "a timid woman," he taunts Deirdre, "It's a poor thing to see a queen so lonesome and afraid." When traditional eloquence will not suffice, he turns to Naisi with more success, voicing the threat of love-weariness. But Fergus makes no impressive impact on the two lovers; their decision is made on grounds beyond his understanding, and his role remains that of emissary until the third act. Even then, as avenger against Conchubor's treachery, his reasoning comes from the world Naisi and Deirdre had rejected seven years earlier, his final lament reminding us only that neither force nor love can halt the passage of time and the inevitability of fate.

Conchubor's folly arises out of ignorance; alone and defeated, he deserves our pity at the end. But with Conchubor sole rival to Naisi the spectrum of love was not complete, nor despite the omnipresence of death was the reality of love sufficiently rooted in the clay and the worms. Almost desperately, Synge sought for a foil to Conchubor, for another aspect of the distortion of love. At first he contemplated developing Ainnle's role so that he became his brother's rival, but that would upset the delicate balance he had achieved through the lovers' quarrel. A harsher, grotesque element was necessary, underscoring the ugliness of time and the violence of unfulfilled, unseemly passion. Finally he introduced Owen, the ragged, wild messenger of Act II who rudely and brusquely reminds Deirdre of the passing of time and inevitability of old age. Coldly rejected by Deirdre, he returns to startle Naisi and finally commits suicide as first casualty of Deirdre's beauty. Synge died before he could work Owen fully into the fabric of his play, but from his notebooks and Yeats's diaries it is possible to ascertain the role this grotesque figure was to carry. In Act I, Yeats reported, "He was to come in with Conchubor, carrying some of his belongings, and afterwards at the end of the act to return for a forgotten knife—just enough to make it possible to use him in Act II." "When Owen killed himself in the second act, he was to have done it with Conchubor's knife."[14] Synge therefore intended Owen to serve as spy for Conchubor and, succumbing to the fatal charm of Deirdre, thus serve as contrast also to Conchubor's other servants, Lavarcham and Fergus. But here passion exceeds all restraint and form, introducing an entirely new note and emphasising a different kind of loneliness. For Owen is an outsider, the freak or madman of nature, perhaps the fool. He may have his origin in Trendorn of the early saga, the stranger hired by Conchubor to kill Naisi; like Trendorn, Owen hates Naisi because Naisi killed his father. He has some affinity also with the tramp of Synge's earlier plays, especially Patch Darcy, the herd of *The Shadow of the Glen* who runs mad in the hills from loneliness. But in *The Aran Islands* we can find further clues. Standing on the shore of the south island Synge noticed among the crowd "several men of the ragged, humorous type that was once thought to represent the real peasant of Ireland . . . there was something nearly appalling in the shrieks of laughter kept up by one of these individuals, a man of extraordinary ugliness and wit." Commenting on "this half-sensual ecstasy of laughter," he reasoned, "Perhaps a man must have a sense of intimate misery . . . before he can set himself to jeer and mock at the world. These strange men with receding foreheads, high cheek-bones, and ungovernable eyes seem to represent some old type found on these few acres at the extreme border of Europe, where it is only in wild jests and laughter that they can express their loneliness and desolation."[15] Here I believe we have the source for Owen's disjointed passion, his wild fits of laughter and sudden action, perhaps even for the folly of his hopeless love for Deirdre. Had Synge finished the play, Owen would perhaps have taken on also more of the character of the Elizabethan fool, who speaks in riddles of great sense and carries with him a haunting reminiscence of another world. But here, in his unfinished state, Owen tells Deirdre nothing she does not already know, nor does the grotesqueness of his imagery rouse in her anything but momentary contempt and a slight uneasiness at the vehemence of his tone. Owen's impact is directed instead towards the audience, lest they overlook the seriousness of Deirdre's earlier confession to Lavarcham, require further assurance of the perfection of the love Deirdre and Naisi have shared for seven years, or seek to identify a climax of action too early in the play. The reality of old age is already a threat to Deirdre, but we may not have grasped its full horror: "Well go take your choice. Stay here and rot with Naisi, or go to Conchubor in Emain. Conchubor's a swelling belly, and eyes falling down from his shining crown, Naisi should be stale and weary." And, in contrast to the lonesomeness of happiness fulfilled, there is the loneliness of love unfulfilled: "It's a poor thing to be so lonesome you'd squeeze kisses on a cur dog's nose." There is something more terrible in this mad folly than in the mistaken folly of Conchubor's solitude. Love can also lead to madness and an undignified death.

Deirdre of the Sorrows was, Synge had claimed, chiefly an experiment to change his hand. In the range of character, depth of passion, and evocation of atmosphere, the play even in its unfinished state proved once again the originality of his genius. At the same time, however, he remained true in treatment of subject and development of theme to the task he originally set himself. As early as April 1904 he had written to Frank Fay, "The whole interest of our movement is that our little plays try to be literature first—i.e. to be personal, sincere, and beautiful—and drama afterwards." And a later jotting in his notebook unconsciously traces his own development as a dramatist: "Dramatic art is first of all a childish art—a reproduction of external experience—without form or philosophy; then after a lyrical interval we have it as mature drama dealing with the deeper truth of general life in a perfect form and with mature philosophy."[16] It would be naïve not to recognise that the pathos of *Deirdre of the Sorrows* is intensified by our knowledge that while Synge was here celebrating both his love and his mature art he was himself close to death. But pathos should not block our awareness of the artistry behind the play, the careful blending of all the notes celebrating love and the glories of the natural world, "the rich joy found only in what is superb and wild in reality." Perhaps the greatest irony lies in our realization that, like the two lovers who just missed perfection of life and love, the artist did not quite achieve perfection of the work. *Deirdre of the Sorrows* remains a superb fragment, a lyric tragedy, in the words of Una Ellis-Fermor, "nobly planned and all but greatly carried out."[17]

Notes

1. All quotations concerning Synge's comments on *The Playboy of the Western World* and the writing of *Deirdre of the Sorrows* are taken from my introduction to *J. M. Synge Plays Book II* (Oxford University Press, 1968).

2. From a letter dated April 1902 in the possession of Major Richard Gregory.

3. See *J. M. Synge Prose*, ed. Alan Price (Oxford University Press, 1966), p. 371; all quotations from Synge's letters to Molly are taken from *Letters to Molly: J. M. Synge to Maire O'Neill*, ed. Ann Saddlemyer, (Belknap Press of Harvard University Press, 1971).

4. In a letter to Stephen MacKenna, January 1904, Synge rejected the concept of "a purely fantastic unmodern, ideal, breezy, springdayish, Cuchulainoid National Theatre," describing a recent production of Yeats's *The Shadowy Waters* as "the most *distressing* failure the mind can imagine," see "Synge to MacKenna: The Mature Years," *Massachusetts Review* (Winter 1964). p. 281. He wrote of Yeats to Molly on 21 August 1907: "I saw a book copy of *Deirdre* at Roberts' yesterday at 3 / 6. There is an extraordinary note at the end giving a page of the

play that he had cut out, and then found that it was necessary after all. He makes himself ridiculous sometimes."

5. This draft occurs on the back of an unfinished letter to Agnes Tobin dated 8 March 1907; for the final version of "Queens" see *J. M. Synge Poems*, ed. Robin Skelton (Oxford University Press, 1962), p. 34.

6. See *Plays Book II*, pp. 393–94, for the complete essay.

7. I have traced the development of Synge's aesthetic theory in "Art, Nature and the Prepared Personality: A Reading of *The Aran Islands* and Related Writings," to be published in 1971 in *Sunshine and the Moon's Delight* a volume of centenary essays edited by Suheil Bushrui and published by Colin Smythe. Two quotations from Synge's notebooks are of particular interest here: *Prose*, p. 35: "All art that is not conceived by a soul in harmony with some mood of the earth is without value, and unless we are able to produce a myth more beautiful than nature—holding in itself a spiritual grace beyond and through the earthly—it is better to be silent." *Prose*, p. 14: "A cycle of experience is the only definite unity, and when all has been passed through and every joy and pain has been resolved in one passion of relief, the only rest that can follow is in the dissolution of the person."

8. In addition to Lady Gregory's and Leahy's translations of the cycle, Synge was also familiar with a manuscript written about 1740 by Andrew MacCruitin, and published in 1898 by the Society for the Preservation of the Irish Language; with the work done on the legend by his professor at the Sorbonne, H. d'Arbois de Jubainville and doubtless knew countless other recent translations, including the cantata by T. W. Rolleston and his friend the composer Michele Esposito. See Appendix C of Maurice Bourgeois, *John Millington Synge and the Irish Theatre* (London: Constable, 1913), Adelaide Duncan Estill, *The Sources of Synge* (Folcroft Press, 1969), pp. 34–41, and Herbert V. Fackler's article on the Deirdre legend in *Eire-Ireland* (Winter 1969), pp. 56–63.

9. Notebook 47, in the possession of Trinity College Dublin.

10. William Empson in *Seven Types of Ambiguity* (London: Chatto and Windus, 1947), pp. 38–42, traces the imagery of the storm and the grave throughout the play.

11. As early as *Riders to the Sea*, Synge developed his themes musically; this can be seen more clearly in his later scenarios where "current" or "motif" is paralleled by character development and plot. Synge tended to choose examples from Elizabethan and French classical dramatists; there are among his papers scene analyses of both *l'Avare and Phèdre*, and he attended lectures on French literature by Petit de Julleville, whose monumental *Histoire du Théâtre en France* he knew well. Synge also acted as advisor for the Abbey Theatre productions of Lady Gregory's translations of Molière, even writing to the *Comédie Française* for copies of their prompt books.

12. See *Prose*, pp. 368–69, also his article "La Vieille Littérature Irlandaise," *ibid.*, pp. 352–55.

13. *Prose*, p. 114, also p. 143 note: "They have wildness and humour and passion kept in continual subjection by their reverence for life and the sea that is inevitable in this place."

14. W. B. Yeats, *Autobiographies* (London: Macmillan, 1955), p. 457 and Yeats's Preface to the published play, *Plays Book II*, p. 179.

15. *Prose*, pp. 140–42.

16. See *Plays Book I*, p. xxvii and *Prose*, p. 350.

17. "John Millington Synge," *The Oxford Companion to the Theatre*, 3rd ed. (London: Oxford University Press, 1967), p. 931.

The Realism of J. M. Synge*

RONALD GASKELL

I

"On the stage," we read in the preface to *The Playboy*, "one must have reality and one must have joy." The aim of this essay is to make clear what Synge understood by reality, to consider how deeply in his plays he accepts it, and to enquire how far his vision of it is dramatic.

What Synge understood by reality can be seen most quickly by a comparison with Ibsen. Ibsen is concerned, almost obsessed, with personal integrity, threatened at once by a heritage of guilt and by insistent social pressures. The essential features of reality in his work are therefore moral conflict and the clash of wills. The life of the body and of the natural world, in which and by which we live, are ignored. For Synge the natural world is present, to the senses or the imagination, at every moment, and present not as a background but in its own right. It is the wildness, not the beauty, of nature that is stressed. If nature is related to man, as in *Riders to the Sea*, it is by the needs of living; for there is nothing theoretic about Synge's economics, as there is nothing sentimental in his awareness of nature. Maybe, says the Tramp in *The Shadow of the Glen*, the young farmer will take Nora with him since Dan is throwing her out: "What would he do with me now? —Give you the half of a dry bed and good food in your mouth." In *The Playboy* this simplicity—Christy's mug of milk by the fire before settling into a clean bed—deepens our enjoyment of the action. The modern literature of towns, as the preface reminds us, is far from "the profound and common interests of life." It is part of our debt to Synge that he brings us back these interests; not least that he brings back to us the reality of the body. Physical action in his plays is energetic, and this delight in the body is immeasurably strengthened by the sensuous pressure of the dialogue.

This has important consequences. For while it is an axiom of naturalistic drama that characters are to be taken as real, the dramatist's conviction of their reality rarely includes more than the mind and the emotions. (This is true not only of Ibsen and Shaw but to a large degree of Chekhov.) Hence

*This essay first appeared in *Critical Quarterly*, 5 (Autumn 1963), and is reprinted with permission of *Critical Quarterly*.

character is commonly defined by intelligence, profession, habits, interests, tastes; more crudely, as in O'Casey, by tricks of speech. In Synge there is almost nothing of this. Since his concern is the whole person (including the body) his conception of character is dynamic: energy counts for more than the marks left by the struggle towards self-determination. Synge, in short, is a dramatist of passion, not of the will; hence his memorable characters are always women—Pegeen, Deirdre, Maurya. Like other naturalistic dramatists, he gives his characters firmness by opposing one to another, but the opposition, as in Pegeen's quarrel with the widow, is of energies rather than traits. Synge is interested in Pegeen as a woman, not just in what makes her different from other women, because he is interested in the total reality of his characters.

This reality is defined by a vivid realisation through their senses of the world about them. It is defined also by their realisation of each other: for speech of such vitality, in its freedom from self-regard, implies appreciation of the reality of others. Where sharper definition is wanted, Synge works for it not by providing his character with a profession to be exploited in clichés or allusions but by a genuine objectivity. So in *The Playboy*, Jimmy (to Pegeen): "What is there to hurt you, and you a fine, hardy girl would knock the head of any two men in the place?" Or the beautiful distancing of Maurya towards the end of *Riders to the Sea*. When we have been brought to regard her as a tragic, almost heroic figure, a few words place her in a suddenly harder light: "It's getting old she is, and broken." Plainly Synge would not have agreed with Yeats that tragedy excludes character. Yeats's essay on "The Tragic Theatre" opens with a superb tribute to *Deirdre of the Sorrows*, yet a glance at Yeats's *Deirdre* is enough to show how different were his aims from Synge's. Yeats, dramatising a mood (the heroic), subordinates his characters to a pervasive lyricism. The exaltation in which Deirdre dies is captured not in her own words but by the lines in which a chorus of musicians acclaims her. In Synge the tragic power of the ending has its source in an awareness of men and women. For it is this that is realised, in dramatic terms, in the quarrel of the lovers which gives their death such poignancy; in the firm presentation of "the squabbling of fools" which Deirdre transcends in her ecstasy (we recognise this ecstasy, as we can't in Yeats, by the solidity of the world transcended); and in the mingling of exalted imagery and rhythms with the commonest facts of everyday. Passion is here not hindered but intensified by the reality of the character it simplifies.

The emotion is held firm by Synge's refusal to focus exclusively on Deirdre (Naisi's two brothers have been flung in the grave that Deirdre is to share with her lover). And emotion in Synge is never something to be enjoyed. The significance of Deirdre's passion, as of Maurya's and Pegeen's, is the sharp definition it gives to a reality harsh with pain and disappointment. Yeats speaks of the "astringent joy and hardness" that was in all Synge did. It is this hardness, affirming the contradictions of experience, that gives us moments of authentic drama: Maurya accepting the death of Bartley, Pegeen burning her lover's leg, Deirdre and Naisi quarrelling by the open grave.

II

The challenge to a writer for whom reality is the life of the passions, the senses and the natural world, comes finally from time and death. For Ibsen, whose deepest concerns are moral, time is the pressure of the past on the present, and death, too frequently, a theatrically effective climax (*Rosmersholm, The Wild Duck, Hedda Gabler*). For Synge, time is the process of change that includes both death and birth.

This sense of time is strong in all his plays. The recognition of what it means to grow old runs deep through *The Shadow of the Glen, The Tinker's Wedding*, and *The Well of the Saints*. In *Deirdre of the Sorrows* it has become the agent of the catastrophe; for Deirdre's decision to return to Ireland is the choice of an abrupt rather than a lingering end to the love she has shared with Naisi. (This motive, significantly, is Synge's; it is not in the legend as told by Lady Gregory, nor in AE's play, nor in Yeats's.) Despite repeated references to "the sorrows were foretold," the decision is scarcely convincing. What seems to be needed, and what Synge would perhaps have ensured had he lived to revise the second Act, is a less plangent mood when the decision is taken, a harder definition of the values for which life can be sacrificed.

Yet even in the text as it stands death is seen for what it is: "a poor untidy thing, though it's a queen that dies." And this realism, intensified by awareness of the beauty of the life to be destroyed, gives the play its dignity. The bitterness of death is at the heart of the last Act, where it isolates Conchubor and the lovers: "I'll say so near that grave we seem three lonesome people, and by a new-made grave there's no man will keep brooding on a woman's lips, or on the man he hates." And it is the grave that forces Deirdre and Naisi into the quarrel from which Naisi rushes to his death.

Synge's awareness of death—it is strong in his lyrics—has nothing morbid about it; it is the counterpart of that joy in life that gives such vigour to *The Playboy*. If death is real, so is birth. (The Aran islander, he noted, can "make a cradle or a coffin.") In *Riders to the Sea* death is defined against birth:

> I've had a husband, and a husband's father, and six sons in this house—six fine men, though it was a hard birth I had with every one of them and they coming into the world—and some of them were found and some of them were not found, but they're gone now the lot of them. . . . There was Patch after was drowned out of a curragh that turned over. I was sitting here with Bartley, and he a baby lying on my two knees, and I seen two women, and three women, and four women coming in, and they crossing themselves and not saying a word.

Maurya's acceptance, not of the death of Michael and Bartley only but of death as the human fate, has been criticised as passive. But in the last few moments of the play there is a going out of her grief to affirm the world in which human life is an episode: "May the Almighty God have mercy on Bartley's soul, and on Michael's soul, and on the souls of Sheamus and Patch, and Stephen and Shawn; and may He have mercy on my soul, Nora, and on the soul of every one is left living in the world." That Christianity is hardly even a hope for her has been made clear:

Nora: Didn't the young priest say the Almighty God won't leave her destitute with no son living?

Maurya: It's little the like of him knows of the sea.

The prayer at the end, then, is only accidentally Christian; but it is essentially religious. And it is the contrast between this religious insight, this broken reverence for the rhythm of life and death, and the pathetic fact of the individual death—the white boards and the deep grave—that makes the end of the play so moving.

In his account of a funeral on the islands, Synge had written:

This grief of the keen is no personal complaint for the death of one woman over eighty years, but seems to contain the whole passionate rage that lurks some-where in every native of the island. In this cry of pain the inner consciousness of the people seems to lay itself bare for an instant, and to reveal the mood of beings who feel their isolation in the face of a universe that wars on them with winds and seas. . . . Before they covered the coffin an old man kneeled down by the grave and repeated a simple prayer for the dead.

There was an irony in these words of atonement and Catholic belief spoken by voices that were still hoarse with the cries of pagan desperation.

If there is irony in the writing of Maury's benediction it is a deeply compassion-ate irony. For her grief is not a despair that rejects death as unintelligibly horrifying, but an exaltation that has accepted death as the final contradition in reality.

III

The integrity of Synge's work, then, is not in question. His vision is consistent and he neither evades nor moderates its pain. Whether this vision is fully dramatic, however, is another matter.

His plays, as he was the first to insist, owe much of their energy to the life of the Aran islands and of the farmers, tramps and tinkers of Wicklow and the West of Ireland: a life that had not only simplicity and passion but emotional subtlety, courtesy and humour. A profound conviction of the value of that life encouraged a dramatic method that is basically representational. The structure of his plays is therefore fairly straightforward; for the most part, the rudimentary structure of the anecdotes on which several of them were based. (This is not to deny that in detail *Riders to the Sea*, for example, is deftly constructed.)

The Playboy, his most complex piece, is firmly put together. Yet the theme, the creation of a hero by the people, is not very obviously dramatic, and the play's success springs rather from the passions Synge can generate by grouping with his hero Pegeen, Shawn Keogh and the Widow Quin. The weakness of the play is, of course, the handling of Old Mahon. ("I fully agree," wrote Synge to Molly Allgood after the first production, "that the third Act wants pulling together.") For the rest there is enough to admire: the control of the comic tone while the "murder" is disclosed, the retention of Christy's miming out his deed till he has a more flattering audience in the second Act, the use of the widow to make plain Pegeen's interest and so encourage Christy to respond to her.

When this has been said, it has to be admitted that the structure, as distinct from the action, contributes little to the play's impact. This is apparent if we put it beside, say, *The Caucasian Chalk Circle* or *The House of Bernarda Alba*. Both these plays have an economy and force, a formal intensity, that *The Playboy* lacks. And this is not simply because Brecht and Lorca have shaped their material more decisively; it is because, while reality means to them very much what it meant to Synge, the way that they see this reality is significantly different. Lorca's vision is inherently dramatic because in the relation of man to the natural world he sees an inescapable conflict between the sexual drive and the conventions imposed on it by society. In Synge, despite his almost feminine sympathy with birth, love is romantic; the obstacles to it in *The Playboy* are slight and in *Deirdre* avoided till the end. Brecht, again, is less passive than Synge. Synge, though he grasps the hardness of the struggle with nature, has no wish to see it altered. Brecht accepts Marx's view that the point about the world is to change it. And change of this kind, achieved by human effort, is potentially dramatic; Synge's feeling for change, as the passing of time, is elegiac.

Synge, of course, is more thoroughly naturalistic than either Brecht or Lorca. But naturalistic drama, no less than any other, must be purposive. If the characters are to be taken as real a play can succeed only if it presents those for whom life is a challenge to action. Synge's indifference to the will, though we may, with Yeats, welcome it as a corrective to Ibsen, makes a fully dramatic play virtually impossible.

This view is supported by a study of Synge's dialogue. Raymond Williams, noting the prevalence of simile rather than metaphor, has drawn attention to the gap between picturesque phrasing and the fully dramatic use of words in, say, Shakespeare. A similar point has to be made against Synge's rhythms. There could clearly be no question of shaping the spoken dialects, on which his writing was based, into verse. The cadences are too long and too distinct to play over a syllabic base or be moulded into stress metre. Nor, though he seems in his earliest notes for the play to have thought of writing *Deirdre* in verse, is there any evidence that Synge could have made himself a verse dramatist. His lyrics, despite his musical training, are rhythmically uninteresting, as are the fragments of his dramatic verse that have been published. The prose of his plays is incomparably more successful. That it has temptations, and that Synge occasionally succumbs to them, is obvious. It provides no discipline such as metre would enforce and so encourages the flamboyant gesture ("Amn't I after seeing the love-light of the star of knowledge shining from her brow?"). More important, the rhythms are not, and perhaps could not be, sufficiently varied to distinguish different characters and different emotions. The strength of the rhythms, to be sure, varies with the strength of the emotion. In the love scene of *The Playboy* the rhythm is perhaps even too strong; Synge's favourite cadence ("with a nosegay in her golden shawl," "in the Owen or the Carrowmore" etc.) appears five times within forty lines. In *Deirdre* the rhythms are stronger throughout Act III, and markedly stronger at the end, than in the first two (unrevised) Acts. But the available rhythmic patterns are limited and for the most part lyrical or meditative. In *Deirdre*, for example, the characteristic falling cadences give a curiously retrospective quality to the emotion, as if the lovers from the beginning were contemplating their own story, already past. Rapid, vigorous exchanges, as between Pegeen and the Widow Quin, are possible; but the tendency is for a speech of any length to be treated as a piece of music by itself, so that the rhythms of a scene don't really carry us forward.

Yeats, in his preface to *The Well of the Saints*, stresses the trouble Synge took to adapt the spoken language to his purpose. "He made his own selection of word and phrase, choosing what would express his own personality. Above all, he made word and phrase dance to a very strange rhythm. . . . Perhaps no Irish countryman had ever that exact rhythm in his voice, but certainly if Mr. Synge had been born a countryman, he would have spoken like that." This judgment, from one who knew Synge intimately, is revealing. For we should not as a rule think to praise a dramatist by saying that his phrases "express his own personality," that "he would have spoken like that." Yet this does define our uneasiness with Synge's dialogue: it is too consistently the expression of "that meditative man."

Compared with the dialogue of Shaw, which is rhetorical, or of O'Casey, which is sentimental, Synge's writing is something to be grateful for in the theatre. For the energy of his phrasing does bring the reality of the senses and the natural world alive to our imagination; and the drama, as he affirmed, is made serious "by the degree in which it gives the nourishment, not very easy to define, on which our imaginations live." Humour, he noted, does this. So also, he might have added, does passion. For the imagination is not a faculty by which we invent a fantasy world, but the faculty that reveals to us the real world, changing, surprising and discordant. And just as humour by its objectivity clears our vision of sentiment, so passion, shearing away self-deception, forces us out of our habit of seeing things not as they are but as we should like them to be.

"On the stage one must have reality and one must have joy." The two are not to be separated, for joy is found in "what is superb and wild in reality." The strength of Synge's plays is the grip that his imagination gives us again on that reality: on the energy of the body, on the passions of men and women, on wind and rain and sun. But the greatest drama offers more than this.

Index

◆